Practical Psychiatry
in the Nursing Home

A Handbook for Staff

CONTRIBUTORS

David K. Conn, M.B., B.Ch., F.R.C.P.(C)
Co-ordinator, Consultation-Liaison Service, Department of Psychiatry,
Baycrest Centre for Geriatric Care, and Assistant Professor, Department
of Psychiatry, University of Toronto

Etta Ginsberg-McEwan, M.S.W.
Director, Department of Social Work, Baycrest Centre for Geriatric
Care

Nathan Herrmann, M.D., F.R.C.P.(C)
Staff Psychiatrist, Sunnybrook Health Science Centre, and Assistant
Professor, Department of Psychiatry, University of Toronto

Alanna Kaye, R.N.
Nurse Clinician, Department of Psychiatry, Baycrest Centre for Geriatric Care

David Myran, M.D., F.R.C.P.(C)
Staff Psychiatrist, Baycrest Centre for Geriatric Care and Lecturer,
Department of Psychiatry, University of Toronto

Dmytro Rewilak, Ph.D.
Staff Psychologist, Baycrest Centre for Geriatric Care

Anne Robinson, R.N.
Nurse Clinician, Department of Psychiatry, Baycrest Centre for Geriatric Care

Joel Sadavoy, M.D., F.R.C.P.(C)
Head, Department of Psychiatry, Baycrest Centre for Geriatric Care,
and Associate Professor, Department of Psychiatry, University of
Toronto

Barbara Schogt, M.D., F.R.C.P.(C)
Formerly Staff Psychiatrist, Baycrest Centre for Geriatric Care

Michel Silberfeld, M.D., F.R.C.P.(C)
Co-ordinator Competency Clinic, Department of Psychiatry, Baycrest
Centre for Geriatric Care, and Assistant Professor, Department of
Psychiatry, University of Toronto

Practical Psychiatry in the Nursing Home

A Handbook for Staff

Edited by

**David K. Conn, Nathan Herrmann,
Alanna Kaye, Dmytro Rewilak,
Anne Robinson, Barbara Schogt**

Hogrefe & Huber Publishers
Seattle • Toronto • Bern • Göttingen

Library of Congress Cataloguing-in-Publication Data

Practical psychiatry in the nursing home : a handbook for staff /
  [edited] by David Conn ... [et al.]
    p. cm.
  Includes bibliographical references and index
  ISBN 0-88937-042-7 : $34.50
  1. Geriatric Psychiatry. 2. Mentally ill aged — Institutional
care. 3. Aged — Mental Health Services. 4. Psychotherapy for the
aged. 5. Nursing home care. I. Conn, David K.
  [DNLM: 1. Homes for the Aged. 2. Mental Disorders — in
old age. 3. Mental Disorders — therapy. 4. Nursing Homes.
5. Psychotherapy — in old age.   WT 150 P895
RC 451.4.A5P69   1991
618.97'689--dc20
DNLM/DLC   91-7101
for Library of Congress   CIP

Canadian Cataloguing in Publication Data

Main entry under title:
Practical Psychiatry in the Nursing Home
Includes bibliographical references and index.
ISBN 0-88937-042-7
1. Geriatric psychiatry — Handbooks, Manuals, etc.
2. Nursing home care — Handbooks, manuals, etc.
3. Aged — Mental Health Services. I. Conn,
David K.
RC451.4A5P73 1991   618.97'689   C91-094266-8

Copyright © 1992, 2nd printing 1993
Hogrefe & Huber Publishers
P.O. Box 2487, Kirkland, Washington 98083-2487
12 Bruce Park Avenue, Toronto, Ontario M4P 2S3

Printed in the U.S.A.

ISBN 0-88937-042-7
Hogrefe & Huber Publishers, Seattle • Toronto
ISBN 3-456-81871-8
Hans Huber Publishers, Bern • Göttingen

Preface

The impetus for this book came from the positive response of staff who attended a seminar series entitled "Practical Psychiatry in Long-term Care," presented by the Psychiatry Consultation-Liaison Team at Baycrest Centre for Geriatric Care in Toronto, Canada, in 1989. In view of the lack of available literature in this area we decided to write a book based on the contents of this course with the addition of several new topics.

Our intention has been to produce a book that is practical, understandable, clinically relevant, "user friendly," and as jargon-free as possible. We hope that the book will be useful for the staff of all long-term care facilities for the elderly, including nursing homes, homes for the aged, chronic care hospitals, and residential centres.

The prevalence of mental disorders in the residents of these facilities is very high and the staff, residents, and their families alike struggle with the problems associated with these disorders on a daily basis. We have aimed this book at all staff members and hope that it will be equally relevant to nurses, nursing aides, physicians, social workers, psychologists, occupational therapists and all the other staff of these facilities.

We are hopeful that the book will be used as a tool for both continuing education of staff and for the teaching of undergraduate students.

The book utilizes clinical case examples, with an emphasis on practical management strategies. We have outlined questions that are frequently asked by staff and have attempted to respond to these questions. The chapters conclude with key points. We have avoided the use of excessive references and a list of suggested reading can be found at the end of each chapter.

The case illustrations are composites of residents seen by the authors. They have been disguised to ensure anonymity. For the most part we have preferred to use the term "resident" rather than "patient" in order to underline the fact that for these individuals the institution is their home, and like all of us they are only "patients" when requiring medical care.

The authors include psychiatrists, nurses, a psychologist, and a social worker. We have tried to emphasize a biopsychosocial model throughout the book and a multidisciplinary approach to the management of these residents.

We are aware that the availability of mental health professionals in long-term care settings is variable, and often minimal. In the majority of institutions front line staff have to "make do" without the help of consultants or staff trained to manage mental disorders. We are hopeful that the ideas and information contained in this book can be utilized by front line staff in their day-to-day management of residents with mental disorders. We have tried to emphasize that for any given problem there may be a variety of potential interventions. Often the best results occur following the introduction of several complementary management strategies. Because many of the problems in long-term care are by their very nature chronic it is easy to slip into a pessimistic or even nihilistic frame of mind. This book tries to show that many of these problems can be managed successfully and that we *can* make a difference.

David Conn
Nathan Herrmann
Alanna Kaye
Dmytro Rewilak
Anne Robinson
Barbara Schogt   *Toronto, January 1992*

ACKNOWLEDGEMENTS

We are indebted to the long-term care residents with whom we have worked, and to their families. They have helped us to formulate our ideas and have given us valuable insights into the world of the institution.

We would like to thank our colleagues at Baycrest Centre for Geriatric Care, who have helped us to understand the often difficult work of the frontline staff.

In addition, we greatly appreciate the efforts of Malerie Feldman, Paula Ferreira, Marci Fromstein, Ruby Nishioka, and Dilshad Ratansi in the preparation of the manuscript.

Finally, we would like to acknowledge the support and enthusiasm of Drs. Christine Hogrefe, Tom Tabasz, and the staff of Hogrefe & Huber with regard to this project.

Table of Contents

CHAPTER

Mental Health Issues in Long-term Care Facilities for the Elderly

1

by David K. Conn

HISTORY

The characteristics of long-term care facilities for the elderly have changed dramatically over the past 100 years. Until this century most facilities for the aged were primitive, badly run, and offered only custodial care.

Institutions for the disabled and infirm date all the way back to the third or fourth century AD [1]. Such facilities developed initially in the Middle East, and over many centuries the concept subsequently spread to Western Europe. By medieval times it was common that the aged and sick were cared for by a variety of religious orders in monasteries, often in remote locations.

In England and Wales, as monasteries disappeared in the 1500s, responsibility for the poor was gradually taken on by the local parishes. Under the Poor Relief Act in 1601, Poor Houses were established for those who were blind, disabled, mentally or physically ill, as well as the destitute. These Poor Houses were also referred to as Work Houses

1

because they were a source of cheap labor. By the nineteenth century between one-third and one-half of the occupants in a typical Work House were elderly or "impotent" persons.

With the development of our modern concept of a hospital in the nineteenth century, the primary emphasis was placed on the treatment of the acutely sick, rather than the chronically ill, and completely separate institutions were established for "the insane." In other institutions, the elderly, the poor, the chronically sick, and the disabled were crowded together in appalling conditions, often with vagrants and the destitute. By the beginning of the twentieth century, there was clearly a growing need for convalescent and chronic care beds. It was only at this point that the modern concept of the nursing home was firmly established, modeled on the general principles of the sanatorium. The early nursing homes were occasionally attached to general hospitals, but more frequently they were built as completely separate institutions, usually some distance from the closest city.

TRENDS

With the growth of the elderly population in modern industrial countries, the number of people receiving care in nursing homes has been rising dramatically. In the United States, for example, the number of beds in such facilities has more than tripled during the past 25 years, and now totals over 1.5 million. This growth in the number of nursing home beds (1963-1985) is shown in Figure 1.

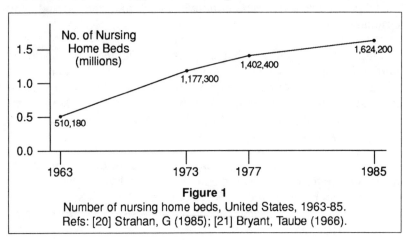

Figure 1
Number of nursing home beds, United States, 1963-85.
Refs: [20] Strahan, G (1985); [21] Bryant, Taube (1966).

The continuing growth of the elderly population in the U.S. is shown in Figures 2 to 5. It is projected that the population 65 years and over will grow at a sustained 1.2% per year until 2010. After 2010, however, the rate of growth will increase in a more striking manner as the Baby Boom generation enters old age.

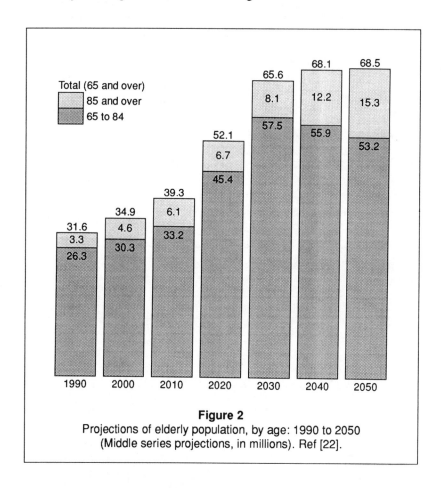

Figure 2
Projections of elderly population, by age: 1990 to 2050
(Middle series projections, in millions). Ref [22].

The phenomenal projected growth of the population 85 years and over is shown in Figure 4. It is of course this age group that is most likely to require long-term care. The continuing increase in life-expectancy at age 65 is demonstrated in Figure 5. Accordingly the projected growth in requirements for nursing home and other long-term care beds is illustrated in Figure 6.

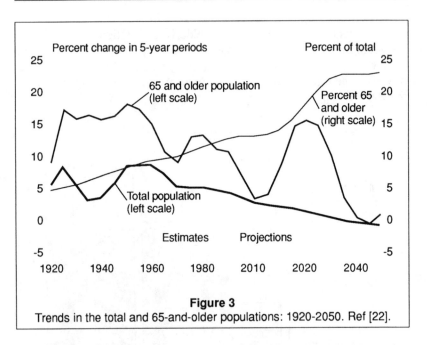

Figure 3
Trends in the total and 65-and-older populations: 1920-2050. Ref [22].

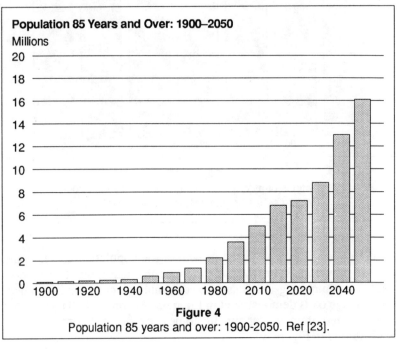

Figure 4
Population 85 years and over: 1900-2050. Ref [23].

There are many important trends in this field which are particularly influenced by these changing demographics. Six of these trends, which will have a critical impact on the future of long-term care include:

- A growth in the physical size of facilities.
- An increase in the availability of higher levels of care.
- A significantly greater percentage of residents with dementia and severe cognitive impairment.
- More residents with psychiatric and behavioral disorders.
- Greater involvement of university programs in nursing homes, with the development of the so-called "teaching nursing home."
- Increased legislation (e.g. OBRA 1987 in the U.S.) to ensure higher standards of care.

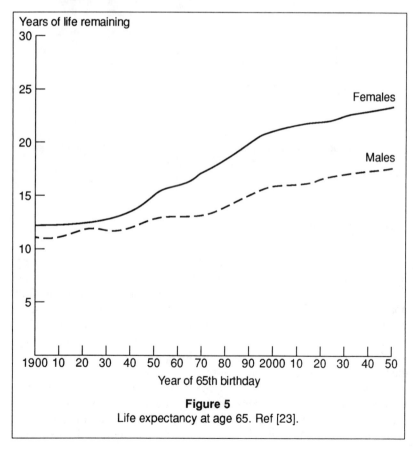

Figure 5
Life expectancy at age 65. Ref [23].

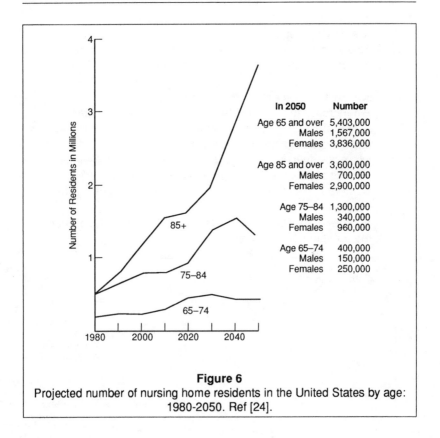

Figure 6

Projected number of nursing home residents in the United States by age: 1980-2050. Ref [24].

THE RESIDENTS

There is considerable evidence that most elderly residents of nursing homes do in fact need a great deal of care and assistance. For example, one recent study found that a remarkable 92% of elderly living in nursing homes were dependent in at least one activity of daily living [2]. Ninety-one percent required assistance in bathing, 78% in dressing, 63% in toileting and transferring, and 40% in eating. It is clear that one's ability or inability to perform the activities of normal daily living contributes substantially to the final decision regarding admission to a nursing home.

As of 1985 there were approximately 19,000 nursing homes operating in the United States, consisting of a total of 1.5 million beds. These institutions are categorized federally as Skilled Nursing Facilities (SNFs) and Intermediate Care Facilities (ICFs). It is estimated that currently, 1 in 10 persons aged 75 and older, and 1 in 5 aged 85 and older are living in nursing homes. Expenditures for nursing home care in 1986 in the U.S. were estimated at 38.9 billion dollars, out of a total of 402 billion dollars in personal health care. In this context, a little over 50% of this expenditure was private spending and the rest was public.

To deal with these powerful demographic and economic forces, various governments are trying new approaches. For example, in Canada the province of Ontario is currently attempting to reform long-term care based on certain key guiding principles, one of which states that:

"an increasing proportion of the elderly and people with physical disabilities who require health and social services will receive them in their own homes, to avoid both inappropriate use of acute care beds and unnecessary growth in the number of extended and chronic care beds."

But in spite of this well-founded goal of attempting to maintain the elderly in the community for as long as possible by increasing the availability of community care and supports, the unstoppable demographic realities we now face, as well as the cumulative ravages of illness and old age, will lead to an increased requirement for long-term care beds, whether or not governments and budget directors accept this situation.

In dealing with these strategic planning issues, it is often suggested that children frequently abandon or ignore their elderly parents, but this is just a myth. In fact families remain the primary source of care for the vast majority of frail parents, and this burden is especially carried by daughters, who are themselves also often trying to care for young children. However, as the demand for care increases, most often as a result of progressive mental impairment, it frequently becomes an impossible burden for the family, and institutional care becomes a necessity

PREVALENCE OF PSYCHIATRIC/BEHAVIORAL DISTURBANCE

Studies suggest that while 80% or more of elderly nursing home residents suffer from some form of mental disorder, only a very small percentage ever receive any care from mental health professionals. During the 1960s hundreds of thousands of psychiatric patients were discharged from state mental hospitals, especially in the USA. This happened partly because of pressure from groups who felt that such individuals should live in the community, and partly because advances in drug therapy allowed even severely ill patients to function at reasonable levels. But many of these former patients, especially those who were elderly, were not able to care for themselves, and as a result ended up being transferred to nursing homes, which were expected to continue the appropriate care and management of these patients, even though such homes were not staffed or funded to provide mental health care.

The U.S. National Center for Health Statistics reported in 1977 that approximately 20% of all nursing home residents had a mental disorder (psychiatric illness or dementia) as their primary source of disability, and that nearly 70%, which was more than 900,000 residents, had a chronic mental disorder which contributed to social dependency, functional impairment, and need for nursing home care [3]. Two thirds of all residents were found to have behavioral problems, most commonly agitation or apathy. In one important study, Rovner and his colleagues found that 76% of their sample of nursing home residents showed at least one problem behavior, while 40% displayed five or more such difficulties [4]. Another study, performed in New York City [5], found that the three most common behavior problems in nursing homes for the aged, were verbal abuse, physical resistance to care, and physical aggressiveness.

Similarly, a recent survey in Ontario, Canada [6] found that the most common behavior problems were agitation, wandering, and depression, whereas the problem of greatest concern for staff was physical aggression. Yet in spite of all these statistics, surveys suggest that fewer than 1% of all patients with a diagnosable mental disorder receive explicit mental health interventions.

In addition to the distinct lack of psychiatric care for nursing home residents, several investigations suggest that psychotropic drugs are overused in this population: 50% to 80% of residents commonly receive psychotropic agents [7,8]. A study of physicians' prescribing practices surveyed the records of 173 nursing homes and revealed that 43% of almost 6,000 residents had prescriptions for a neuroleptic [9]. Incredibly, the average dose per resident turned out to be directly related to the size of the nursing home, and the size of the prescribing physician's caseload. It is clear that more research is needed in order to determine the appropriate use of these medications.

COMMON PSYCHIATRIC AND EMOTIONAL PROBLEMS

It appears that the majority of residents with psychiatric problems in the nursing home setting suffer from some form of organic mental syndrome. The most common of these syndromes is dementia, and the most common cause of dementia is Alzheimer disease, followed by multi-infarct dementia. Dr. Alzheimer himself, in his initial description of dementia, emphasized the development of behavioral disturbances. His descriptions included paranoid delusions, hallucinations, unfounded jealousy, hiding of objects, and screaming. Dementing disorders are often associated with disruptive behavior, including physical and verbal aggression, anger, paranoid ideation, wandering, insomnia, and incontinence. A recent study of 126 demented patients [10] found that 83% of them exhibited one or more such behavior problems.

Depression is another common mental problem in the nursing home setting. Depressive symptoms occur in approximately 15% of the elderly in the general community, although the prevalence rate for major clinical depression is probably 2% to 4%. In contrast, studies suggest that between 15% and 25% of nursing home residents have symptoms of major depression, but that up to 50% have depressive symptoms of lesser severity [11]. The recognition and diagnosis of depression is particularly important because it is a treatable condition; unfortunately, on occasion untreated depression can lead to extreme morbidity and ultimately to death.

DIAGNOSTIC CLASSIFICATIONS

The diagnoses used in this book are based on the American Psychiatric Association's diagnostic system, entitled DSM-IIIR [12]. It is a multi-axial system with axis I containing the major psychiatric diagnosis, axis II containing personality traits and disorders, axis III the medical illnesses, axis IV the level of psychosocial stress, and axis V the level of functioning of the individual. Table 1 lists common DSM-IIIR diagnoses seen in long-term care residents.

Table 1
Common Psychiatric Diagnoses in Residents of
Long-Term Care Facilities

- Dementia
- Delirium
- Organic mood syndrome
- Organic delusional syndrome
- Organic personality syndrome
- Major depression
- Dysthymic disorder
- Adjustment disorder
- Personality Disorder

MODELS OF CARE

The "biopsychosocial" model, in contrast to the biomedical approach, is the model of choice in both geriatrics and psychiatry. In formulating a clinical situation, it is often helpful to categorize etiologi-

	Biological	Psychological	Social
Predisposing			
Precipitating			
Perpetuating			

Figure 7
The biopsychosocial model: A grid for formulation.

cal factors into biological (physical), psychological, and social categories, as illustrated in Figure 7. The category "social" includes both cultural and environmental factors. This model then allows for the design of treatment interventions aimed at a variety of factors.

CASE ILLUSTRATION

Mrs A, an 89-year-old widow, had been admitted to the nursing home 2 months previously. She was born in England, emigrated to Canada shortly before the First World War, and had worked as a secretary prior to her marriage to a tailor. They had a "solid," happy marriage, and two children. Mr A had died one year earlier of a stroke. Mrs A was having difficulty functioning in her own apartment, and was neglecting herself to the point that finally her daughter arranged for an application and placement at the home. Mrs A had not adjusted well to the new environment, and had been weepy, distressed, and agitated at times. She appeared unmotivated and disinterested in activities and programs. She was sleeping poorly, not eating, and stated clearly that she wanted to die. Her daughter was away in Florida, and her son lived out of town. Mrs A had a past history of hypothyroidism and of postpartum depression. Her own mother was described as having had "bad nerves," and her son had required treatment for depression. Mrs A had a history of losses early in life, including the death of her mother when she was 8 years old. She was cared for by an aunt until her father remarried, and she subsequently had a poor relationship with her stepmother. Mrs A described frequent episodes of mild depression for many years but never sought professional help. It was worthy of note that the unit itself was under some stress due to illness among the staff, including the head nurse. There was also some disruption on the floor because of renovations that were underway.

Comment

In order to understand the possible reasons for Mrs A's depression and grief it is helpful to use the framework described in Figure 7.

This approach can be helpful both in understanding the situation and in developing a management plan. In the case of Mrs A, predisposing factors for depression include a biological vulnerability based on a positive family history of mood disorder, and a previous history of hypothyroidism. She is also psychologically predisposed because of her early life losses, especially the death of her mother, and deprivation. Major precipitants include her recent admission to the institution and the death of her husband 1 year earlier, producing an "anniversary reaction." Recent problems on the unit may also have led to less available support from staff. Factors which could perpetuate the depression include her poor adjustment to the home, her apparent inability to develop new relationships, and her long-standing history of depression. Management steps based on our approach would include medical investigations, such as thyroid function, antidepressant medication, supportive psychotherapy, and attempts to encourage her to participate in recreation programs. With the introduction of appropriate treatment, the return of her daughter from vacation, and the restabilization of the unit, her prognosis would probably be good.

In some institutions models which favor one or another professional orientation, such as a "social work model" or a "nursing model," are preferred. It is the conclusion of the authors of this book that a biopsychosocial approach, which attempts to understand a resident's problems from a variety of different perspectives, makes the most sense. Inherent in any model of nursing home care is an acceptance of reasonable goals, and an emphasis on "care not cure." Lawton tries to define "the good life" for nursing home residents, and outlines the components of such an experience, which include behavioral competence, psychological well-being, and quality of life and of the objective environment [13]. These are translated into goals of health, happiness, satisfaction with daily life, and a comfortable environment.

WHAT ARE THE COMPONENTS OF GOOD CARE?

Attempts to understand and support the biological, psychological, and social needs of the resident provide a solid foundation for good care. Edelson and Lyons emphasize the need to individualize care and promote a sense of mastery in the residents in order that they can feel a sense of trust in and some control over their environment [14]. They stress in particular the importance of understanding the meaning in the impaired resident's behavior. They also point out that an understanding of "the system" is critical and that an institution is like a living organism.

One must battle against nihilism, cynicism, and resistance to change which is often present in geriatric institutions. Borson and colleagues note that long-term care "emphasizes maintenance of functional capacity, delaying the progress of disease when possible, and the creation of a safe, supportive environment that promotes maximal autonomy and life satisfaction. The over-arching philosophy of good long-term care is the preservation of dignity and purpose in the face of dependency and decline" [15].

POTENTIAL PROBLEMS IN THE CARE OF NURSING HOME RESIDENTS

There has been growing public criticism regarding care in nursing homes. A series of books with titles such as Warehouses for Death have presented searing indictments of nursing home care [16]. There have been accounts of mistreatment and abuse of the elderly, poor medical/nursing care, and even greed, particularly in the private sector. In spite of this, considering the funds available, the staff of the majority of nursing homes do an admirable job under trying conditions. However, there are still problems to be solved, and these problems include:

- Poor staff/resident ratios
- Lack of qualified professional staff
- Low morale among staff
- Poorly designed and aging facilities
- Lack of commitment from society and government to direct appropriate funds to this population.

WHAT ARE SOME OF THE SPECIAL PROBLEMS ENCOUNTERED IN THE NURSING HOME SETTING?

Behavior Problems

One of the major challenges for staff is the management of disruptive behaviors, especially those resulting from dementia and other organic mental syndromes. Although control of these problems can be difficult to obtain, very specific pharmacological, psychological, behavioral, and environmental modifications can often be quite helpful. Several chapters in this book will addres this approaches.

Relocation

There has been a considerable interest in the issue of the impact of relocation, i.e., simply changing one's place of residence, and conflicting literature has developed with regard to the potential dangers of moving an elderly person into an institution. Some research has suggested that relocation per se is dangerous. Other studies suggest that relocation is only a serious problem when individuals are moved without their knowledge and participation. There is evidence to suggest that orientation of the person to the nursing home ahead of time will decrease the stress of relocation.

Roommate Incompatibility

Most of the adults admitted to an institution are accustomed to their privacy. The prospect of sharing living quarters with a complete stranger would be unappealing to most of us. In spite of this, most nursing homes do not have the luxury of predominantly private rooms. Private rooms are often sought after like gold dust. One of the difficult tasks for administrators can be the distribution of private rooms, and staff often spend a considerable amount of time trying to decide on the best combination of roommates.

Death and Dying

For caucasian Americans, the nursing home is now the second most common place in which to die. Staff often become emotionally attached to residents over a number of years and it can be difficult when death finally arrives. Birkett [17] notes that there are a variety of different categories of residents who die in nursing homes including:

- Patients who are severely demented and whose consciousness is impaired.
- Patients who are physically ill but whose need for specific medical measures cannot be established.
- Patients who are critically ill but for whom hospital care would have a negative effect or whose lives would not be prolonged by medical measures.
- Patients whose lives might be saved by medical measures at a higher level of care but this care is withheld because of concurrent illness, the patient's advanced age or poor quality of life, or as a result of the patient's expressed wishes.

Decision-making with regard to the degree of medical interventions to be undertaken can be problematic. When the resident is no longer competent, family members or other substitute decision-makers are asked to make decisions. It is important to know the family ahead of time and to have been able to establish a route of communication to the family spokesperson. Sometimes families have difficulties reaching a consensus and meetings are necessary to clarify the wishes of the family members.

HOW CAN STAFF DETECT BEHAVIORAL PROBLEMS THAT MAY REQUIRE INTERVENTION?

With increased education of staff in the nursing home setting the early recognition and even prevention of some psychiatric/emotional problems may be possible. There is no doubt that for illnesses such as depression early intervention may be critical. A variety of screening instruments such as the Geriatric Depression Scale [18] and the Folstein Mini-Mental State Exam [19] may be of particular help, and can be easily administered by most staff members following a short period of training, and this is discussed in some detail in Chapter 2. Most importantly, staff should rely on their own experience, judgement, and vigilance to determine when intervention is necessary. This book attempts to guide the staff member at the bedside with some basic information regarding the assessment and management of these problems.

FUTURE DIRECTIONS IN NURSING HOME CARE

Future directions will include the development of newly designed facilities that offer a more appropriate physical environment for the elderly impaired resident. There is a new movement towards the involvement of academic institutions in nursing homes, and the term "teaching nursing home" has become popular. This will offer exciting new opportunities for us to develop a greater understanding of the kinds of problems experienced by residents and their families in the nursing home setting. These developments will hopefully generate interesting improvements in clinical care, education, and ultimately in the development of new research initiatives for this rapidly growing population. The authors of this book particularly hope that extra funding will be available to increase the availability of mental health professionals in the long-term care setting.

KEY POINTS

- The prevalence of mental disorders in residents of long-term care facilities is at least 80%.

- Common problems include depression and behaviors associated with dementia, such as verbal and physical aggression, wandering, and physical resistance to care.

- Very few residents ever receive care from mental health professionals.

- The biopsychosocial model of care is helpful both in the understanding of the problems and in the planning of individualized care.

- Staff vigilance and the use of screening instruments can facilitate the early recognition and prevention of psychiatric/emotional disorders.

REFERENCES

1. Forbes, W.F., Jackson, J.A., Kraus, A.S. (1987). *Institutionalization of the elderly in Canada.* Toronto: Butterworth.
2. Hing, E. (1987). *Use of nursing homes by the elderly: Preliminary data from the 1985 national nursing home survey.* Advance data No. 135. National Center for Health Statistics, Hyattsville, MD.
3. U.S. National Centre for Health Statistics. (1979). *The national nursing home survey: 1977 Summary for the United States.* Vital and Health Statistics, Serial 13, Number 43. Washington, DC: U.S. Government Printing Office.
4. Rovner, B.W., Kafonek, S., Filipp, L., Lucas, M.J., Folstein, M.F. (1986). Prevalence of mental illness in a community nursing home. *American Journal of Psychiatry*, 143:1446-1449.
5. Zimmer, J.A., Watson, N., Treat, A. (1984). Behavioral problems among patients in skilled nursing facilities. *American Journal of Public Health*, 74:1118-1121.
6. Conn, D.K., Lee, V., Steingart, A., Silberfeld, M. (1990). *A survey of*

psychiatric services to nursing homes and homes for the aged in Ontario. Presented at Annual Meeting, The Gerontological Society of America, Boston, MA., November 19, 1990.

7. Glasscote, R.M., Beigel, A., Butterfield, A., et al. (1976). *Old folks at homes: A field study of nursing and board-and care homes.* Joint information Service of the American Psychiatric Assoc. and the National Assoc. for Mental Health, Washington, DC.

8. Prien, R.F. (1980). Problems and practices in geriatric psychopharmacology. *Psychosomatics,* 21:213-223.

9. Ray, W.A., Federspiel, C.F., Schaffner, W. (1980). A study of antipsychotic drug use in nursing homes: Epidemiological evidence suggesting misuse. *American Journal of Public Health,* 70:485-491.

10. Swearer, J.M., Drachman, D.A., O'Donnell, B.F., Mitchell, A.L. (1988). Troublesome and disruptive behaviors in dementia: Relationships to diagnosis and disease severity. *J. Am. Geriatr. Soc.,* 36:784-790.

11. Katz, I.R., Lesher, E., Kleban, M, Jethanandani, V., Parmelee, P. (1989). Clinical features of depression in the nursing home. *International Psychogeriatrics,* 1:5-15.

12. American Psychiatric Association. (1987). *Diagnostic and statistical manual of mental disorders* (3rd Ed., revised). Washington, DC: American Psychiatric Association.

13. Lawton, M. P., (1983). Environment and other determinants of well-being in older people. Robert W. Kleemeier Memorial Lecture. *Gerontologist,* 23:349-357.

14. Edelson, J.S., Lyons, W. (1985). *Institutional care of the mentally impaired elderly.* New York: Van Nostrand Reinhold Company.

15. Borson, S., Liptzin, B., Nininger, J., Rabins, P. (1987). Psychiatry and the nursing home. *American Journal of Psychiatry,* 144:1412-1418.

16. Baum, D.J. (1987). *Warehouses for death: The nursing home industry.* Don Mills, ON: Burns and MacEachern.

17. Birkett, D.P. (1988). The life-threatened patient in the long-term care facility. In Klagsbrun, S.C., Goldberg, I.K., Rawnsley, M.M., Kutscher, A.H., Marcus, E.R., Siegel, A. (Eds). *Psychiatric aspects of terminal illness.* Philadelphia: The Charles Press.

18. Yesavage, J.A., Brink T.L., Rose, T.L., Lum, D., Huang, V., Adey, M., Leirer, V.O. (1983). Development and validation of a geriatric depression screening scale: A preliminary report. *Journal of Psychiatric Res,* 17:37-49.

19. Folstein, M.F., Folstein, S.E., McHugh, P.R. (1975). "Mini-Mental State:" A practical method for grading the cognitive state of patients for the clinician. *Journal of Psychiatric Res*, 12:189-198.
20. Strahan, G. (1985). *Nursing home characteristics: Preliminary data from the 1985 National Nursing Home Survey.* Advance data 131. Hyattsville, MD: National Center for Health Statistics.
21. Bryant, E., Taube, C. (1966). *Utilization of institutions for the aged and chronically ill. United States: April-June 1963.* Hyattsville, MD: National Center for Health Statistics.
22. U.S. Department of Commerce: Bureau of the Census. (1989). *Population profile of the United States.* Series P-23. No. 159. Washington, DC: U.S. Government Printing Office.
23. U.S. Department of Commerce: Bureau of the Census. (1983). *America in Transition: An aging society.* Series P-23. No. 128. Washington, DC: U.S. Government Printing Office.
24. Brody, J.A., Foley, D.J. (1985). Epdemiologic considerations. In: E.L. Schneider, et al., (Eds.). *The teaching nursing home.* New York: Raven Press.

SUGGESTED READING

1. Borson, S., Liptzin, B., Nininger, J., Rabins, P. (1987). Psychiatry and the Nursing Home. *American Journal of Psychiatry*, 144:1412-1418.

    A well written overview of the important psychiatric issues in the nursing home setting.

2. Schneider, E.L., Wendland, C.J., Zimmer, A.W., List, N., Ory, M., (Eds.) (1985). *The teaching nursing home: A new approach to geriatric research, education, and clinical care.* New York: Raven Press.

    An excellent multiauthored text on care, education, and research in the nursing home.

CHAPTER

The Mental Status Examination

2

by Barbara Schogt and Dmytro Rewilak

The Mental Status Examination (MSE) provides an organized approach to observing and describing important aspects of an individual's mental functioning. It is based on observations that are made at a particular point in time regarding the individual's appearance, behavior, feeling, and thinking.

Skilled professionals make numerous observations about the residents with whom they work. Whether contact with a resident is a casual greeting in the hall or a more formal work-related interaction, the opportunity to make observations is always present. Based on their training, experience, and prior knowledge of the resident, staff interpret these observations to assess changes in the resident, to guide further information gathering, and to make management decisions. Mental status data are most helpful when they are placed within the context of other available clinical information,including the individual's sociocultural background, medical history, and current physical and laboratory status. A comprehensive understanding of the resident both guides interviewers and observers as they perform the MSE and provides a background against which to interpret observations.

It is important to adopt an organized approach to making and recording these naturally occurring observations for the following reasons:

The MSE guides and sharpens observational skills. By following a mental checklist of areas that need to be assessed, the observer becomes more attentive and is less likely to omit important areas in gathering information. There is also less likelihood of confusing the process of observing and recording data with the process of interpreting and analyzing these data. For example, to observe that, "Mrs P seems a bit off today," is to give a general impression that something may be wrong with her. Much more information is made available, however, if the observer identifies what it was about Mrs P that made him or her say that she seemed "off." The observer may have noticed a change in Mrs P's appearance, such as a deterioration in her usually meticulous grooming, or a change in her behavior such as increased irritability. Mrs P may have expressed uncharacteristically gloomy feelings or shown evidence of rambling speech and disorganized thinking. Each of these observations suggests different possibilities, resulting in different courses of action to investigate further why Mrs P is "a bit off."

The MSE facilitates communication of information. The use of a standard approach to assessing residents and recording observations has several practical consequences:

- It is easier for members of the staff to understand and build on the observations made by others.
- It is easier to identify changes in a resident's condition over time.
- The observations provide a basis for making comparisons between residents or groups of residents.
- An accurate record is established that, apart from its clinical value, may be useful for research and/or administrative purposes.

This chapter describes the components of the MSE (see Table 1). Concepts relating to mental functioning are defined and case examples are used to illustrate important points. Our goal is to provide the professional working within a long-term care setting with the information necessary to perform and record an accurate and clinically useful MSE. The chapter also includes a brief discussion of standardized assessment instruments and their role in a clinical setting. Two case examples of complete MSE's are presented at the end of the chapter.

| **Table 1** |
| Components of the MSE |

- Behavioral observations
- Mood and affect
- Thought
- Perception
- Cognition

GENERAL CONSIDERATIONS

Before proceeding with a detailed description of each component of the MSE, a few general questions should be addressed.

When and How Should Information Be Gathered?

As noted above, every contact with a resident provides an opportunity for information gathering. Much of the mental status data can be gathered unobtrusively, in a nonthreatening manner. Sometimes, however, questions have to be posed that are more difficult to weave into the course of a routine interaction. Posing such questions can be associated with considerable discomfort for caregivers, and residents may perceive the inquiries as jarring, intrusive, and threatening to their self-esteem. Prior contact and especially the presence of a good rapport with the resident can facilitate the gathering of this information. Even when assessing someone for the first time, however, the examiner can introduce potentially threatening material without disturbing the flow of the interaction. Examples will be given later in the chapter.

The organization shown in Table 1 is the one used when recording a MSE and is useful to keep in mind as a mental checklist when assessing residents, but the information may be gathered in any order. This flexibility helps reduce the anxiety sometimes associated with the MSE, both for staff and residents.

How Comprehensive Should the MSE Be?

The MSE ranges from a cursory 5-minute survey of cognitive functioning to a detailed evaluation that is administered by a psychologist and requires several hours. The amount of detail required depends on the purpose for which the information is to be used. For example, assessing a resident's cognitive potential for rehabilitation following a stroke is a much more complex task than establishing that an individual has become disoriented following an increase in medication.

The comprehensiveness of the MSE also depends on what the resident can tolerate. A formal MSE, especially the evaluation of cognitive (intellectual) functions, requires that the resident be able to participate in an interview situation. In the case of a highly agitated individual, questions may have to be kept to a minimum or avoided altogether, as the information necessary to manage the situation can be gathered on the basis of observation alone.

How Should Information Be Recorded in the Chart?

The chart is used by staff as a source of information and a vehicle for communication. It is also a legal document. Mental status information is most informative when it is recorded in the form of descriptions, using quotations in the resident's own words, rather than as interpretations by the observer. For example, co-workers learn more from an entry in the chart that states, "Mrs T was afraid that her coffee had been tampered with, but she ate her sandwich and took her medication" than from the entry, "Mrs T is paranoid." Judgmental, pejorative, and critical comments are inappropriate and have no place on the chart, but sensitive information must be recorded, especially if not having a record of the information places others at risk. To write that, "Mr G behaved in his usual rude and offensive manner," is both inappropriate and uninformative. However, recording that, "Mr G grabbed me by the arm, tried to kiss me as I bent over to give him his medication, and used sexually explicit language," provides important clinical information to other caregivers.

COMPONENTS OF THE MSE

Behavioral Observations

The MSE is usually introduced with a general description of the resident. This includes observations about the individual's appearance, verbal and non-verbal behavior, and attitude.

Appearance

When observing and describing appearance, attention to detail and the liberal use of adjectives allows the observer to paint a picture of an individual that brings that individual to life in the minds of others. Visual cues play a major part in the initial impression we form of others. The person's general appearance (e.g., height, weight, complexion, state of health) and details of self-care (e.g., grooming, make-up, clothing) are involved in creating this impression. Especially in long-term care settings, where changes in residents are so gradual as to be almost imperceptible, a glance back in the chart to a description recorded several years earlier provides useful clinical information.

Behavior

An accurate description of non-verbal behavior is particularly relevant in working with the elderly. The overall level of activity can range from agitation, restlessness and pacing to a slowing, where movements are hesitant, delayed, or almost absent. Gait, a crucial variable in determining the level of independence, also deserves comment and may be described, for example, as unsteady, stiff or shuffling. Abnormal postures and movements, such as various tremors and facial movements, are frequently seen in this population.

Speech

Difficulties in communication that may affect other sections of the MSE are noted here. These can include language barriers in non-native speakers, hearing impairment, and speech that is unintelligible because it is too soft, hoarse, or poorly articulated.

Attitude

Included in the general description is an impression of the way in which the resident relates to the observer. The resident's attitude may be friendly, suspicious, demanding, hostile, overly familiar, inattentive, or withdrawn. It must be kept in mind that many variables affect the resident's attitude, including characteristics of the caregiver, and the circumstances of the interaction. All caregivers, for example, have their bad days when they may be too tired, busy or preoccupied to respond to those around them in their usual manner. Residents will pick up these fluctuations in staff and their own responses will be affected accordingly.

Some residents seem to create an atmosphere of chaos around them. Staff working with a resident like this may find themselves developing strong views that contradict those of coworkers and result in major conflicts centred around the resident. Intense feelings of anger and helplessness are evoked in caregivers. This problem is discussed in detail in Chapter 8, "The Resident with Personality Disorder." For the purpose of the MSE, it is important for observers to learn to monitor their subjective responses to residents and use these reactions as a valuable source of data.

Mood and Affect

An individual's dominant feeling state over a period of hours, days, or even weeks is called mood. Affects are the various emotions displayed by the individual in the course of an interaction. Miss J may have an overall mood of depression but display anxiety, fear, and irritability as well as sadness during a particular interview. These affects may be conveyed through tone of voice, gesture, facial expression, physiological reactions to emotion, such as crying or flushing, and content of speech.

Affects can be classified not just according to type, but also according to quality. Emotions may be experienced intensely or be shallow and less deeply felt. Lability of affect refers to rapidly fluctuating emotional states. Subjective feelings can be elicited by asking questions such as, "How would you describe your feelings?" It is also important, however, to watch for nonverbal emotional behaviors such as facial expressions and postures that may be at odds with what the individual is saying about his or her feelings. When Mr M whispers with tears in his eyes that everything is fine or Mrs E mutters through clenched teeth that she is not at all angry, their words clearly are not the whole story.

The question of suicidal ideation must be addressed whenever the interviewer has even the slightest concern in this area. Not just depressed individuals, but also those who are frightened, anxious or apparently resigned to their fate may be suicidal. Many clues, other than those available through the mental status, can alert staff to the risk of self-harm or suicide. These are discussed in Chapter 6, "The Suicidal Resident."

Asking people whether they are suicidal can be uncomfortable. Society has traditionally regarded the taking of one's own life as taboo and in contravention of religious and natural laws. Suicide is associated with fear and shame. Moreover, some caregivers believe that by enquiring into suicidal ideation they can drive residents to commit suicide because they are giving the residents ideas they never had in the first place. This belief is not borne out through clinical experience. The majority of individuals who have suicidal thoughts welcome the opportunity to share their frightening, isolating feelings with others. People who are not suicidal will say so and are rarely resentful or threatened by having been asked. When inquiring into suicidal ideation, the topic may be approached gradually, beginning with such questions as, "Have you ever felt your life was not worth living?," moving to, "Have you ever felt so low that you wanted to end your life?," and finally posing more direct questions, "Do you have any thoughts of killing yourself?" If suicidal thoughts are present, the resident should then be asked whether the thoughts are accompanied by a wish or intent to die, whether any suicide plans have been made, and, if so, whether the means are available to put the plan into action.

Encountered less frequently than suicidal ideation are thoughts of harming others. If there is any suspicion that such thoughts or plans may exist, however, the question must be explored in the same way as that of suicidal ideation.

An inquiry into the somatic functions that are often disturbed in mood disorders is sometimes included in this section of the MSE. These include changes in sleep, appetite, weight and libido (sex drive). Clearly, in an ill, elderly population, any findings in this area will be confounded by the many disorders other than depression that can interfere with these functions. This point is dealt with in Chapter 5, "Depression and Other Mood Disorders".

Thought

In assessing the individual's thinking, attention is focused on two main areas. These are the individual's thought process (how the individual thinks) and thought content (what the individual thinks).

Thought process

Access to what others are thinking comes primarily through their speech. Abnormalities in thought process are reflected in disturbances in the rate, quantity, and form of speech. Excessively rapid or slowed speech, lack of spontaneous speech, and speech limited to one word answers are examples of disturbed thought process. Circumstantial speech refers to a pattern of responding to questions in an overinclusive manner. A tangential response is one in which the original question is never answered and the individual, through a series of associations, ends up talking about an unrelated topic. Thinking may be disorganized to an even greater degree, resulting in a complete loss of logical connections between ideas. Individuals may jump from topic to topic without following any apparent pattern or connect words through rhyming. In its most extreme form, disorganized thinking results in speech that consists of a series of apparently random words. Because abnormal thought process can result in speech that sounds bizarre, it can be extraordinarily difficult for the listener to quote, even minutes after hearing it. It is useful to jot down an example immediately so that the quote can be recalled for later charting. Disorders in thought process occur in illnesses such as schizophrenia and mania. They must be distinguished from the disturbed communication resulting from brain lesions such as strokes and tumors.

Thought content

The content of thought can be disturbed in a variety of ways. Individuals can become preoccupied with a particular idea or subject. Obsessions (repetitive unwanted thoughts) and phobias (irrational fears), although recognized by their sufferers as being illogical, exert considerable control over mental life and behavior. Miss L, for example, experiences a compulsion (an uncontrollable impulse) to wash her hands, because she cannot rid herself of the obsessional idea that, as soon as she touches something, she is contaminated. Even though she knows it makes no sense, Miss L scrubs her hands to the point where they bleed and she experiences great anxiety whenever she cannot get to a sink. Mrs R, who has had a lifelong fear of heights and elevators, has had to settle for a less favourable room on the ground floor so that she can walk to the dining room and participate in activities without having to confront her fear.

Delusions

Another example of disturbed thought content are false beliefs that the individual does not recognize as irrational. These are called delusions. The ideas are so fixed, that the person cannot be talked out of them even when presented with logical evidence that refutes the ideas. Delusions may be disorganized and fleeting or highly structured and held for many years. There may be a single delusional belief such as the idea that a spouse is having affairs. In other cases an elaborate system of beliefs is created to encompass the individual's entire world, with new information constantly being incorporated into the delusional belief system. For example, Mrs O says, "There is a conspiracy to take control of this building. The telephones are bugged, they are listening through the vents, and now they have bribed the cleaning staff. I know that, because for the last three days they have started cleaning at the other end of the hall and they never used to do that."

The presence of a delusion is indicative of psychosis (loss of touch with reality). Other manifestations of psychosis include the disorders of thought form described above and perceptual disturbances (see below). Psychotic symptoms can occur in many different disorders, including delirium, dementia, schizophrenia, and mood disorders.

Asking residents whether they have delusions can feel awkward. The interviewer may feel threatened by exploring a realm of ideas that in layman's terms would be called "crazy." Many psychotic individuals reveal their delusional beliefs spontaneously or behave in a manner that clearly suggests that they are out of touch with reality. In other cases, however, the delusions begin to emerge only after careful questioning by the interviewer. Examples of questions eliciting information about delusions include, "Do you have any ideas that might seem unusual to others?," "Have you ever thought people might be trying to harm you in some way?," and "Have you ever thought that you were special and in some way different from other people?"

Some psychotic people are uncomfortable discussing their delusions. In these cases, the interviewer may still suspect that an individual has delusions although the delusions have not been identified.

When deciding whether a belief meets the criteria for a delusion, the observer must remember that certain religious and cultural ideas held by large groups of people are considered irrational in other societies. For example when Mrs G accuses Mrs O of having caused her fall by placing "the evil eye" on her, Mrs G's background must be considered before concluding that she is suffering from a persecutory delusion.

Perception

Perception is the complex process of obtaining information about the world. It begins with sensations, but involves many other variables as well. For example, a child sees that he has cut himself but is not aware of any pain until he sees blood and hears his parent's concerned response. Information received by the child through his visual, tactile, and auditory senses is interpreted at a higher level to form the perception of a cut that hurts. The perceptual process may be distorted in a number of different ways.

Illusions

These are formed when a real stimulus is misinterpreted. For example, Mr F, who is hard of hearing, has the repeated experience of hearing his name mentioned, as he walks by groups of people engaged in conversation. Miss G, who is suffering from toxic levels of medication, misinterprets the image of the duvet flung over the chair as a man sitting in her room. Sensory deficits as well as higher level cognitive difficulties increase the risk of developing illusions.

Hallucinations

These are perceptions that occur in the absence of any appropriate external stimulus. They may involve any sensory modality. Mrs C may hear voices accusing her of being an unworthy person, Mr R sees little people running through his room, and Mrs D smells a horrible odor emanating from the vents.

Illusions and hallucinations vary not just in their content and in the sensory modality involved, but also in how they are understood by their sufferers. At times, individuals recognize that their perceptions are distorted but are frightened nevertheless. At other times, individuals develop delusional interpretations of the abnormal perceptions. Mrs D for example, may interpret the horrible odor as evidence of a plot to poison her or drive her out of the institution.

Information regarding abnormal perceptual experiences is elicited with questions like, "Have you ever had an unusual experience such as hearing voices when nobody was there, or seeing something that nobody else could see?" When abnormal perceptions occur is important since hallucinations can occur in the absence of any neurological or psychiatric disturbance. It is not unusual for people to experience abnormal perceptions as they are falling asleep or waking up. Hallucinations occurring at other times usually suggest the presence of a mental disorder.

Cognition

Cognition refers to the mental processes involved in the acquisition, processing, and utilization of knowledge or information. The assessment of cognitive functions is an important component of the MSE. These functions are listed in Table 2.

Table 2 Cognitive Functions
• Attention and concentration • Language • Memory • Abstraction • Constructional ability • Praxis • Insight and judgement

General comments

As noted earlier in the chapter, the comprehensiveness of the cognitive assessment depends on the purpose for which the information is being gathered and the resident's ability to tolerate the assessment. Being confronted with evidence of cognitive impairment can be painful both for the impaired resident and for staff who have worked closely with the resident on a daily basis, sometimes for many years. Because of this, there may be a tendency to gloss over or even omit this part of the MSE in order to protect everyone involved. When residents respond to the cognitive assessment with outrage that someone would dare to ask them "silly questions" or try to dodge questions by joking or by distracting the interviewer, this is often an indication that there are problems in the area of cognition that need to be pursued if at all possible.

Care should be taken in every case to prepare residents for this part of the assessment. If this is not done residents become understandably upset when someone begins asking them, apparently out of the blue, if they know where they are and whether they can do some arithmetic. The following example illustrates one way of introducing the cognitive assessment in a non-threatening manner:

INTERVIEWER: Mrs A, you mentioned earlier that you have noticed some difficulty in remembering names.

MRS A: That's right. It's so annoying. They come back to me eventually but at the time I feel so silly.

INTERVIEWER: Have you noticed any other problems with your memory or thinking?

MRS A: Well, not really...but I do worry about it sometimes.

INTERVIEWER: Maybe we can look into this problem a bit further. I'd like to ask you a few questions now to check your memory and your thinking....

Occasionally, even when a careful approach has been taken, an impaired resident will become anxious and distressed when faced with a task he or she cannot do. This kind of response is referred to as a catastrophic reaction, and requires that the resident be reassured and the cognitive assessment be postponed to a more appropriate time.

A number of factors affect performance on the cognitive assessment. Some of these include intelligence, level of education, cultural considerations, sensory deficits, fatigue, pain, anxiety, poor motivation, an altered level of consciousness, and a noisy or otherwise distracting environment. These factors should be considered both in the administration of the cognitive assessment and in the interpretation of its results.

Impairment in one area of cognition affects the efficiency of other cognitive processes. This interdependancy of cognitive abilities needs to be borne in mind when administering and interpreting test data. If, for example, an individual cannot attend to what is being said because of pain, or is unable to comprehend spoken language as a result of a stroke, it will not be possible to assess that person's memory accurately, since memory tests require a capacity for sustained attention and intact language capabilities.

Attention and concentration

Attention is the foundation of cognition. It usually is tested early in the course of the assessment since impairments in this area will result in problems throughout the cognitive assessment. These problems may be attributed mistakenly to other impairments if the attentional deficit has not been identified.

Attention may be disturbed as a result of a decreased level of consciousness. A note is made, therefore, whether the individual is alert or drowsy.

Excessive distractibility is another form of attentional disturbance, reflecting limitations in the individual's span of attention. This aspect of attention is tested through digit recall. The interviewer recites a series of random numbers at a rate of one digit per second and asks the resident to repeat the series back to him. The length of the series is increased each time the resident gives a correct response. Different numbers are used on every trial. The task can be made more demanding by asking the resident to repeat the series backwards. Now, the individual not only has to keep the series of digits in mind, but he also has to mentally juggle the digits around. Normal individuals are able to repeat five digits forwards and four backwards.

A measure of concentration is the subtraction of serial sevens. The individual is asked to subtract seven from 100, then keep subtracting seven from each succeeding answer.

Language

Language functions are also tested early in the cognitive assessment. Aphasic disturbances, disorders of language comprehension and/or expression, are distinguished from dysarthrias, problems with the mechanical articulation of speech (e.g., slurring).

Throughout the assessment, the interviewer makes note of the individual's spontaneous speech. Problems in spontaneous speech include word-finding difficulties, circumlocutions, word substitutions, and impaired fluency.

Testing of repetition involves asking the individual to repeat single words, phrases, and sentences of increasing complexity. Individuals with language difficulties may omit words and alter word sequences. Individuals with dysarthria slur and stumble over words.

Screening for possible comprehension deficits requires the resident to respond to a series of "Yes-No" questions (e.g., "Does a bird fly?") and commands of increasing complexity such as, "Point to the door," and, "Close your eyes and open your mouth." To test for higher order deficits, the resident can be given a construction such as, "If the lion and the tiger have a fight and the tiger kills the lion," then asked the question, "Who is killed?"

Difficulties in naming are identified by asking residents to name objects that are pointed out to them. Failure to recall high frequency words such as chair and pencil indicates a greater degree of impairment than difficulty with low frequency words such as shoelace and key-chain. It is useful to test naming in different linguistic categories (e.g., colors, actions, letter).

Aspects of oral and written language are tested by asking residents to read aloud, explain the content of what they have read, copy sentences and write spontaneously.

Memory

Memory is classified into three types: immediate, recent, and remote. Immediate memory, referred to as short-term memory by psychologists, is the process of holding events, objects, or ideas in immediate awareness without necessarily committing them to memory. A good example of immediate memory is the operation of locating a phone number in the directory, keeping it in mind and dialling it without retaining it. Clinically, it can be examined through recall of digits which has already been described in the section on attention.

Recent memory is the ability to learn new information. Orientation to place and time requires registration and retention of new information on an ongoing basis and depends on the intactness of recent memory. Residents are asked to give their exact location, the day of the week, date, month and year. While incorrect responses may suggest an impaired ability to learn new information, they could reflect the resident's restricted contact with the outside world. A simple test of recent memory involves presenting the individiual with three or four unrelated words or objects until he has learned them and asking him to recall them after a five and 20 minute delay. If the individual has difficulty recalling the items spontaneously, providing him with cues (e.g., "The third one was a vegtable.") might assist his recall. If he benefits from cueing, this might suggest problems retrieving rather than storing new information.

Remote memory involves the recall of information that has been known for a long time. It can be tested by questions about birthdays, names of family members, famous political figures and actors, and important historical events. General knowledge questions are sometimes asked, but it is important to bear in mind that the resident's background and education will influence responses.

Abstraction

The ability to think at an abstract level is a good indicator of overall intellectual functioning. Residents are asked to give similarities between two items (e.g., an apple and an orange, or a statue and a poem), or to interpret proverbs. Like general knowledge, interpretation of similarities and proverbs is influenced by the individuals educational and cultural background.

Constructional ability

Copying a two- or three-dimensional figure, such as two intersecting pentagons or a cube, requires the ability to perceive the visual stimulus, plan the drawing, and then execute it. Residents who have problems with this task may show other manifestations of impaired visuospatial functioning, such as difficulty finding their way around the institution.

Clock drawing is a frequently used measure of constructional ability. The resident is asked to draw a clock, place all the numbers in their correct position, and set the hands for 10 minutes after 11. Should the resident have difficulty spontaneously drawing the clock, he is presented with a predrawn circle and then asked to put in the numbers and set the time. Clock-drawing is sensitive in picking up a number of abnormalities (e.g., constructional deficits, spatial neglect, planning difficulties) that are differentially related to different neurological conditions.

Praxis

Praxis is the ability to perform voluntary purposeful movements. The inability to do so, in the absence of any sensory, motor, or comprehension deficits, is called an apraxia. The resident may be able to perform an activity automatically (e.g., blowing out a match), but begins to experience difficulty when he tries to place the movement under conscious control. In the typical examination for disorders of praxis, the resident is asked to make symbolic movements (e.g., blow a kiss), use actual objects, and pantomime the use of objects without the real object (e.g., using a comb) both to imitation and to command.

Insight and judgement

Insight involves the capacity to understand a situation, and judgement is used in planning a response. One way of assessing these abilities is by asking residents how they understand relevant aspects of their situation (e.g., their institutionalization or an illness) and how they plan to respond, based on that understanding.

THE ROLE OF STANDARDIZED ASSESSMENT INSTRUMENTS IN THE MSE

Many questionnaires, scales, and tests have been developed to assess different areas of mental status functioning. As long as these are not used as the sole basis for making diagnostic and management decisions, they can enrich the clinical assessment by providing additional and corroborating information. A number of cautionary statements need to be made, however, regarding their use in clinical settings.

Assessment instruments are best used as an adjunct to, and not a replacement for, the clinical assessment. When used, care should be taken that the instrument was developed for clinical as opposed to research or epidemiological purposes, that it is reliable, and that standards are available for the population to which it is being applied. The application in the elderly of depression instruments, such as the Hamilton Depression Rating Scale [1] and the Beck Depression Scale [2], has been criticized; some of the symptoms used as evidence of depression in a younger population, such as loss of appetite and sleep disturbance, are common in the elderly for reasons other than depression. The Geriatric Depression Scale [3] is a scale that has been developed specifically for the rating of depression in the elderly. It focuses on the cognitive and affective features of depression and consists of 30 yes/no items. Higher scores are associated with more severe levels of depression. The scale is listed in the Appendix to this chapter.

The Mini-Mental State Examination (MMSE) [4] is a widely used and practical tool that screens for cognitive impairment and takes 5 to 10 minutes to administer. The maximum score that can be obtained is 30, and scores of less than 21 are highly correlated with the presence of cognitive impairment. This score, however, must be interpreted in light of the individual's cultural and educational background. The MMSE is included in the Appendix to this chapter.

CASE ILLUSTRATIONS

Case 1

Mr G was lying on his bed. His sparse gray hair was un-combed, he was not wearing his dentures, and his stained pyjama top was half undone. He looked pale and sweaty. He was short of breath and rolled his head from side to side moaning. When first addressed, he appeared startled and suspicious, his eyes darting from one interviewer to the other. After the purpose of the meeting was explained, he became calmer but continued to startle easily and was constantly distracted by noises in the hall.

He appeared anxious and fearful. He was not feeling suicidal. Mr G's thinking was rambling and difficult to follow. He seemed to be preoccupied with the idea that bad people were coming to take him away and kill him, although it was not clear who these people were or where they would take him. He did not express any other delusional ideas. When he heard the medication cart rolling down the hall, he said "It's them! They're coming! I know it!," but he was reassured when told that it was only the medication cart. There was no evidence that he was suffering from hallucinations.

Mr G was disoriented to time, thinking it was shortly after breakfast when it was eleven o'clock at night. He identified the year as 1947 and could not tell the examiner where he was. He was unable to perform serial sevens, but was able to list the days of the week backwards until Friday at which point he was distracted by a car honking outside. Given his impaired concentration and agitated state, further cognitive testing was not attempted.

Comment

On the basis of the MSE and data from his history, physical exam and laboratory status, Mr G was diagnosed as having a delirium (see Chapter 4, Delirium) resulting from pneumonia. The mental status data would predict that he will become very frightened and possibly put up a struggle when the ambulance attendants arrive to transfer him to hospital, but that he may respond positively to reassurance and a calm explanation of what is happening.

Case 2

At the time of the examination, Miss J was sitting in her room, staring down at her hands. She was neatly dressed in a tweed skirt and silk blouse. Her slight, brittle-looking frame was dwarfed by the armchair in which she sat. She had little interst in her surroundings and avoided eye contact during the meeting, responding to questions with brief answers, speaking so softly that at times she was barely audible.

Miss J appeared deeply depressed. She became tearful when talking about her past life, especially her mother. She expressed feelings of hopelessness, worthlessness, and guilt. She wished her life were over and admitted to having thoughts about killing herself, but did not think she had the courage to act on her thoughts. Her appetite was poor, she had lost weight and was no longer sleeping well at night. There was no evidence of a thought or perceptual disorder.

Miss J participated reluctantly in the cognitive assessment, sighing frequently and complaining that she was too tired. She was oriented except to the exact date. She refused to continue subtracting serial sevens after two correct subtractions and recalled two out of three objects after 5 minutes. She copied two intersecting pentagons without difficulty, and wrote the sentence, "I am sad." Miss J felt she was beyond help, but did agree to participate in the treatment plan that was discussed with her.

Comment

The above is a description of a depressed individual (see Chapter 5). The treatment plan was based not only on the MSE, but also on information regarding previous episodes of depression, and the absence of abnormal findings on a recent physical examination.

KEY POINTS

- The purpose of the MSE is to observe and describe mental functioning.

- Most mental status data can be gathered unobtrusively during the course of routine interactions with the resident.

- Clinical judgement is used in determining how detailed the MSE should be. The decision is based on the purpose for which the information is being gathered, and what the resident can tolerate.

- When doing an MSE it is useful to refer back to a mental checklist of the major areas that need to be covered (see Tables 1 and 2).

REFERENCES

1. Hamilton, M. (1967). Development of a rating scale for primary depressive illness. *British Journal of Social and Clinical Psychiatry*, 6:278.
2. Beck, A.T., Ward, C.H., Mendelson, M., Mock, J., Erbaugh, J. (1961). An inventory for measuring depression. *Archives of General Psychiatry*, 4:53.
3. Yesavage, K., Brink, T.L., Rose, T.L., Lum, O., Huang, V., Adey, M., Leirer, O. (1983). Development and validation of a geriatric depression screening scale: A preliminary report. *Journal of Psychiatric Research*, 17:37.
4. Folstein, M.F., Folstein, S.W., McHugh, P.R. (1975). "Minimental state." A practical method of grading the cognitive states of patients for the clinician. *Journal of Psychiatric Research*, 12:189.

SUGGESTED READING

1. Leon, R.L., Bowden, C.L., Faber, R.A. The Psychiatric Interview, History and Mental Status Examination. In M.J. Kaplan & B. J. Saddock (Eds.), *Comprehensive Textbook of Psychiatry*, Vol. 1, 5th Ed. pp. 449-461. Baltimore: Williams and Wilkins, 1989.

Provides an excellent overview of how to conduct a thorough mental status examination.

2. Strub, R.L., Black, F.W. *The Mental Status Examination in neurology*. Philadelphia: F.A. Davis, 1977.

Offers more comprehensive and detailed information on the assessment of cognitive abilities.

APPENDIX 1: THE MINI-MENTAL STATE EXAMINATION*

* Ref [4] Folstein, Folstein, McHugh, (1975).

Patient _____
Examiner_____
Date _____

Max.   Score
Score

Orientation

5   ( ) What is the (year) (season) (date) (month) (day)?
5   ( ) Where are we? (state) (country) (town) (hospital) (floor)

Registration

3   ( ) Name 3 objects: 1 second to say each.
       Then ask the patient all 3 after you have said them.
       Give 1 point for each correct answer.
       Then repeat them until he learns all 3.
       Count trials and record.
       Trials _____

Attention and Calculation

5   ( ) Serial 7's. 1 point for each correct. Stop after 5 answers. Alternatively, spell "world" backwards.

Recall

3   ( ) Ask for the 3 objects repeated above.
       Give 1 point for each correct answer.

APPENDIX 1 (Cont'd)

Language

9   ( )   Name a pencil, and watch. (2 points)
Repeat the following "No ifs, ands or buts." (1 point)
Follow a 3-stage command:
"Take a paper in your right hand, fold it in half, and put it on the floor." (3 points)
Read and obey the following:
Close your eyes (1 point)
Write a sentence (1 point)
Copy design (1 point)

Total score
ASSESS level of consciousness
along a continuum _____

            Alert   Drowsy   Stupor   Coma

INSTRUCTIONS FOR ADMINISTRATION OF THE MINI-MENTAL STATE EXAMINATION

Orientation

Ask for the date. Then ask specifically for parts omitted, e.g. "Can you also tell me what season it is?" One point for each correct.

Ask in turn "Can you tell me the name of this hospital?" (town, country, etc.). One point for each correct.

Registration

Ask the patient if you may test his memory. Then say the names of 3 unrelated objects, clearly and slowly, about one second for each. After you have said all 3, ask him to repeat them. The first repetition determines his score (0-3) but keep saying them until he can repeat all 3, up to 6 trials. If he does not eventually learn all 3, recall cannot be meaningfully tested.

INSTRUCTIONS FOR ADMINISTRATION OF THE MINI-MENTAL STATE EXAMINATION (Cont'd)

Attention and Calculation

Ask the patient to begin with 100 and count backwards by 7. Stop after 5 subtractions (93, 86, 79, 72, 65). Score the total number of correct answers.

If the patient cannot or will not perform this task, ask him to spell the word "world" backwards. The score is the number of letters in correct order. E.g., dlrow = 5, dlorw = 3.

Recall

Ask the patient if he can recall the 3 words you previously asked him to remember. Score 0-3.

Language

Naming: Show the patient a wrist watch and ask him what it is. Repeat for pencil. Score 0-2.

Repetition: Ask the patient to repeat the sentence after you. Allow only one trial. Score 0 or 1.

3-Stage Command: Give the patient a piece of plain blank paper and ask him to carry out the command. Score 1 point for each part correctly executed.

Reading: On a blank piece of paper print the sentence "Close your eyes" in letters large enough for the patient to see clearly. Ask him to read it and do what it says. Score 1 point only if he actually closes his eyes.

Writing: Give the patient a blank piece of paper and ask him to write a sentence for you. Do not dictate a sentence, as it is to be written spontaneously. It must contain a subject and verb and be sensible. Correct grammar and punctuation are not necessary.

Copying: On a clean piece of paper, draw intersecting pentagons, each side about 1 in., and ask him to copy them exactly as they are. All 10 angles must be present and the 2 pentagons must intersect to score 1 point. Tremor and rotations are noted.

Estimate the patient's level of sensorium along a continuum, from alert on the left to coma on the right.

APPENDIX 2: GERIATRIC DEPRESSION SCALE*
* Ref [3]Yesavage, Brink, Rose, et al., (1983).

Instructions

These questions are about your everyday mood, attitudes and feelings. I would like to know how you have been feeling over the past week, including today. As I read them to you, please answer "Yes" or "No."

1. Are you basically satisfied with your life? . . . . yes/*no*
2. Have your dropped many of your activities and interest? . . . . *yes*/no
3. Do you feel that your life is empty? . . . . *yes*/no
4. Do you often get bored? . . . . *yes*/no
5. Are you hopeful about the future? . . . . yes/*no*
6. Are you bothered by thoughts you can't get out of your head? . . . . *yes*/no
7. Are you in good spirits most of the time? . . . . yes/*no*
8. Are you afraid that something bad is going to happen to you? . . . . *yes*/no
9. Do you feel happy most of the time? . . . . yes/*no*
10. Do you often feel helpless? . . . . *yes*/no
11. Do you often get restless and fidgety? . . . . *yes*/no
12. Do you prefer to stay at home, rather than going out and doing new things? . . . . *yes*/no
13. Do you frequently worry about the future? . . . . *yes*/no
14. Do you feel you have more problems with memory than most? . . . . *yes*/no
15. Do you think it is wonderful to be alive now? . . . . . . yes/*no*
16. Do you often feel downhearted and blue? . . . . *yes*/no
17. Do you feel pretty worthless the way you are now? . . . . *yes*/no
18. Do you worry a lot about the past? . . . . *yes*/no
19. Do you find life very exciting? . . . . yes/*no*
20. Is it hard for you to get started on new projects? . . . . . . *yes*/no
21. Do you feel full of energy? . . . . yes/*no*
22. Do you feel that your situation is hopeless? . . . . *yes*/no
23. Do you think that most people are better off than you are? . . . . *yes*/no
24. Do you frequently get upset over little things? . . . . *yes*/no
25. Do you frequently feel like crying? . . . . *yes*/no
26. Do you have trouble concentrating? . . . . *yes*/no

27. Do you enjoy getting up in the morning? . . . . yes/*no*
28. Do you prefer to avoid social gatherings? . . . . *yes*/no
29. Is it easy for you to make decisions? . . . . yes/*no*
30. Is your mind as clear as it used to be? . . . . yes/*no*

N.B. Responses associated with depression are in bold italics.

Suggested Ratings: Normal: 0 -10
Mild depression: 11-20
Moderate to severe depression: 21-30

The instruments presented in Appendices 1 and 2 are reprinted with the permission of Pergamon Press, Oxford, UK from the *Journal of Psychiatric Research*.

CHAPTER

Dementia   3

---

by Nathan Herrmann

Residents with dementia demonstrate cognitive impairment that is
persistent, progressive, and affects the way in which they function.
Cognitive impairment refers to a loss of previous mental abilities and
can include problems with orientation, concentration, memory, language, calculation, insight, and judgement. Impairment of functioning
refers to a change in social or occupational functioning, or a reduced
ability to perform the activities of daily living including grooming,
dressing, feeding, and toiletting. Although dementias are best known
for the disturbance of memory, staff in long-term care are often more
concerned about the accompanying behavioral problems such as agitation, wandering, shouting, and suspiciousness.

Between 5% and 10% of people over age 65 and 20% of people
over 80 years of age will suffer from dementia. These figures, which
demonstrate how the risk of developing the illness increases with
advancing age, are likely to be underestimates. Studies have shown the
prevalence rates in nursing homes to be in excess of 50%, making
dementia the most common mental disorder affecting this population.

DIAGNOSIS

At the present time, the diagnosis of dementia is made clinically on the basis of the history and clinical examination. Many diagnostic classification systems exist, the most commonly used in North America being the Diagnostic and Statistical Manual of the American Psychiatric Association third revised edition (DSM-IIIR). The DSM-IIIR diagnostic criteria for dementia are listed in Table 1.

Table 1
Diagnostic Criteria for Dementia

A. Impairment of short- and long-term memory
B. At least one of the following:
    1. impairment of abstract thinking
    2. impaired judgement
    3. disorder of language (aphasia)
    4. inability to recognize and use common objects (agnosia and apraxia)
    5. inability to copy designs (constructional deficits)
    6. personality change
C. The disturbance in A and B significantly interferes with work or usual social activities or relationships with others.

Adapted from DSM-IIIR, American Psychiatric Association, 1987.

The presence of impaired memory is essential for a diagnosis of dementia. Short-term memory impairment refers to an inability to learn new information and can be tested by asking the person to recall 3 objects after 5 minutes. Long-term memory impairment is indicated if the person is unable to recall personal information or items of general knowledge that were known previously. The resident must also show other evidence of cognitive impairment such as impaired judgement, inability to think abstractly, speech and language difficulties, and the inability to recognize or correctly use common objects. The resident's personality may change (e.g., a previously quiet and withdrawn person may become outgoing and rude) or become accentuated (e.g., the somewhat suspicious resident may become completely paranoid). The diagnosis of dementia requires that these features significantly interfere with the resident's social activities, relationships with other people, or daily functioning.

Several short, simple, easily administered tests are available to screen for cognitive impairment. The Mini-Mental State Examination (MMSE, see Appendix 1, Chapter 2) is a reliable and valid measure of cognitive impairment that can be performed in 10 minutes by any staff member (see Chapter 2). Although screening exams like this help to identify cognitive impairment, the diagnosis of dementia should not be based on test scores alone, but also on the resident's history and functional status.

Alzheimer Disease

Approximately 50% of people with dementia have Alzheimer disease. This progressive illness usually begins in mid- to late life, and becomes increasingly common with aging. Some people die within one year of diagnosis, while others may survive for five to ten years. The disease progresses through a number of stages. Initially these residents may have trouble with short-term memory, forgetting appointments or misplacing belongings. They may experience difficulty with speech, frequently searching for the correct word, or have problems naming objects. In the early stages the residents may be aware of their difficulties, and begin to restrict their activities or become depressed. As the illness progresses, the memory problems become much more severe, while speech becomes more vague and less grammatically correct. Residents often lose track of time and become disoriented. Their ability to read, write, and calculate is impaired at this stage. They may lose the ability to use common objects or perform common tasks (referred to as "apraxia"). This often leads to further dependence on staff. Insight is usually lost at this stage, and residents may complain of their belongings being stolen, or of seeing intruders in their rooms. In the final stages of Alzheimer disease residents become almost totally dependent. They may be incontinent, bedridden, and totally unable to feed themselves. Speech, if present, is fragmented, garbled, and incomprehensible. Death usually results from the physical deterioration and infections such as pneumonia or a urinary tract infection that occur at this stage.

The diagnosis of Alzheimer disease is made on the basis of the criteria outlined previously, and only after other causes of dementia have been ruled out. There are no laboratory tests or x-ray methods that specifically identify this illness as a cause of dementia, and a definitive diagnosis can only be made at autopsy. Microscopic examination of the brain reveals several characteristic changes including neuronal loss, senile plaques, and neurofibrillary tangles. The brain is shrunken or "atrophied." Brain atrophy can be seen on computerized tomography

(CT) scans while the person is alive, but it is not specific for Alzheimer disease, and may occur in normal elderly.

The cause of Alzheimer disease is not known. There are families with many cases of the disease, suggesting that it may be an inherited illness. The finding that most people with Down syndrome eventually develop the characteristic pathology of Alzheimer disease has led to a genetic hypothesis. Some investigators have implicated environmental toxins such as aluminum, while others have proposed a viral etiology. At the present time there is no agreement about what causes Alzheimer disease.

Other Dementias

Although Alzheimer disease represents at least 50% of dementias, other causes need to be considered (Table 2). Dementia caused by repeated small strokes (referred to as multi-infarct dementia) and dementia secondary to chronic alcohol abuse are common causes. Many neurological illnesses such as Parkinson disease, Huntington disease, and multiple sclerosis are also associated with dementia.

Table 2
Causes of Dementia

- Alzheimer disease
- Multi-infarct dementia
- Alcoholic and other toxic dementias
- Pick disease
- Normal pressure hydrocephalus
- Dementias with metabolic disturbances:
  — Thyroid disease
  — Vitamin deficiency
- Dementia with other neurologic illness:
  — Parkinson disease
  — Huntington disease
  — Wilson disease
  — Multiple sclerosis
- Infectious dementias:
  — Syphilis
  — Jakob-Creutzfeldt disease
- Dementia from head trauma
- Dementia from brain tumors
- Dementia syndrome of depression

Some dementias are potentially reversible, including dementia secondary to vitamin B12 deficiency, thyroid disease, and chronic drug use (e.g., over-the-counter medications with antihistamines). Psychiatric disorders, most notably depression, can present with cognitive impairment and other manifestations of dementia. The dementia syndrome of depression, sometimes referred to as "pseudodementia," is reversible with adequate treatment for the depression (see Chapter 5).

BEHAVIORAL DISTURBANCES IN DEMENTIA

Behavioral disturbances in persons with dementia are common and are often the reason why families have decided on institutionalization. They are difficult for staff to deal with and frequently lead to psychiatric consultation. Table 3 provides a list of some of the typical behavioral disturbances associated with dementia.

| **Table 3** |
| Behavioral Disturbances in Dementia |

Agitation	Catastrophic reactions
Restlessness	Incontinence
Wandering	Phobias/fears
Mood disorder	Shouting/screaming
Delusions	Sleep disturbances
Misidentification syndromes	Sundowning
Hallucinations	Disinhibition
Rage and violence	Sexual behaviors
Compulsive/repetitive/bizarre behaviors	

Mood Disturbances

Depression in people with documented dementia has only recently been identified as a common treatable form of excess morbidity. The diagnosis is based on mood, changes in sleep and appetite, and changes in activity and energy. Because many of these signs and symptoms can occur in demented patients without depression, staff should be vigilant for recent changes in any of these areas that could signify the coexistence of these two disorders.

Displays of inappropriate affect are occasionally associated with dementia. Residents may show excessive tearfulness, laughter, or crying that is abruptly turned on and off, or affect that is incongruous with their underlying mood. These behaviors, referred to as "emotional incontinence," "pathological laughter/crying," or "pseudobulbar affect," are sometimes associated with depression, but can also occur as a direct result of injury to the brain (e.g., stroke). Residents with this type of inappropriate affect may not have any of the other signs and symptoms of a depressive illness.

Psychomotor Disturbances

Changes in the activity levels of demented residents are common and bothersome. Some residents become withdrawn, slowed down, and want to spend the day lying in bed or sitting in a chair. At the other extreme are the agitated residents who wander and require constant redirection and attention from staff.

Agitation

Agitation can present in many ways ranging from direct expressions of anxiety, to repetitive shouting or screaming, to displays of aggression and rarely violence. Agitation can be triggered when residents experience frustrations and stresses which overwhelm them. Episodes of acute agitation are referred to as "catastrophic reactions," and occasionally lead to aggression. Seemingly minor events, such as being unable to string beads in an activity group or being bathed, may provoke aggressive, agitated reactions in residents who are unable to verbalize their frustrations.

Psychosis

Delusions and hallucinations frequently coexist and may occur in more than 25% of residents at some stage of the dementia. The delusions of dementia tend to be fleeting, poorly structured, and often involve themes of belongings being stolen, or of being the victims of persecution. The delusions, which are secondary to brain injury, can also be viewed as psychological defenses. The resident who cannot find his glasses may feel "better" believing they have been stolen, rather than admitting his memory is failing. When a resident believes she is the victim of persecution, the implication is that she must be an important person who inspires jealousy. Occasionally the delusions are more elaborate and involve the institution, staff members, or other residents.

Hallucinations are most commonly visual or auditory and may involve seeing people or animals, or hearing voices or noises. The hallucinations may or may not be frightening or disturbing to the resident.

Sexual Disturbances

While many residents with dementia lose interest in sex, some do not. The disinhibition and lack of social judgment that accompanies dementia may lead to masturbation and disrobing in public, or even solicitation of sex from staff or other residents.

MANAGEMENT

There are several general principles which can facilitate the management of residents with dementia.

Expectations and Goals

The primary goal in dealing with cognitively impaired individuals is to help them function at the highest level physically, emotionally, and intellectually, for as long as possible. This goal implies that the cognitive impairment and behavioral disturbances must be acknowledged by staff so that expectations are neither too high nor too low. The staff needs to recognize that disturbed behavior is a direct expression of the underlying brain disease; this prevents behavior from being interpreted as "manipulative" or "attention-seeking," and the resident from being labeled as a "bad" person. The resident's premorbid personality and functioning also need to be considered in order to establish reasonable and realistic expectations.

CASE ILLUSTRATIONS

Case 1

Mr A was a 72-year-old resident with a history of a stroke which affected the right side of his body and caused problems with his speech. He was reasonably self-sufficient in his daily activities, and even organized a weekly trip by taxi to a local pub. Mr A constantly argued with the nursing staff and his physician, demanding more of the medications which had been prescribed for him. On several occasions he had left the home to get prescriptions for these medications from unknowing physicians in the community. Staff had confronted him several times to explain the danger of taking too much medication, but the behavior persisted. Frustrated, the team and nursing home administration threatened him with discharge if he could not abide by the home's rules. He was referred for a psychiatric consultation that revealed significant cognitive impairment. His level of comprehension was poor, and his behavior was ritualistic and repetitive. He repeatedly stated that his doctors had told him the medications were essential for his health, which led him to erroneously conclude that "if some was good, more was better." With a better understanding of Mr A's impairment the staff redesigned a management plan which took his cognitive deficits into account and was successful in resolving the conflicts.

Comment

This case demonstrates how unrealistic expectations helped to pit the staff against the resident. Because Mr A appeared intact in many respects, the staff underestimated his cognitive impairment which was affecting his insight and judgement with respect to medication. They interpreted his behavior as manipulative, and responded by threatening him with discharge. Once his deficits were acknowledged, his behavior was reinterpreted as a manifestation of damage secondary to a stroke, and team members were then able to modify their expectations and communication patterns in a way that made effective intervention possible.

Communication

Because dementia can significantly affect the ability of residents to comprehend language and express themselves, a consideration of communication is essential. Staff should speak slowly, in short clear sentences, and be concrete, avoiding ambiguous messages. Questions should be structured in a way that limits choices and allows the resident to respond with "yes/no" answers. Non-verbal communication can be useful and may include gesturing, emotional inflection in the voice, and the use of touch. The resident should be allowed ample time to respond. A resident's inability to communicate is a source of frustration that can result in agitation and anxiety. Supportive comments, such as "This must be very frustrating for you...." often reduce agitation by validating the resident's distress.

Consistency and Structure

Residents with dementia have difficulty tolerating change and adapting to new situations. For the cognitively impaired elderly, the long-term care institution can provide consistent care within the context of a structured environment and a daily schedule. This combination is often sufficient for controlling agitation and other disorders of behavior.

Case 2

Mr B was an 86-year-old widower with Alzheimer disease who was admitted to hospital with pneumonia. He was agitated, often striking out at staff when they attempted to care for him. Although his pneumonia cleared quickly, his family decided to place him in a nursing home. While awaiting placement, he was moved several times within the hospital. On each occasion he became acutely agitated and would often require physical restraints and tranquilizers. Following transfer to the nursing home, he was a major management problem because of his verbal abuse, shouting, and aggressive behavior. A psychiatric consultation was requested which identified change of environment as the precipitant of his episodes of acute agitation. This predictable pattern was discussed with the staff who agreed to view the ensuing couple of weeks as a period of adjustment for Mr B. He was placed on a structured daily schedule, which involved care by a consistent primary nurse, and careful monitoring of his activities to avoid over-stimulation. A neuroleptic was prescribed as needed for episodes of severe agitation. Over the next month his behavior settled and he adapted well to the daily routine without the need for continued medication.

Comment

This case demonstrates how change of milieu acted as a precipitant for agitated behavior, while consistency and structure was used as an important therapeutic intervention to reduce Mr B's troublesome behavior.

Focus on Strengths and Abilities

In order to maximize functional capacity and independence, care
plans should be tailored to the residents' remaining strengths and
abilities, rather than focusing only on their disability. Tasks of daily
living can be broken down into steps that allow residents to perform the
components they are still able to do. For example, while some residents
may be unable to choose suitable clothing, they may be able to dress
themselves. Other residents may not be able to use a knife to cut food,
but may be able to use a spoon and a fork. Residents who have lost the
ability to speak coherently may still be able to sing well. Detailed
knowledge of the resident's premorbid personality, skills, and interests
enhances the effectiveness of this approach.

Case 3

*Miss C, a 72-year-old woman with a 3-year history of demen-
tia, was agitated, wandered most of the day, and slept poorly
at night. Knowledge that she had been a professional tennis
player and instructor for many years helped the team to devise
a schedule which included allowing her to hit a tennis ball
against a wall in a secluded courtyard for a period of time each
day. This activity helped to reduce her daytime agitation and
improve her sleep at night.*

Comment

This case demonstrates how knowledge of Miss C's premorbid
skills and interests was used to devise a personalized and
effective treatment intervention. This approach is not only
helpful for the resident, but also provides insight for staff into
the rich life and history of the cognitively impaired resident
they work with each day.

Other Treatment Considerations

The management of residents with dementia requires a consideration of their cognitive impairment, functional disability, and behavioral
disturbances. At the present time a diagnosis of dementia implies that
cognitive impairment is progressive and permanent. There are no

medications currently available which have proven ability to arrest or reverse the cognitive impairment to a useful degree. The best management for these problems are the general measures outlined above as well as careful monitoring for intercurrent medical and psychiatric illness. Even relatively minor illnesses such as respiratory or urinary tract infections may precipitate delirium and significantly impair a resident's functioning.

The management of behavioral disturbances always requires a multi-modal approach that includes environmental manipulations, behavioral or psychological interventions, and use of medications. Although psychoactive medications should not be regarded as the "treatment of last resort," their use requires careful consideration, as there is ample evidence of their overuse and abuse in long-term care settings. The elderly, and particularly those with underlying brain disease, have an increased sensitivity to the effects of these medications. Staff should constantly monitor their usefulness and be vigilant for adverse side-effects. Continuous reappraisal and regular attempts to withdraw these medications are indicated. Because dementia is a progressive illness and behaviors occurring at different stages of the illness may vary, all management strategies require constant reevaluation.

Case 4: Dementia, Agitation and Aggression

Mr D, an 80-year-old resident, had a 5-year history of progressive memory loss, disorientation, and speech difficulties. He could no longer recognize his wife, and referred to the staff as if they were his long-time business associates. Mr D was agitated and often struck out at nursing staff. He would walk into other residents' rooms and frighten them with his loud aggressive speech.

What kind of information would be useful in designing a care plan for this gentleman?

Mr D's wife indicated that prior to the onset of the dementia, he was an action-oriented person who was always busy. He controlled a leather-goods company and was a workaholic. He had a large circle of male friends and tended to have a low opinion of women. His only pastime was listening to classical music.

Based on this information, an appropriate care plan was devised. Whenever possible, male nurses and attendants were used. Exercise and walking were encouraged. In activity group, Mr D was given leather and tools for a simple crafts activity, meant to be reminiscent of his previous work. His wife brought in a tape recorder with a collection of his favorite symphonies. He was also encouraged to wear a small portable cassette tape-player with headphones during the day, as the sounds of classical music seemed effective in reducing his agitation.

Can the violent outbursts be controlled?

The staff were asked to observe all episodes of violence and record the precipitants, the nature of the act, and the consequences for the resident. It became apparent that the violence was limited to occasions when he was showered or bathed. Using a male attendant during these interactions helped reduce the agitation. At other times, when female nurses bathed him, the knowledge that this was a particularly difficult time for Mr D helped staff to anticipate the agitation and avoid injury.

Can anything else be done to control agitation?

There are residents with dementia whose agitation and aggressive outbursts remain a significant problem despite all interventions. In Mr D's case the behavioral strategies were supplemented by treatment with a neuroleptic. Because his agitation was worse during the day, a non-sedating neuroleptic, perphenazine, was chosen and started in low doses. After several months of treatment, the agitation improved and the neuroleptic was withdrawn.

Comment

This case demonstrates how the management of agitation and aggression involves multiple modalities including consistency, structure, knowledge of premorbid personality, behavioral interventions, and medications.

Case 5: Dementia and Wandering

Mrs E, an 84-year-old widow with multi-infarct dementia, had been a resident in the nursing home for over 2 years. From the time of admission she tended to wander around the floor in an aimless manner, often entering other residents' rooms and lying down on their beds.

What kind of care does the wandering resident require?

The primary consideration for a resident who wanders is to ensure their safety. Ideally, a resident like Mrs E, who is a known wanderer, should be on a floor which can be locked or monitored with an alarm system, and is designed to allow for wandering in a non-restrictive and obstruction-free manner. Where this type of structure is unavailable, other measures are required. The residents should wear brightly coloured, reflective identification shirts. Slippers and shoes should be checked on a regular basis to ensure stability. The resident may require constant supervision to avoid falls when walking on floors that are polished and wet. Doors to the nursing station and storage rooms should always be closed, as open doors are a magnet to the wanderer. Regularly scheduled, supervised walks should be part of their daily program.

Can anything be done to stop her from wandering into other residents' rooms?

A large brightly coloured disk was placed on Mrs E's door, and she was trained to direct her attention to it. Each time a staff member accompanied her to her room they pointed out the disk. When she was found in other residents' rooms the staff showed her that there was no disk on the door. After several weeks, this simple behavioral intervention reduced her tendency to wander into other rooms.

Can wandering ever become a serious problem?

Mrs E's wandering began to escalate again over a period of several months. She became increasingly agitated and anxious, and paced the halls in a frantic manner. The time spent wandering increased dramatically until she spent all her waking hours pacing. She appeared exhausted, dehydrated, and had lost 15 pounds in an 8-week interval.

What can be done to manage wandering when it becomes a threat to health?

Because Mrs E was only sleeping 2 to 3 hours a night, a minor tranquillizer was started. Oxazepam 15 mg was chosen because of its relatively short half-life. Although her sleep improved slightly, her wandering continued unchanged. She was drowsier during the day which led her to stumble several times. The Oxazepam was therefore discontinued and a neuroleptic, thioridazine, was started. Thioridazine was chosen because it has less potential to cause tremor and stiffness ("Parkinsonian-like" side-effects) than other neuroleptics. Her wandering continued unchanged, but her falls became more frequent as a result of drug-induced orthostatic hypotension. The neuroleptic was discontinued and an antidepressant was started. Trazadone was chosen because of its sedating effects and low incidence of side-effects. The wandering and agitation showed a gradual but significant reduction over a period of weeks, and she stopped losing weight.

Comment

This case demonstrates how pharmacological intervention is potentially problematic in residents such as Mrs E. Medications that were meant to decrease the wandering, all had serious side-effects which placed her at greater risk for falling. Because Mrs E's wandering had increased dramatically over a short period of time, it was considered a possible behavioral manifestation of depression, requiring treatment with an antidepressant. In general, pharmacological intervention should be avoided in wanderers. When indicated however, it should be initiated and monitored closely for side-effects.

Case 6: Dementia, Shouting, and "Sundowning"

Mrs F, an 87-year-old resident, had a long-standing history of memory loss and disorientation that led to placement in a nursing home. She required a lot of assistance with activities of daily living. Mrs F spent most of the day standing in front of the nursing station shouting, "Nurse, where am I?" She would become increasingly agitated at night and spent several hours screaming, "Help, Help!" after being put to bed. Her shouting disturbed the other residents and irritated the staff because of its repetitive nature.

What specific behavioral disturbances does this resident display?

There are many causes for shouting and screaming in dementia. Mrs F had a long history of being disoriented, and expressed her fear and frustration about not recognizing where she was by shouting. The repetitive nature of the shouting was interpreted as evidence of perseveration, the pathological repetition of speech or actions caused by damage to specific areas of the brain. Her shouting and agitation increased markedly at night, a behavioral phenomenon known as "sundowning." The decreased sensory stimulation (less lighting, noise, and activity) increased her disorientation in the evenings and resulted in an increase in her agitation as well.

How can shouting be managed?

The staff were reminded that Mrs F's shouting was perseverative and related to her underlying brain disease. It was not manipulative, and would therefore require some tolerance on the part of the staff. To manage her disorientation, a bulletin board was placed in her room with the date, the name of the nursing home, and her name in large letters. A bold-faced clock was placed in her room to orient her to the time of day. The staff also scheduled regular brief interactions with her each hour, aimed at reorientation and providing empathic support. When she would call out between these scheduled interactions she was reminded that a staff member would see her at "the regularly appointed time."

Are there any techniques to manage sundowning?

Mrs F's daytime schedule was modified to assist her to become more active and avoid afternoon naps. She was allowed to remain near the nursing station and encouraged to watch television or listen to the radio until it was time for sleep. A radio playing soft music was also placed in her room. These interventions reduced her repetitive verbalizations during the day, but she continued to shout immediately after being put to bed. A minor tranquillizer lorazepam 0.5 mg was given half an hour before bedtime and was effective in decreasing her shouting at night.

Comment

Shouting, like many disturbing behaviors in residents with
dementia can have different etiologies. Treatment planning
must therefore follow a detailed assessment of the likely causes
for a particular behavior. For Mrs F, shouting appeared to be
related to problems with orientation, so management was focused on techniques to help reorient her.

Case 7: Dementia, Depression, and Paranoia

*Mr G was a 76-year-old married gentleman with a long history
of numerous strokes and progressive intellectual decline. His
wife reluctantly placed him in a nursing home when he became
incontinent of urine. On admission he presented as a pleasant
somewhat withdrawn gentleman who tended to isolate himself
in his room. His speech was vague and fragmented. His wife
visited daily, and Mr G was always tearful after each visit. One
month after his admission his wife became ill and was hospitalized. Mr G became more withdrawn and spent more time in
bed. His appetite decreased and he lost weight. Occasionally
staff found him crying in his room, but, when questioned, he
denied crying or feeling depressed. He became more suspicious of the staff, and would barricade his door with furniture
at night.*

*Is this resident depressed, or is he just adjusting to his recent admis-
sion?*

On admission Mr G was noted to be somewhat withdrawn, but
he seemed to make a fair adjustment to the home. It is not
uncommon for residents with dementia to be tearful following
family visits, a pattern which may persist for many months after
admission.   His behavior changed dramatically, however,
when his wife's visits stopped. He was more tearful, had
decreased energy, was more withdrawn, and began to eat
poorly. All these features make the diagnosis of depression
likely. The denial of depression may have been related to his
difficulty understanding and expressing himself, a common
problem in diagnosing depression in residents with dementia.
For Mr G, the denial may also have been related to another

feature of his illness, the paranoia. Psychiatric consultation revealed that Mr G believed that he was in jail, and that his wife had been executed by the nursing home staff. He barricaded his room to protect himself from attack.

How are depression and paranoia managed in residents with dementia?

The management of psychiatric disturbances like depression should be based on the same principles as for cognitively intact individuals. Management begins with a recognition that residents with dementia are at least as likely to develop depression as cognitively intact residents. Although in Mr G's case there appeared to be an obvious precipitant (i.e., his wife's hospitalization) it was still important to review his medical status for other conditions that can precipitate depression (e.g., another small stroke).

Treatment for Mr G began with the prescription of an antidepressant and a neuroleptic. The neuroleptic was essential because the paranoia and fear were interfering with his care, making it impossible for the staff to intervene with psychological, social, or recreational therapies.

A family meeting was arranged, in which Mr G's children were asked to increase the frequency of their visits while their mother was in hospital. The staff attempted to get Mr G to speak to his wife on the telephone, but he refused insisting that it was just a trick to confuse him. After about 10 days on the neuroleptic he appeared less suspicious, and began to weep openly for his wife.

The staff met with him for regularly scheduled sessions during which they explained his wife was ill and in hospital. They continuously repeated empathic comments such as, "It must be very difficult for you to be here in the nursing home, while your wife is sick in hospital." The staff began to gradually integrate him into ward activities. Over the next four weeks, he became less tearful, less withdrawn, and started eating more. He no longer thought his wife had been killed, but stated that he thought she had died.

Comment

The management and outcome of this case demonstrate several important principles. Pharmacological intervention was an essential prerequisite for the implementation of other dimensions of the multimodal management approach. As soon as possible, family intervention was requested. Psychotherapeutic interventions were frequent but brief because of the resident's inability to tolerate lengthy interactions. Psychotherapy provided support and validated his feelings about his wife. He was gradually integrated into the ward activities.

The biopyschosocial approach to Mr G's problems was effective in treating his depressive symptomatology and reducing his fear and paranoia. Despite the improvement in his emotional state Mr G continued to believe incorrectly that his wife had died. This firmly held, fixed belief was less distressing to him than his earlier belief that she had been killed, but was still clearly delusional in nature. The underlying dementia may have contributed to the development of this psychotic symptom, and may help to explain why it persisted even after treatment.

"He's getting better. He can remember everything now except getting married."

HERMAN COPYRIGHT. 1978. (FIRST TREASURY). Jim Unger.
Reprinted with permission of Universal Press Syndicate.

KEY POINTS

- Dementia is the most common mental disorder affecting residents in long-term care.

- Residents with dementia will demonstrate cognitive impairment that significantly impairs their daily functioning and their relationships with other people.

- Residents with dementia show behavioral disturbances such as agitation, depression, delusions, hallucinations, wandering and aggression, that can significantly affect their care and their quality of life.

- Alzheimer disease is the most common cause of dementia, but there are other causes, some of which are potentially treatable.

- The general principles of management of residents with dementia include: a) setting realistic goals and expectations, b) providing consistent care within a highly structured environment, and c) constructing care plans that utilize a resident's remaining strengths and abilities.

- The management of specific behavioral disturbances must be comprehensive. Treatment considerations include environmental manipulations, behavioral or psychological interventions, and drug therapy.

- Residents with dementia have an increased susceptibility to side-effects from psychoactive drugs; drug therapy must be closely monitored and reevaluated at regular intervals.

SUGGESTED READING

1. Ropper, A.H. (1979). A rational approach to dementia. *Canadian Medical Association Journal*, 121:1175-1188.

This comprehensive article reviews the differential diagnosis of dementia and related laboratory investigations.

2. Hutner-Winograd, C., Jarvik, L.F. (1986). Physician management of the demented patient. *Journal of the American Geriatrics Society,* 34:295-308.

This excellent article reviews all aspects of management including diagnosis and assessment, environmental and behavioral techniques, and pharmacological interventions.

3. Burnside, I. (1988). Nursing care. In: L.F. Jarvik, C.H.Winograd, (Eds). *Treatments for the Alzheimer patient,* pp 39-58. New York, Springer.

The management of dementia is reviewed from a nursing perspective. The author discusses assessment of the patient, environmental aids, communication, and special care needs.

4. *The Journal of Clinical Psychiatry.* Volume 48, May 1987 Supplement.

This issue of the journal was dedicated to the behavioral and psychiatric disturbances associated with dementia, and their management.

CHAPTER

Delirium   4

by Barbara Schogt and David Myran

People suffering from an acute physical illness sometimes experience a mental disturbance characterized by a wandering of the mind. These people seem to be in a world of their own, often unable to tell whether it is night or day, what meal they have just had, and sometimes even where they are. Such people can be in a state of frenzied excitement, perhaps as a result of hallucinations, while several hours later they become withdrawn and stuporous. They may suddenly respond to familiar caregivers as if they are hostile strangers or misidentify strangers as long-lost relatives.

These symptoms are the result of an acute disturbance of brain function precipitated by a physical illness and they constitute the syndrome of delirium.

There are a number of reasons why it is important for those working in long-term care settings to be familiar with the identification and management of delirium:

Delirium Is Common

The elderly are more likely than younger people to have multiple illnesses and to be on many different medications. They are also more likely to be demented and to have limited cognitive reserves. These factors make them vulnerable to delirium.

Delirium Is Serious

Unrecognized and untreated, the underlying disease processes that give rise to delirium can lead to serious illness or even death. In the elderly, delirium may be the only evidence that a person has developed an acute medical problem. For example, all the usual signs and symptoms of myocardial infarction may be absent in an elderly person. However, a sudden change in the person's mental status (i.e., delirium) points to a need for medical investigation. In the course of that investigation the silent myocardial infarction may be identified.

Delirium Gives Rise to Behavior Problems

Delirium can be an extremely frightening experience for both residents and staff. Although delirious individuals may be withdrawn and drowsy to the point of stupor, they can become extremely agitated and sometimes violent. The behavior can pose a risk to staff, other residents, and to the delirious person himself.

Delirium Is Often Reversible

If properly identified and managed, delirium is often fully reversible. With the correction of underlying medical problems, the symptoms of delirium usually resolve and the resident is restored to his baseline level of functioning. There is perhaps no other behavioral disturbance that can be so dramatic, challenging, and treatable.

Delirium has been best studied in the general hospital where there is a concentration of acutely and critically ill people with very high rates of delirium. Yet there is evidence that even in this setting, delirium is often missed. Less is known about delirium in long-term care settings. Although residents in these settings are for the most part neither critically nor acutely ill, they are nevertheless at high risk for developing delirium. They are old, often frail, and demented, and on many medications that may have to be juggled repeatedly in an effort to maintain a fragile homeostasis. This chapter will focus on the identification and management of delirium in the long-term care setting.

WHAT IS DELIRIUM?

Until Lipowski's work in 1980, there was a great deal of disagreement about the definition of delirium [1]. Terms such as "acute confusional state," "acute brain failure" and "senile delirium" were poorly defined and used interchangeably with delirium. This hampered communication, education, and research.

With the advent of the DSM-III, delirium came to be defined more rigorously [2]. Delirium is a syndrome. A syndrome is a cluster of signs and symptoms that tend to occur together in such a way as to produce a recognizable and discrete diagnostic entity.

Delirium is organic. The term "organic" is used to indicate that a syndrome results from physical illness that can be identified clearly using routine diagnostic techniques. Nearly every physical illness and many different medications can produce the syndrome of delirium in elderly people. The other major organic brain syndrome affecting the elderly is dementia, in which a physical disease process can also be demonstrated although often not until autopsy, (See Chapter 3, Dementia). Organic brain syndromes are differentiated from disorders such as schizophrenia, anxiety disorders, and personality disorders, where a physical basis has been much more elusive and difficult to establish.

The DSM-IIIR criteria by which the organic brain syndrome of delirium can now be diagnosed consistently and reliably are listed in Table 1. Many different cognitive functions are affected simultaneously, so that delirium is often said to be characterized by global cognitive impairment.

A hallmark of the disorder is that it affects the individual's ability to focus, maintain, and shift attention. This symptom may be somewhat familiar, albeit in a milder form, to readers who have struggled with a complex task while suffering from extreme fatigue. The mind has a tendency to wander until it is jogged abruptly, and with considerable effort, back to the task at hand. While in such a state, people often startle easily and may become very irritable.

Table 1
Diagnostic Criteria for Delirium

A. Reduced ability to maintain and shift attention.

B. Disorganized thinking.

C. At least two of the following:
1. Reduced level of consciousness
2. Perceptual disturbances: misinterpretations, illusions or hallucinations
3. Insomnia or daytime sleepiness
4. Increased or decreased psychomotor activity
5. Disorientation to time, place, or person
6. Memory impairment

D. Clinical features develop over a short period of time and tend to fluctuate over the course of a day.

E. Either 1 or 2.
1. Evidence of a specific organic factor(s) judged to be etiologically related to the disturbance; or
2. In the absence of a specific factor, an etiological organic factor can be presumed if the disturbance cannot be accounted for by any nonorganic mental disorder.

Adapted from DSM-IIIR, American Psychiatric Association, 1987.

In delirium, thinking is affected and speech becomes rambling and incoherent. Level of consciousness, orientation, and memory can all be impaired during delirium, and hallucinations may occur. The disturbances in activity level and the sleep-wake cycle can be particularly troublesome in an institutional setting.

Another characteristic feature of delirium is that, unlike most psychiatric disorders, it can develop acutely in a period of hours to days. The delirious individual's mental status can fluctuate markedly over the course of a single day from apparently normal during so called "lucid intervals," to stupor, or frenzied hyperactivity.

The time course of an episode of delirium is quite variable but tends to be measured in days to weeks rather than months. With correction of the underlying medical problems, delirium begins to resolve and can often do so remarkably quickly. However, particularly in elderly people, some of the symptoms may linger for a long time.

How Does Delirium Begin?

While most psychiatric disorders develop gradually, delirium does so in hours to days. Even before florid symptoms are present, staff who know the resident will often have a sense that the resident is not him- or herself. The resident may also voice concerns that something is wrong without being able to easily identify what it is. By attending to these complaints, staff can heighten their level of observation. A mental status screening done at this time would be useful and might reveal deficits not previously present. Even if the mental status examination is normal or unchanged, it can provide a recent baseline against which any subsequent deterioration can be measured.

There may be other subtle warning symptoms such as worsening sleep, increasing restlessness, irritability, nightmares, and daytime sleepiness before the delirium progresses to its full-blown state.

What Are the Implications of the Fluctuating Course?

Even when delirium is well established, its clinical picture can be very puzzling to those who are not familiar with its fluctuating course. The fluctuations although not universally present, can be quite dramatic.

During lucid intervals the resident may appear normal, although cognitive deficits can be demonstrated on mental status screening.

Agitation, if present, often occurs at night when the resident is most likely to misinterpret visual stimuli and when opportunities for reassurance and reorientation are less readily available. As a result, symptoms reported during the night shift might not be present or as obvious the next morning. This could lead to the symptoms being dismissed as transient or simply attributed to "a bad night," until the larger picture of ongoing fluctuation and uncharacteristic behavior begins to emerge. This points to the importance of keeping delirium in mind whenever a resident displays a new behavioral disturbance.

The fluctuation of symptoms also has important implications for management. An individual who is calm and apparently "normal" after a stormy night cannot be assumed to have recovered from the delirium. The possibility of re-emergence of agitiation and disruptive behavior, especially the following night, should be considered when planning staffing needs. A sustained period of return to baseline mental status is necessary before staff can safely relax their vigilance.

WHAT IS THE MENTAL STATUS IN DELIRIUM?

There is no unique mental status picture in delirium. Different residents present with different abnormalities and even the same resident can display enormous variation over the course of an episode. Nevertheless, certain general observations can be made regarding the mental status in delirium.

Appearance

A sudden dramatic change in the appearance of a resident can be an important clue in the diagnosis of delirium. The individual who is ordinarily appropriately dressed may suddenly appear dishevelled and inappropriately or partially attired. Make-up may be poorly applied, buttons and flies may be undone, hair uncombed, and dentures left by the bedside.

Psychomotor Behavior

As already noted, delirious individuals have difficulty attending to external stimuli. At times they will appear to "tune out," look apathetic, and be unaware of what is happening around them. They may sit or lie listlessly for hours at a time.

Conversely, a delirious person may become hyperalert, responding to all stimuli but without being able to do so in a selective manner. Such residents will look tense. Their eyes will dart around the room as they are distracted by the slightest noise. They startle easily and are often as unable to attend to a conversation as the listless residents. Moreover, they may become very fearful and agitated. Lipowski points out that the individual showing the exaggerated fear response, (sometimes called hypervigilance), and angry outbursts is the one more likely to be noticed and to receive staff attention, while the individual who is quietly delirious and appears apathetic may remain unattended and untreated [1].

Delirious residents may be seen picking at things on their clothes and bedding or pointing towards things in a distressed fashion. This is evidence that they are responding to internal stimuli (see "Perceptual abnormalities" below).

Affect

The affect displayed by the delirious resident is labile and characterized by rapid shifts and variability. The individual may appear anxious, apathetic, excited, or depressed. Sudden unprovoked outbursts of anger, sometimes associated with violence towards self or others, may occur. These exaggerated and unpredictable emotional responses can make management difficult.

Thought Process and Content

Thinking is fragmented and disorganized. The resident may shift rapidly from topic to topic. The delirious resident may experience the world around her as hostile and threatening. Delusions are frequently present and may cause anger or fear. The delusions tend to be simple and transient, changing rapidly in response to environmental stimuli. Most of them are thought to arise out of the perceptual distortions described below.

Occasionally there is a preoccupation with sexual themes that can be associated with disinhibited behavior. The resident may also confabulate in response to questions, weaving elaborate tales around events that may never have taken place.

Perceptual Abnormalities

Perceptual abnormalities are very common in delirium, and usually arise when the individual misinterprets ordinary environmental stimuli. These illusions are frequently visual but may occur in other sensory modalities. Familiar objects and faces become distorted and frightening. A shadow can appear as a menacing monster with a life of its own. Voices and noises may sound unusually grating, or muffled and remote.

Delirious individuals exist in a twilight state drifting in and out of sleep. It may become difficult for them to distinguish dreams from reality and the experience may resemble a "living nightmare." It is not surprising that many develop delusional explanations for these terrifying experiences and become very fearful. Innocuous sounds in the hall become evidence of attacking soldiers, perhaps recalling a childhood experience. Familiar caregivers are seen as imposters. Much of the violence in delirium is a defensive lashing-out at perceived attackers.

Cognition

Assessment of cognitive functions may not be possible if the resident is too agitated or stuporous to participate in a focused task. However, if testing is possible, it can help confirm the diagnostic impression formed on the basis of the rest of the mental status.

Delirious residents are globally impaired. Language and speech are affected; word-finding difficulties and problems with articulation may occur. Orientation and memory are affected by the attentional problems. There is usually disorientation to time, including time of day and often to place as well. The resident will perform poorly on tests of recent memory although long-term memory is usually intact. Praxis is affected resulting in difficulty with constructional tasks.

Insight is almost always impaired and faulty judgement may lead residents to act impulsively and at times dangerously.

FROM WHAT OTHER DISORDERS MUST DELIRIUM BE DIFFERENTIATED?

There are a number of conditions commonly encountered in the long-term care setting that may be confused with delirium:

Physical Discomfort

Residents who are unable to put physical distress into words, perhaps as a result of dementia or stroke, may present with a sudden onset of severe agitation resembling delirium. Obvious sources of discomfort such as thirst, hunger and pain (e.g., from a fracture or uninary retention) must be considered and ruled out. Unlike the more persistent symptoms of delirium, those caused by acute physical discomfort are usually relieved as soon as the physical problem is addressed.

It should be kept in mind that delirious residents may also be impaired in their ability to tell staff about physical symptoms and pain may exacerbate fear and agitation in delirium.

Dementia

Given the high prevalence of dementia among nursing home residents, it is important that staff in these settings be able to differentiate between delirium and dementia. This can be quite difficult, because individuals whose cognitive reserves are limited by dementia are more vulnerable to developing delirium than the general population. Delirium is therefore frequently superimposed on dementia.

In dementia, residents are normally alert and relatively stable in their capacities from day to day. The demented resident may become progressively more impaired but this is usually a very gradual process. Moreover, the demented resident does not show dramatic fluctuations in mental status over the course of a single day. They are less likely to experience perceptual distortions and difficulties with sleep. The memory problems in dementia are primary rather than secondary to attentional difficulties as in delirium.

A longitudinal knowledge of the resident and his baseline mental status is crucial to recognizing delirium when it is superimposed on dementia. A sudden change in the mental status of a demented resident may indicate the onset of delirium and should always prompt further investigation.

Depression and Mania

Although apathetic delirious individuals can sometimes appear depressed, depression has a much more gradual onset and is not usually associated with global cognitive impairment. A recent history of dysphoric mood and a past history of depression are also more suggestive of depression than delirium. The importance of past history underscores the need for a thorough intake history when a resident first enters the nursing home.

Mania may be difficult to differentiate from agitated delirium, especially since mania can also develop quickly. The absence of global cognitive impairment in mania, and the presence of a past history can help establish this diagnosis.

Paranoid Disorders and Schizophrenia

Residents with paranoid disorders and schizophrenia may have delusions and hallucinations resembling those in delirium. These disorders generally have a more gradual onset, are not characterized by a fluctuating course or global cognitive impairment, and are often associated with a past history of psychiatric disability. The delusions in these disorders tend to be more complex and stable than those in delirium. The hallucinations in schizophrenia are often auditory while delirium is typically characterized by visual hallucinations.

WHAT CAUSES DELIRIUM?

By definition, delirium has a physiological basis. There are a myriad of diverse biological factors that can stress brain function to the point of decompensation and ensuing delirium. Delirium in the elderly is often complex and produced by many different factors acting simultaneously. Sometimes the physical cause or causes are known or easily identified. However, delirium is often the first sign that something is wrong and necessitates a thorough search into possible etiological factors. Some of the causes of delirium are listed in Table 2.

Table 2
Causes of Delirium

Category	Examples
Intracranial problems	Strokes, vasculitis, post-ictal states, meningitis, space-occupying lesions such as tumors and subdural hematomas
Systemic illness	Cardiovascular disease such as myocardial infarction and congestive heart failure, renal or hepatic failure, respiratory insufficiency, anemia, diabetes, and other endocrine disorders
Infection	Generalized sepsis, pneumonia, urinary tract infections, meningitis
Toxic/metabolic	Medications, alcohol, electrolyte problems, acid-base disturbances, and hypoxia
Deficiency states	Folate, thiamine, and iron deficiency
Trauma	Head injury, surgery, burns

At first glance, the list in Table 2 may look overwhelming. Moreover, the investigation of many of these conditions is beyond the scope of the long-term care setting and would require transfer to a general hospital. However, there are certain principles than can guide the preliminary investigation into the causes of an episode of delirium.

A thorough review of the resident's medical history will reveal areas of particular vulnerability. The resident may have a history of recurrent urinary tract infections, unstable diabetes, or partially compensated congestive heart failure. When a newly admitted resident develops delirium shortly after admission, a withdrawal state must always be suspected. Less commonly, newly admitted residents become delirious when they begin to take prescribed medications regularly with which they were non-compliant at home.

In the absence of such clues, it is useful to keep in mind that "common things are common." Toxic states induced by medication and infection are particularly likely to be contributing factors in delirium. After medications have been reviewed with regard to the chronology of changes in dose and the introduction of new medications, the resident should be taken off all non-essential drugs. Numerous different medications can act or interact with other medication to produce delirium. Table 3 lists some categories of medication that are frequently implicated. Especially prominent are drugs that have anticholinergic effects including many over-the-counter hypnotics, antihistamines, psychoactive drugs such as neuroleptics and antidepressants, and certain antiparkinsonian agents (e.g., amantadine). Even eyedrops containing anticholinergic agents can be absorbed systemically and have been implicated in delirium. Many residents are on more than one medication with anticholinergic effects. Often some of these medications can be discontinued or replaced with others that are less anticholinergic (see Chapter 9, Pharmacology). Other commonly used medications that frequently produce delirium are benzodiazepines, digoxin, and cimetidine.

The resident may be able to identify symptoms of physical illness if interviewed during a lucid interval. A complete physical examination is essential, although it may be difficult to perform if the resident is uncooperative.

Baselines laboratory investigations such as those listed in Table 4 should be done.

Table 3
Medications That Can Cause Delirium

Category	Examples
Analgesics	Salicylates, opiates (e.g., codeine)
Anticonvulsants	Barbiturates, carbamazepine, phenytoin
Antihistamines/ decongestants	Many over-the-counter preparations
Anti-parkinsonians	Amantadine, benztropine, levodopa
Cardiac medications	Digitalis, antiarrhythmics, anti-hypertensives
Gastrointestinal medications	Antidiarrheal agents, antinauseants, antispasmodics, cimetidine, and to a lesser extent ranitidine
Psychoactive medications	Antidepressants, antipsychotics, lithium, benzodiazepines, and other sedative hypnotics
Other	Antineoplastic agents, anesthetics, antidiabetic agents, some antibiotics

Table 4
Baseline Laboratory Investigations

- Complete blood count with differential
- Erythrocyte sedimentation rate
- Blood chemistry: electrolytes, blood urea nitrogen, creatinine, glucose, calcium, phosphate, liver enzymes
- Urinalysis
- Chest X-ray

WHO SHOULD BE WATCHED MOST CLOSELY FOR DELIRIUM?

- Residents who have just been admitted from the community or from a hospital are particularly vulnerable. Unsuspected alcohol, benzodiazepine or barbiturate dependence may be un-masked and withdrawal syndromes may occur.

- Residents who are placed on new medications or on higher dosages of their regular medications may become delirious.
- Any acutely ill resident can develop delirium. In this situation, even though the resident's underlying illness is known, awareness that the resident may become behaviorally unstable can guide the level of observation and other aspects of the management plan.
- Residents who have had a previous episode of delirium are especially likely to respond to future biological stressors with delirium.

HOW IS DELIRIUM MANAGED?

While investigating and treating the underlying physical causes of delirium, the treatment team will have to cope with the stormy course that delirium may take. Several general principles can be followed.

Approaching the Delirious Resident

When interacting with delirious residents it is important to remember that they may be very confused and frightened and that they may perceive any approach as an attack. When entering the room it is best to get a sense of the resident's mental status before any physical contact takes place. Speaking clearly, slowly and in a direct manner, staff can introduce themselves, gently orient the resident and explain in simple terms the purpose of their visit (e.g., taking vital signs). Sometimes it becomes obvious at this point that residents are too agitated to be touched, while at other times they can be reassured and approached. Abrupt movements and loud noises should be avoided since they are perceived as hostile.

While in the resident's presence, staff and visitors should avoid holding discussions among themselves as these are likely to be misinterpreted. It is extremely important to remember that even a stuporous resident may be able to hear everything that is said. There is sometimes an unfortunate tendency to talk about people who look like they are "out of it" as if they are not there. Residents can be deeply hurt by things they were not meant to hear and remember the comments long after the delirium has resolved.

Helping Delirious Residents Understand What is Happening to Them

"Going crazy" is something everyone fears; in delirium that fear becomes a reality. It can be very reassuring for residents to hear that a medical problem is causing a disturbance in the way the brain works and that the frightening symptoms will eventually go away. This is best conveyed during lucid intervals and may need to be repeated later in the course of the delirium as the ability to retain information may be impaired.

Optimizing the Resident's Environment

Environmental factors can contribute to the onset of delirium and seriously aggravate its symptoms. Change is bad for delirious residents. It will cause further disorientation and increase residents' sense that their world is out of control. Whenever possible, room changes should be avoided and staff continuity maintained. Familiar faces, voices, and objects can be reassuring and reorienting. As in dementia, clocks and calendars are helpful.

The level of sensory input has to be monitored carefully. Too much light and noise and too many people can create panic. It may be necessary to limit the number of people in the room at any one time and the number of different visitors who can come on a particular day. However, sensory deprivation can also exacerbate the resident's fears, so that adequate lighting and regular human contact are important.

Supportive Measures and Ongoing Monitoring

Adequate intake of fluid and nutrition must be maintained. Residents who are inactive should be mobilized to prevent the development of pressure sores and deep vein thromboses. Hyperactive residents have to be protected against injuries and exhaustion. Constant observation may be required.

Delirious residents are medically ill and may require frequent monitoring of vital signs, laboratory tests, and treatment interventions. The importance of any procedure must always be weighed against the risk of further aggravating an already agitated resident. Ideally, flexibility should be preserved so that necessary interactions take place when the resident is relatively calm.

Involving Family

Family members need to be given an explanation and ongoing reassurance that the puzzling and frightening changes taking place in the resident arise out of physical problems. They often have great trouble coping with the hostile, bizarre, and embarrassing ways in which the resident may behave.

Psychoactive Medications

Psychoactive medications can help manage the behavioral disturbance accompanying delirium. It should be stressed that, except in cases of withdrawal delirium, these medications are used for symptom control only and do not treat the underlying medical problems that are causing delirium.

In most cases of delirium, an antipsychotic medication, preferably one with minimal anticholinergic effects such as haloperidol, is the treatment of choice for agitation and behavioral disturbance. An exception to this rule occurs in delirium secondary to alcohol or barbiturate withdrawal in which a long-acting benzodiazepine such as diazepam would be optimal.

It may be possible to predict the need for medication early in the course of delirium and avoid a crisis. If a resident is highly agitated on the night the delirium begins, it is likely that the behavior will recur and possibly escalate on subsequent nights. In this case, the use of a regular dose of neuroleptic given early in the evening, before the agitation begins, would be far more effective than trying to administer a p.r.n. dose to a frenzied resident at 11:30 p.m.

Psychoactive medications should be discontinued when the delirium has resolved so that side effects associated with the long-term use of these drugs are avoided.

Physical restraints should be used only as a last resort as the experience of being held down will only add to the delirious resident's terror. Whenever residents have been physically restrained, a specific protocol should be followed to monitor the resident's status and to ensure that there is adequate circulation, and mobilization of restrained limbs. A more appropriate means of achieving behavioral control, usually through the use of psychotropic medications should be initiated at the same time. Careful charting of the team's actions and the reasons for these actions is recommended. Restraints are never a substitute for constant observation.

"Hospital regulations. You gotta wear the straps while I read the bill."

HERMAN COPYRIGHT, 1978. (First Treasury). Jim Unger.
Reprinted with permission of Universal Press Syndicate.

Transfer

At some point in the course of treatment, transfer to a general hospital may have to be considered. Sometimes the etiology of the delirium remains obscure despite adequate initial investigation and management. The resident's condition may deteriorate and require investigation and treatment that are beyond the scope of a long-term care facility. Occasionally a transfer is necessary when the resident's behavior exceeds the bounds of what the setting can cope with.

It is important to involve family in this decision as not transferring the resident may lead to deterioration or death within days or weeks. In some cases the decision to transfer for further investigation has to be weighed against the difficulty the delirious resident will experience in relocating to a new environment. The resident's overall prognosis and expected quality of life can also be a factor in the decision, especially since delirium is extremely common in the terminally ill.

WHAT IS THE RECOVERY PHASE LIKE?

The prognosis of delirium varies from rapid and complete recovery to death. Clearly this will depend on the nature of the underlying medical problems. There is evidence that when these problems are identified and treated early in the course of delirium there is a better prognosis for recovery from the symptoms of delirium.

Although the duration of an episode of delirium is usually measured in days to weeks, it is not uncommon for an individual to take much longer to reintegrate. This is especially true for the elderly. Symptoms of cognitive impairment may linger for months before a new baseline is established. Serial mental status examinations may show a very gradual improvement, and an eventual return to the previous level of functioning, although some residents may be left with permanent deficits. Staff and family may assume that there has been complete recovery once the more florid symptoms of delirium have resolved. This can lead to unrealistic expectations being placed on the resident. However, it is important not to conclude that the resident has become demented as gradual improvement can continue for months.

The resident's memory of what took place during the delirium is usually incomplete. Many will say it was like a bad dream. It is important to give recovered residents an opportunity to discuss the experience and express their feelings about it. Particularly in cases where aggressive and sexually disinhibited behavior has occurred, the resident may be deeply ashamed. If residents do not remember these disruptive incidents, it serves no purpose to remind them. Fears regarding the chances of a recurrence of the delirium may also have to be addressed.

CASE ILLUSTRATIONS

Case 1

Mrs H was a 76-year-old widowed woman who had always been pleasant and co-operative with staff. She showed signs of mild memory impairment. She had a number of medical problems, all of which were well controlled, including diabetes mellitus, hypertension, osteoarthritis, and hypothyroidism. She required a walker for amubulation as a result of osteoarthritis in her hips. Much of her time was spent socializing with other residents and she attended crafts programs regularly.

Over a period of several days, the staff noted changes in the resident which at first were quite subtle. While she slept well she complained of increased restlessness and seemed irritable in the mornings. She refused to go to her usual activities and remained in her room. She also appeared to react with an abnormal degree of irritability when questioned as to whether she was feeling well. She stated uncharacteristically that she didn't think it was anyone's business. On the third night her sleep was disrupted and she became agitated and shouted for help stating that she had seen someone at the foot of her bed. She had thrown a glass of water at this figure.

Staff were able to settle her but noted that she still looked frightened and vigilant and appeared to mistake one of the staff for her deceased mother. The resident appeared improved in the morning but over the course of the day she developed a fever and began to complain of shortness of breath. She no longer recognized staff and on one occasion believed she was on a boat cruise and that the nurse handing out medication was a purser.

At this point, the nursing staff put the resident on close observation and the physician in charge of the resident's care was called. On the basis of the clinical exam the physician suspected that the resident had a pneumonia. She was transferred to a general hospital where she was assessed in the emergency room and found to be hypoxic and suffering from left lower lobe pneumonia.

In hospital, the resident was placed on oxygen and started on intravenous antibiotics. She appeared more settled and coop-

erative and less short of breath. On the first night she was in hospital shouts were heard coming from her room. The resident was swinging her I.V. pole and had pulled out her I.V. She believed that she was in a jungle and that a snake was attacking her. Several nurses were required to restrain her and the attending physician was asked to reassess her. The resident was placed on a low dosage of haloperidol consisting of 1 mg p.o. b.i.d. and was kept on constant observation. Her family came to the hospital the next day from out of town and were shocked by the fact that she couldn't recognize them and kept shouting, "Stop staring at me." Later in the day the resident was observed to be more herself and was taken out of the posey restraint and ambulated. The next 2 days were uneventful and the resident was taken off of constant observation. She remained distractible and had no understanding of why she was in hospital. She had some awareness that she had been through a very frightening time but had difficulty believing the accounts of her condition and behavior over the past few days. She alternated between disbelief and embarrassment.

When the resident returned to the nursing home where she had been living it was noted that she was not as bright as she had been prior to the illness. She found that she had difficulties with her concentration and memory. She would frequently ask the staff and her family if she was suffering from Alzheimer disease. She seemed less confident and appeared to require more reassurance and guidance from the staff.

Her relatives were quite concerned about her and on several occasions wondered if she was going to need transfer to another unit where she could have more supervision.

The staff reassured the family that the resident appeared to be improving slowly and that it was premature to make any changes until her status plateaued. After 5 months the resident appeared to be much her usual self.

Comment

This case illustrates a situation encountered quite frequently in residents who have mild cognitive impairment that pre-dates the onset of their delirium. The first manifestations of a serious physical illness may be mental status changes rather than the more usual physical signs and symptoms. Even after Mrs H has recovered from the acute phase of the delirium, subtle deficits in her mental status and functioning linger for many months. Staff are able to reassure Mrs H and her relatives because they are familiar with the protracted course that an episode of delirium can have in this population, and because in monitoring Mrs H's mental status carefully, they are able to document a gradual improvement in her condition.

Case 2

Mr W was an 87-year-old man with mild dementia. He had been through a difficult period of adjustment since his admission to the nursing home several months earlier. He was critical of staff, impatient with his room-mate and plagued by insomnia.

One night at 3:00 a.m., he awakened, put his clothes on over his pyjamas, and went to the dining room for breakfast. When staff tried to orient him he exploded in anger and accused them of trying to make him look like a fool. He refused to go back to bed and paced the halls until morning. Staff who changed his sheets noticed that, for the first time since admission, he had been incontinent of urine.

On reviewing his chart, the team noted that he had been started on oxazepam 30 mg qhs for insomnia 5 days earlier. Mr W was not very cooperative upon physical examination and refused to answer mental status questions complaining bitterly that this was an infringement of his rights.

The oxazepam was discontinued. However, 2 weeks later, Mr W had deteriorated further. He appeared dishevelled, swore at staff, and shook his fist at them whenever they tried to approach him. During the afternoon he slept for hours snoring loudly and moaning restlessly in his sleep. At night he paced the halls and refused to go into his room demanding that cleaning staff get rid of the bugs in his room.

Prior to the delirium, Mr W had been physically healthy and although assessment had been difficult since the delirium had started, a fairly complete physical examination and baseline laboratory tests did not reveal any abnormalities.

The team called Mr W 's daughter who lived in another city to communicate their concern about him and to discuss their decision to transfer him to a general hospital. During this conversation it emerged that 3 weeks earlier, the daughter, who had been concerned about her father's insomnia, had left him some of the pills she used for the same problem. Fourteen tablets of flurazepam were recovered from Mr W's room.

A week later, Mr W began to improve. Soon he was back to his premorbid level of functioning.

Comment

Medications are a very common cause of delirium in the elderly. In those cases where there is no apparent physical illness to account for the mental status changes, it is especially important to review the medications carefully. Mr W's case also points to the need for staff to keep in mind the possibility of self-medication with substances ranging from alcohol and over-the-counter medications, to prescription drugs obtained outside the institution.

KEY POINTS

- Delirium is an organic brain syndrome characterized by a rapid onset, a fluctuating course and global cognitive impairment.

- Delirium is produced when one or more biological factors stress brain function to the point where decompensation occurs.

- If a resident's behavior and/or cognitive status undergo a sudden change, consider delirium after eliminting obvious physiological factors such as pain, thirst, or hunger.

- Demented individuals are particularly vulnerable to delirium. Any sudden deterioration in a demented resident may represent a delirium superimposed on dementia.

- If the biological factors underlying the delirium can be corrected, recovery from the delirium is usually rapid and complete, although some symptoms may linger for months, especially in the elderly.

- As medications are so often implicated in delirium, all nonessential medications should be discontinued in the absence of other etiological possibilities.

- Delirious residents are often very frightened. They should be approached in a calm, reassuring manner and cared for in a restful, familiar environment.

- Psychoactive drugs may be required to manage the disruptive and violent behavior that sometimes occurs.

- Transfer to a general hospital may have to be considered.

REFERENCES

1. Lipowski, Z.J. (1980). *Delirium: Acute brain failure in man.* Sprinfield, IL: Charles C. Thomas.
2. APA. (1980). *Diagnostic and statistical manual of mental disorders,* third edition. Washington, DC: American Psychiatric Association.

SUGGESTED READING

1. Fawdry, K., Berry, M.L. (1989). The Nurse's role: Fear of senility in managing reversible confusion. *Journal of Gerontological Nursing,* 15(4):17-21.

    This paper is a sensitive exploration of managing delirium and its sequelae from a nursing perspective.

2. Lipowski, Z.J. (1982). Differentiating delirium from dementia in the elderly. *Clinical Gerontologist,* 1(1):3-10.

This paper provides a useful guide to a difficult diagnostic area.

3. Lipowski, Z.J. (1989). Delirium in the elderly patient. *New England Journal of Medicine*, 320:578-582.

A comprehensive overview of delirium in the elderly.

4. Seltzer, B., Mesulam, M.M. (1988). Confusional states and delirium as disorders of attention. In. F. Boller, J. Grafman, G. Rizzolatti, H. Goodglass, (Eds.), *Handbook of neuropsychology*, Volume I, pp. 165-174. Amsterdam: Elsevier.

A detailed look at delirium with emphasis on neuropsychological aspects.

CHAPTER

Depression and Other Mood Disorders

5

---

by David K. Conn and Alanna Kaye

"Coming in here is the last stop, it's the end of the road" ...
A nursing home resident.

When an elderly person enters an institution, there is invariably some degree of sadness. Of course not everyone who feels sad suffers from a depressive illness. The term "depression" is used in a variety of situations to denote either a feeling, a mood, a symptom, a reaction, or an illness. The terms "clinical depression" or "major depression" refer to a depressive illness. It is important that staff are alert to the possibility that a resident may be suffering from major depression as this is an eminently treatable condition. Without treatment there may be considerable suffering with a decreased level of physical and cognitive functioning and in severe cases a potential risk of suicide. Table 1 outlines the criteria used to make a diagnosis of major depressive episode from the DSM-IIIR [1].

Table 1
DSM-IIIR Diagnosis of Major Depression

Either depressed mood or loss of interest or pleasure (not due to a physical illness) for at least 2 weeks and representing a change from previous functioning with at least five of the following:

1. Depressed mood most of the day, most days
2. Markedly diminished interest or pleasure
3. Significant change in weight or appetite
4. Insomnia or hypersomnia
5. Psychomotor agitation or retardation
6. Fatigue or loss of energy
7. Feelings of worthlessness or excess of inappropriate guilt
8. Diminished ability to think or concentrate or indecisiveness
9. Recurrent thoughts of death or suicidal ideation

Absence of an organic factor initiating or maintaining the disturbance. The disturbance is not "uncomplicated bereavement."

No prolonged delusions or hallucinations before mood symptoms developed or after they remitted.

Not superimposed on schizophrenia, schizophreniform disorder, delusional disorder, or psychotic disorder.

Adapted from DSM-IIIR, American Psychiatric Association, 1987.

What Symptoms and Signs am I Likely to See in a Clinically Depressed Patient?

Although residents may report a persistent depressed mood, it is not infrequent for the person to minimize or even deny the presence of depressive feelings. Other feelings such as nervousness or irritability may be reported. Frequently there is a marked change in behavior with a loss of motivation and interest in usual activities. The person may withdraw from social interactions, slow down, almost to the point of immobility, or conversely become highly agitated and restless. Some of the classical symptoms of a depressive illness, such as changes in sleep, appetite, weight, and energy can also be caused by physical illness, and it is therefore critical, although difficult at times, to differentiate between those attributable to a physical illness and those caused by depression. In the elderly, depressive thinking may be the best clue to the presence of underlying depression, especially if this presents a distinct change. The person may view themselves, the world and the future in totally negative terms, feeling hopeless, helpless and worthless, often with associated feelings of guilt and self-blame. When severe, the person may dwell on thoughts of death and develop suicidal ideation.

Are there other Forms of Depression Besides Major Depression?

There are several other forms of depression. The term "dysthymic disorder" is used to describe a more chronic and usually less severe form of depression. This form of depression may persist for many years and some individuals may describe having had feelings of depression for much of their lives. It is not clear whether this disorder is a subtype of major depression or whether it is a separate entity related in part to an individual's personality structure. Transient depressions can occur following a major life event and are referred to as adjustment disorders with depressed mood. This is common in newly admitted nursing home residents. Although not in the DSM-IIIR the terms "demoralization" and "existential depression" are sometimes used to describe individuals suffering from a depression related to difficult life events. If an "organic" factor, for example, a stroke is judged to be the cause of a depression, a diagnosis of organic mood disorder is made. A bipolar affective disorder is indicated if the individual has a history of mania or hypomania. When symptoms of depression are present it is important to try to establish a diagnosis of the type of depression in order to determine the most appropriate management strategies.

EPIDEMIOLOGY OF DEPRESSION IN THE ELDERLY

There is considerable debate as to whether the elderly are more at risk for major depression than younger adults. When strict definitions of major depression are applied, the prevalence appears to be between 2% and 4% in the general population. Community studies report depressive symptoms in 10% to 15% of the general population. Comparisons of the elderly with younger adults show that teenagers and younger adults may have the highest levels of reported symptoms. However, 20% to 30% of medically ill patients and an even higher percentage of patients and residents in long-term care report significant depressive symptoms. A recent study of nursing home residents in Philadelphia using DSM-IIIR diagnostic criteria suggested that 18% to 20% of this population have significant levels of depression [2]. A study of patients in a chronic care hospital in Toronto found that 35% of patients able to complete rating scales had scores in the depressed range [3]. Interestingly, in the latter study feelings of sadness were equally present in both depressed and non-depressed institutionalized patients. Two-thirds of the depressed medical patients had a previously unrecognized diagnosis of depression. This finding highlighted the need for greater awareness of the degree of depression in institutionalized geriatric patients with chronic medical illness.

IS DEPRESSION IN THE ELDERLY DIFFERENT?

There is debate about whether depression in the elderly is distinct from depression in younger adults. Although more research is needed it appears that depression in the elderly is characterized by less frequent complaints of depressed mood, more cognitive symptoms and signs, more hypochondriasis, less guilt, and more frequent completed suicide.

DIFFERENTIAL DIAGNOSIS

Psychiatric Disorders

As mentioned above if depression is present the diagnosis may include major depression, bipolar affective disorder, adjustment disorder with depressed mood, dysthymic disorder or organic mood disorder.

It is important to differentiate the depressive disorders from other conditions that resemble depression: anxiety disorders such as agoraphobia, panic disorder, generalized anxiety disorder, or post-traumatic stress disorder, and other psychiatric disorders such as paranoid disorders and hypochondriasis which can present with depressive features or may coexist with a depressive disorder.

Grief

A grief reaction following the loss of a spouse or other relative can often present with depressive symptoms and may progress to a significant depressive illness. In the acute phases it can be difficult to differentiate grief from depression. The process of grief is discussed later in this chapter.

Physical Illness

Various physical illnesses, whose main symptoms are weakness, lethargy, or pain can resemble depression. A good example is the post-viral syndrome in which the individual is overwhelmed with fatigue and is unable to perform the normal activities of daily living.

Neurological Disorders

The majority of patients in the nursing home setting will have some form of underlying brain disease that can mimic depression. Patients with Parkinson disease look and sound depressed. They typically have a blank emotionless facial expression and their speech is monotonous and barely audible. Damage to many different areas of the brain may result in dysprosody, which is an inability to communicate one's emotional state through voice pitch, voice inflection, posture, and mimicry. Consequently, patients with dysprosody may sound depressed, when they are not, or may actually be depressed, but be unable to adequately express their feelings.

Other patients with brain lesions can present with pathological crying or emotional lability which can be mistaken for depression. These patients complain that they cannot control their emotions and find that they will cry spontaneously or in response to any emotional thought or feeling. Some patients with frontal lobe damage or subcortical dementia may present with apathy and psychomotor retardation. It should be noted that, although the above conditions can mimic depression, depression may coexist with these presentations. Depression is especially common following stroke and in Parkinson disease, for example.

OTHER PRESENTATIONS OF DEPRESSION WORTH NOTING

Masked Depression

The term "masked" depression refers to a depressive illness characterized primarily by physical complaints such as headache or abdominal pain. Residents with masked depression usually report vegetative signs of depression, negative depressive cognitions, anxiety, and agitation. When confronted with the suggestion that they might be depressed, however, they typically deny it and focus entirely on their physical symptoms. Masked depression frequently responds well to antidepressants.

Dementia Syndrome of Depression (Pseudodementia)

Some patients with a picture of dementia actually have a depressive illness which, once treated, leads not only to an improvement in depression but also to normal cognitive functioning. Clues to this particular presentation include patients who highlight their failures, worry about their memory, have a short rapidly progressive history, perform inconsistently on testing, and have an equal impairment of recent and remote memory. Most clinicians find that this is a rare syndrome and that the more common presentation is of a coexisting depression and dementia. The syndrome may in fact be an early warning signalling the beginning of a dementing process.

Delusional Depression

Severe forms of depression can be associated with delusions that are typically somatic or persecutory. These delusions are usually mood-congruent, that is, the content is consistent with depressive themes of guilt, disease, death, nihilism, or deserved punishment. Associated features include ruminations and agitation. Residents with delusional depression will often require transfer to a psychiatric unit for optimal care.

FACTORS IN LONG-TERM CARE

Loss is an important factor in the development of depressive feelings. For many elderly people the move into an institution is perceived as a loss of home, independence, decision-making, freedom, and privacy. Sadness in response to this situation can be considered normal. These feelings are exacerbated by other losses that can occur in association with institutionalization. Often there has been a loss of a spouse or other close relatives and friends as well as a developing illness or disability. Sensory deprivation from failing hearing or eyesight may result in feelings of isolation from the world. An important aspect regarding the move into an institution is the degree to which the elderly person has been able to participate in the choice of institution and in the process of moving. If individuals have the cognitive and emotional capacity to participate in the process and have had the opportunity to orientate themselves to the institution ahead of time, then they may feel more in control of the situation. Perceiving oneself as being in control contributes to the reduction or allaying of feelings of helplessness and depression.

WHAT CAUSES DEPRESSION?

Various biological, psychological, and social factors have been proposed as causative agents in depression. The development of depression as a result of several contributing factors has been termed a "Final Common Pathway."

Possible biological etiologies include a genetic vulnerability, a functional deficiency of monoamine neurotransmitters such as norepinephrine and serotonin, circadian rhythm desynchronization, specific relationships to medical illnesses (e.g., strokes), and abnormal neuroendocrine functions. These potential biological etiologies may overlap and be interrelated.

A variety of psychological factors have been described in the precipitation of depression. As mentioned above, the elderly often experience multiple losses which can in turn contribute to the development of depression. The loss of loved ones, in particular, leads to grief, which can develop into a full blown major depression. A history of earlier losses predisposes an individual to the later development of depression. Erikson conceptualized the psychology of later life as a conflict of "integrity versus despair" [4]. He pointed out that as older persons try to come to terms with their life there is either an acceptance, and ultimately a sense of integrity, or despair about lost opportunities. Cognitive theories of depression assign a central role to dysfunctional or negative thoughts. Behavioral theories suggest that depression results from a social skills deficit which prevents individuals from receiving positive reinforcement from important others in their environment. Important social factors contributing to the development of depression include lack of family support, lack of friends, and deprivation such as poverty.

DEPRESSION AND PHYSICAL ILLNESS

Physical illness is another contributing factor to the development of depression in the elderly. There are four possible relationships between medical illness and depression:

- Depression may be a presenting complaint related to an underlying and as yet undiagnosed medical disorder, such as carcinoma
- Physical symptoms may at times arise from an underlying depression in which there is virtually no complaint of a depressed mood (e.g., masked depression, often presenting as headache or other pain)
- Depression and physical illness may occur together and be directly related
- Depression and physical illness may coexist but be essentially unrelated

Table 2 lists some of the medical illnesses and medications which are frequently associated with depression.

Table 2
Medical Illnesses and Medications Often
Associated With Depression

Neurological
- Stroke
- Parkinson disease
- Hydrocephalus
- Multiple sclerosis
- Cerebral neoplasms
- Head-injury

Endocrine
- Hypothyroidism
- Hyperthyroidism
- Cushing Syndrome
- Addison Disease

Collagen-vascular diseases

Carcinoma-lymphoma

Viral illness
- Hepatitis
- Influenza
- Mononucleosis

Medications
- Methyldopa
- Propranolol
- Corticosteroids
- L-dopa
- Cimetidine
- Barbiturates

GRIEF

The process of grief after the death of a loved one varies considerably. If death occurs after a lengthy illness, during which the process of dying has been evident, the family has the opportunity to begin grieving prior to the death. In these instances of anticipatory grief, death may be accepted as an inevitable part of life or even as a timely release for the dying. In situations of sudden death or where levels of denial are high, the grief process cannot begin until the individual has died.

Parkes describes four stages of grief: 1. initial numbness, 2. protest and searching, 3. disorganization and despair, and 4. acceptance and reorganization of a new life [5]. The initial stages of numbness can last from days to weeks. The person may deny all feelings and feel as though in a dream. This state may be interspersed with overwhelming feelings of distress and episodes of crying. During the stage of protest and searching, the person feels anxious and pines. He/she is in a state of high physiological arousal with uncomfortable physical sensations such as tightness in the chest, hollowness in the stomach, and generalized weakness, and has a strong desire to see and hear the lost person, which commonly results in illusions or, on occasion, hallucinations.

The stage of disorganization and despair is characterized by apathy, aimlessness, and feelings of hopelessness. It is difficult to establish plans or new goals. Symptoms of depression such as insomnia, loss of appetite, and energy are common, and, if severe and persistent, may require treatment with antidepressant medication. Although there is rarely a clear ending to the process of grief, most individuals eventually reach a point of acceptance and can begin to live life and experience pleasure again. Nevertheless, anniversaries, birthdays, and holidays often precipitate exacerbations of grief feelings.

Many people need support and assistance during the process of grief recovery. This support most often comes from relatives and friends but health professionals and clergy can also be of assistance. At times it is helpful to simply spend time with the individual: listening, accepting, reassuring, and gently encouraging. It is considered to be important for the bereaved to go through the pain of grief and to express all their feelings about the deceased, a process that is referred to as "grief work." For some, widow's or widower's support groups are invaluable.

Grief can become atypical or complicated as when the person withdraws totally, feels excessively guilty or angry, experiences severe anxiety or panic attacks, or shows no signs of grief whatsoever. In these cases a referral to a psychiatrist is advisable as it is important to rule out an underlying major depression or other psychiatric illness.

HOW SHOULD RESIDENTS WITH DEPRESSION BE MANAGED?

Individuals with major depression respond best to a combination of medication and psychotherapy. As the cases below will illustrate, a variety of interventions may be necessary.

Pharmacologic treatment of depression usually involves tricyclic antidepressants. The choice of medication is usually made according to target symptoms and likely side effects. Antidepressants usually take several weeks to work but once they do the response to treatment is often dramatic. Appropriate antidepressants for the elderly include desipramine, nortriptyline, doxepin, and trazodone. A newer antidepressant, fluoxetine, may also be of value in this population of patients. The severely agitated or psychotic patient with depression may require a neuroleptic. The role of medications in the management of depression is discussed in Chapter 9.

For the seriously depressed patient who is unresponsive to medication and/or whose life may be endangered, a trial of electroconvulsive therapy (ECT) may be indicated. Unilateral ECT administered to the non-dominant hemisphere causes less post-ictal confusion than bilateral and is probably equally effective. Patients requiring ECT would normally require transfer to a psychiatric inpatient unit.

Supportive psychotherapy and more specific approaches such as cognitive therapy can be of particular benefit to the depressed resident. Group therapies can also be helpful, although it may be difficult to get the seriously depressed resident to participate. Psychotherapeutic techniques are discussed in Chapter 11.

Patients with less severe forms of depression such as an adjustment disorder with depressed mood generally do not respond well to antidepressants. These individuals usually require support, time, and sometimes psychotherapy to help in the recovery process. In the nursing home situation the most likely time for an adjustment reaction is the period following admission. It is important during this time to let the resident know that the staff understand this kind of reaction.

The resident should be encouraged to form new relationships and to participate, where possible, in programs.

MANIA (BIPOLAR AFFECTIVE DISORDER)

The cardinal symptoms of mania are listed in Table 3. The person with mania is generally agitated, euphoric, or cantankerous and irritable, and is often awake much of the night.

Table 3
DSM-IIIR Diagnosis of Manic Episode

A distinct period of abnormally and persistently elevated, expansive, or irritable mood.

During the period of mood disturbance, at least three of the following symptoms have persisted (four if the mood is only irritable) and have been present to a significant degree:

1. Inflated self-esteem or grandiosity
2. Decreased need for sleep, e.g., feels rested after only 3 hours of sleep
3. More talkative than usual or pressure to keep talking
4. Flight of ideas or subjective experience that thoughts are racing
5. Distractibility, i.e., attention too easily drawn to unimportant or irrelevant external stimuli
6. Increase in goal-directed activity or psychomotor agitation
7. Excessive involvement in pleasurable activities which have a high potential for painful consequences

Mood disturbance sufficiently severe to cause marked impairment in occupational functioning or in usual social activities or relationships with others, or to necessitate hospitalization to prevent harm to self or others.

No delusions or hallucinations for as long as 2 weeks in the absence of prominent mood symptoms.

Not superimposed on schizophrenia, schizophreniform disorder, delusional disorder, or psychotic disorder.

Absence of an organic factor initiating or maintaining the disturbance.

Adapted from DSM-IIIR, American Psychiatric Association, 1987.

A significant proportion of elderly patients, especially males, with bipolar affective disorder have evidence of an organic brain disorder or history of a neurological insult. A variety of medical illnesses and drugs are believed to precipitate secondary mania (organic mood syndrome). These are listed in Table 4. It is probable that those who develop secondary mania have a particular vulnerability to mood disorders. Sometimes individuals can display features of both depression and mania, which is termed a "mixed bipolar disorder."

Table 4
Medical Illnesses and Medications Associated With Mania

Medical illnesses
- CNS stroke/cerebral neoplasms (esp. right hemisphere)
- Multiple sclerosis
- Encephalitis
- Syphilis
- Head injury
- Hyperthyroidism
- Uremia
- Hemodialysis

Medications
- Corticosteroids
- Thyroxin
- Levodopa
- Bromocriptine
- Sympathomimetics
- Amphetamines
- Cimetidine

HOW SHOULD RESIDENTS WITH MANIA BE MANAGED?

Residents with severe mania can be very difficult to manage in the nursing home setting, however less severe mania (hypomania) is generally managable without transfer. Treatment generally involves lithium carbonate in combination with a neuroleptic for treatment of agitation and insomnia. The elderly appear to require lower levels of lithium to control their affective illness. Lithium levels of 0.4 to 0.8 mEq/l will generally be sufficient but must be individualized. Lithium levels should be monitored carefully as the elderly are much more susceptible to lithium toxicity and it appears that some elderly patients can develop toxicity at relatively low levels, e.g., 1.0 mEq/l. The cognitively impaired elderly are especially vulnerable to developing neurotoxicity.

CASE ILLUSTRATIONS

A number of case vignettes are presented to help the reader understand the variety of potential presentations of depression. In each case a different management approach was required. Case 1 describes a woman with a relatively acute episode of depression that responded well to treatment. Following this, several cases of chronic depression are described because these types of cases are common and present the treatment team with particular difficulties. There are a number of predictors of chronicity of depression. These include coexisting medical illness, long duration of current or previous depressive episodes, dysthymia or "double depression," (the latter referring to an acute depression in addition to dysthymia), and associated personality disorders.

Case 1: Masked Depression, Responsive to Treatment

Mrs A, an 82-year-old retired school teacher, began to deteriorate shortly after admission. She had been a widow for 8 years and had one daughter. She withdrew from social contacts and described severe headaches, constipation, and pain in her abdomen. A full medical workup was negative. She completely denied any feelings of depression, saying that she "wasn't crazy," and found it difficult to describe any emotions. She was, however, distressed, and felt that she should be left alone to die. Her appetite was decreased and she had lost 8 pounds over a 2-month period. Her sleep was broken and restless. She was able to give a clear account of her life and had evidently always been a fiercely independent woman who hated to rely on others. She confided that she had never wanted to go into a nursing home, but that she could no longer manage at home any more and refused to be a burden to her daughter. She nevertheless complained that her daughter was only visiting twice a week.

The difficulty in assessing Mrs A was in determining whether her symptoms represented an adjustment disorder with depressed mood or a major depression. She was started on an antidepressant, nortriptyline, with the dose increasing to 40 mg per day, and was seen for a half hour of supportive psychotherapy each week. After approximately 10 days of treatment, she noted that her headaches had diminished. She was feeling less worried and was surprised that her appetite was picking up. She gradually began to talk to some of the other residents and noted that her sleep was improving. She started to attend the exercise group and the arts and crafts programs. Within a month her daughter felt that her mother was back to her usual self.

Comment: Can patients who deny being depressed actually suffer from a depressive illness?

Elderly patients often are reluctant to admit to psychological or emotional distress, considering this to be a stigma and a sign of weakness. As a result, "masked depression" whose primary presenting symptom is physical pain, is relatively common in elderly patients. It is extremely important, therefore, for staff to be vigilant to the possibility of an underlying depressive illness.

Case 2: Depression, Paranoid Delusions, and Dementia

Mr L, a 90-year-old widower, was admitted to a home for the aged following his second wife's death. He had always been an active, social man who now thought that the Home would give him the opportunity to continue his social activities. He had no children from his first marriage, but had become extremely close to his stepsons. Some time before this, Mr L learned that one of his stepsons was in hospital following a stroke. His status and prognosis was unclear at that time. Mr L responded to the news by becoming increasingly agitated and seeking staff out incessantly with many somatic complaints. He was eating poorly, losing 2 kilograms within a week, and had difficulty falling asleep. In time, he began expressing fears that his food was being poisoned by certain staff members who had joined together in a plot to kill him. Antidepressants and major tranquilizers were not effective in reducing the psychotic symptoms. He was then transferred to an inpatient psychiatric unit and he ultimately required a course of nine ECT treatments. He recovered significantly from the psychotic symptoms and returned to the home.

Mr L, however, never completely regained his previous level of independence and remained fearful, requiring direction and reassurance that staff would always be available to him. Despite his fear of falling, he would go to the main dining room or would sit for brief periods in the lobby, a pastime he had previously enjoyed. Within 3 months, the staff noticed that he was becoming more agitated and refusing to go off the floor, except with his stepson who had recovered by this time. His delusions of being plotted against resurfaced. Medications were used unsuccessfully in an attempt to decrease the agitation, delusions, and depressive symptoms of sleeplessness and weight loss. He began to voice feelings of helplessness and hopelessness in the face of the onslaught of his "attackers." He became passively suicidal wanting to kill himself but unable to think of means to accomplish this. Another inpatient admission was arranged. It became necessary to certify him as his delusions now encompassed the hospital staff and he had become increasingly frightened, refusing to agree to the admission.

He was beginning to show signs of memory loss, and word-finding difficulties which contributed to his sense of suspiciousness. The inpatient staff, after much deliberation, felt that Mr L's depressive episodes were a response to his chronic delusions and increasing dementia. Mr L was vulnerable to his interpretations of the world which he now saw as threatening and malevolent. His medications were carefully titrated and were effective in decreasing some of the agitation associated with the delusions.

After Mr L returned to the nursing home, staff witnessed his increasing dependence, continued fear of being poisoned, and increasing memory loss. The agitation decreased further with his debilitation but the delusions remained fixed. The staff, once considered to be his friends, had to contend with his repeated accusations of poisoning and "torturing." They were able to understand his illness, however, and continued to give him ongoing supportive care.

Comment: Why were Mr L's symptoms so persistent?

In addition to depression Mr L also had paranoid delusions and dementia. His deteriorating cognitive state compounded the other problems and because of a low tolerance to neuroleptic medications it was not possible to use an adequate dosage. In addition, persistent paranoid symptoms are notoriously difficult to treat and it is difficult for staff to accept that there are some individuals with psychiatric problems whose symptoms are essentially incurable. In spite of this the care and support offered to Mr L was crucial and did make his difficult existence somewhat more tolerable. Techniques such as reassurance, frequent interactions, and a gentle, non-confrontive approach are often effective in decreasing fear and promoting trust.

Case 3: Chronic Depression and Somatization

Mrs B, an 80-year-old divorced woman, was admitted to a nursing home when she could no longer manage on her own effectively. Although she was only mildly cognitively impaired, she had several physical ailments including heart disease, numerous past surgical procedures, arthritis, and mild diabetes. She was placed on a minimal care floor since she was capable of doing most of her care herself.

Mrs B described herself as having been an outgoing and happy person. She was proud of her role as hairdresser to "the Queen of Rumania." She fell in love at the age of 21 and married her "one true love." Five years later her life was shattered with the onset of World War II. Her husband was taken away and subsequently died, her daughter was "shot in (her) arms," and she was in prison camps for close to 5 years. During this time, she described horrific conditions and experiences including experiments without anesthesia, beatings, deaths of friends and family. She managed to survive, met her second husband, and settled in Israel. She subsequently gave birth to two children who both died of TB. Unable to cope, she and her husband emigrated to Canada. After several years she discovered that her husband was having an affair. She left him and lived on her own until admission to the nursing home.

Not long after her admission, staff became aware of her excessive demands and reacted to her imperious attitude toward them. Interviews revealed chronic depression related to her past experiences and grief over the many losses she had faced. She tended to focus on somatic concerns, describing in detail her various maladies, pains, and sleeplessness. A tricyclic antidepressant was started at night in order to ameliorate her sleeping difficulties and improve her mood. A nurse-clinician saw her on a weekly basis for the next 3 years. Staff meetings were held weekly for 6 weeks for the nurses to examine the reasons for her behavior and to facilitate care planning. A strong supportive component was necessary throughout the sessions since her unabating demands, attitude of entitlement, and derogatory personal comments tried the patience of staff working with her.

Over time, the staff realized that Mrs B's demands represented her "need to be treated as a somebody." The somatic complaints were her way of communicating psychic pain. Her treatment became a delicate balance between investigating her complaints, treating her symptoms when indicated, and reassuring her when no changes to her mental status were apparent. She tended to interpret decreased interventions as a lack of caring and would hurl intense accusations at medical and nursing staff that they were not "doing anything," until they relented. The myriad of medications, tests and surgeries she had undergone in the past were a testimony to her strength and ability to get what she perceived she needed. Dilemmas arose frequently over whether a new or intensified symptom warranted further investigation. The staff became attuned to her and were able to discern minute changes in behavior which were often correlated with actual changes in her physical status.

As the staff grew to know and understand Mrs B, they were less likely to take her suspicious accusations personally and used humor as a method of interacting with her. Her time was more structured and her routines became more predictable. Although her moods and corresponding demands fluctuated, she was finally able to form attachments, go on outings, and participate in programs, and at times was able to describe her accomplishments with a sense of self-worth. When she died 7 years after admission, staff were able to discuss the pride they felt in caring for this warm but difficult woman.

Comment: How can Mrs B's difficulties be explained?

Mrs B had a history of numerous psychic traumas and losses. It was difficult to fully comprehend the psychological effects of these events. At times Mrs B seemed to exaggerate her symptoms and even embellish her history, which staff found difficult to understand. Because of deprivation during her life she used physical symptoms as a way of gratifying her dependency needs. Her more rewarding relationships were ultimately with health care professionals. As the staff grew to understand Mrs B, their tolerance of her behavior increased and they were able to provide her with the care she desired.

Case 4: Depression and Cancer

Mr A, a 78-year-old married man, decided to live in the same nursing home as his wife, an Alzheimer victim, and moved in several months following her institutionalization. He was a warm, quiet man who generally kept to himself and would rarely venture off the floor except for meals and short visits with his wife. About a year after his admission, staff became concerned about his lack of motivation, increased isolation, sudden weight loss, and tearfulness. The psychiatric team was called in to assess the possibility of an acute depression. An interview revealed a tall emaciated-looking man who was able to engage quickly and openly. He described past episodes of depressive and psychotic-like symptoms in his earlier years, which had been treated effectively with perphenazine 4 mg per day. He had been on this medication for many years and had refused to have it discontinued. He was tearful when describing his experience of having a wife who was dementing. He reported a decrease in appetite, energy, and sleep; poor concentration; and pains in the upper left abdominal quadrant. The psychiatric team recommended investigation of his pain, and doxepin 25 mg qhs. A nurse-clinician began weekly supportive psychotherapy sessions aimed at helping him cope with his current life situation.

A week later, Mr A described a "miraculous cure" after taking the doxepin for 2 nights. He stated that his sleep, appetite, and mood had improved significantly. The miracle was short-lived, however, and by the next week he began to apologize, saying "I know you and the doctor are trying to help me but I don't think the pill is working." The dosage of the antidepressant was increased. In the meantime, investigations of the left-sided pain proved negative. Since Mr A continued to lose strength and weight and was not responding well to antidepressants, he was transferred to a psychiatry inpatient unit. Despite pharmacotherapy, milieu therapy, and interactional therapy, he became increasingly focused on the pain. He was adamant that there was something physically wrong and that his depression was related to the pain he was experiencing.

Teasing out organic pain from psychic pain was difficult. Mr A's lack of progress, and the nagging possibility of a malignancy prompted reinvestigation. This time, CT scan of the abdomen revealed a pancreatic tumor. Mr A, his family, and the staff experienced mixed emotions as a result of the diagnosis — sadness at the prognosis but relief that there was a physical reason for the pain and depression. Mr A was more at peace now that at last his pain was "heard" and there would be a response to relieve his suffering.

Comment: When should it be suspected that "somatic" symptoms are due to physical illness?

The term "somatic" should be used with caution as it can lull us into a false sense that we can "explain away" certain physical complaints. Physical causes should always be ruled out. However, practical problems include the cost and risks associated with over-investigation and the fact that some diseases such as carcinoma can be difficult to identify in the early stages. It is important to remember that physical illnesses often present initially with emotional symptoms.

Case 5: Bipolar Affective Disorder, Dementia

Mrs C was an 89-year-old woman with a 52-year history of mood disorder. She had had several psychiatric admissions in the past requiring treatment with ECT for depression. Over the 4 years prior to admission, she had become increasingly cognitively impaired and had been diagnosed as having Alzheimer disease. At the time of her admission to the nursing home, she scored 13/30 on the Folstein Mini-Mental State Exam (MMSE). She continued to have frequent episodes of mood change. Although she was significantly demented, the charac-

ter of these mood shifts was clearly that of a bipolar disorder. When she was manic she was irritable and abusive towards nursing staff particularly during the night. She would persev- erate on themes related to sex and money and insisted on telling all visitors to the unit that she had absolutely no interest in sex. She was managed with lithium levels ranging from 0.4 to 0.6. On one occasion her lithium level increased to a level of 0.9 and she became quite withdrawn and delirious. A lowering of her level resulted in a reduction of her confusion.

Comment: What approaches should be taken in the management of the manic patient?

Pharmacological management is critical and it is particularly important to ensure that the resident receives enough medica- tion to promote adequate sleep. The patient with mania is easily over-stimulated and it is important, therefore, to try to reduce excessive sensory stimulation. Some behaviors may be quite bizarre. For example, one nursing home resident would, when manic, empty all of the local newspaper boxes and deliver "free" newspapers to the residents in the institution. In general, a clear setting of limits is necessary to manage the disruptive behaviors of the manic resident. This may require the involve- ment of the nursing home administrator. Although generally not a major issue in a nursing home setting, it should be noted that residents with mania often have poor judgment and may be incompetent to manage their own financial affairs. Once the acute manic episode has been brought under control it is important to monitor the lithium levels closely and to find an optimal level for the individual resident.

KEY POINTS

- Depression can be subdivided into major depression, dyst- hymic disorder, adjustment disorder with depressed mood, and organic mood disorder.

- If there is a history of mania or hypomania a diagnosis of bipolar affective disorder is made.

- Diagnosis may be difficult in the elderly. Neurological and other medical illnesses can mimic depression. Elderly individuals with a depressive illness tend to complain less frequently of actually experiencing a depressed mood.

- Many medical illnesses and medications can precipitate depression.

- Major depression represents a final common pathway, that is a non-specific response to a variety of biological, psychological, and/or social factors.

- Treatment approaches should therefore include medication, psychotherapy, and social modalities as indicated. Treatment is often highly effective and therefore rewarding for all involved.

REFERENCES

1. The American Psychiatric Association. (1987). *Diagnostic and Statistical Manual of Mental Disorders*, 3rd Edition, Revised. Washington, DC: The American Psychiatric Association.
2. Katz, I.R., Lesher, E., Kleban, M., Jethanandani, V., Parmelee, P. (1989). Clinical features of depression in the nursing home. *International Psychogeriatrics*, 1:5-15.
3. Sadavoy, J., Smith, I., Conn, D.K., Richards, B. (1990). Depression in geriatric patients with chronic medical illness. *International Journal of Geriatric Psychiatry*, 5:187-192.
4. Erikson, E.H. (1959). Identity and the life-cycle. *Psychological Issues, Monograph 1*. New York: International Universities Press.
5. Parkes, C.M. (1972). *Bereavement*. New York: International Universities Press.

SUGGESTED READING

1. Murphy, E. (1986). *Affective disorders in the elderly*. Edinburgh: Churchill Livingstone.

A useful review of the affective (mood) disorders in the elderly.

2. Rodin, G., Voshart, K. (1986). Depression in the medically ill: An overview. *American Journal of Psychiatry*, 143:696.

An excellent overview of the relationship between depression and physical illness. Well referenced.

3. Blazer, D.G. (1989). Affective disorders in late life. In: E.W. Busse, D.G. Blazer, (Eds.). *Geriatric Psychiatry*. Washington DC: American Psychiatric Press.

Focuses on epidemiology, differential diagnosis and treatment. Also a good source for further references.

CHAPTER

The Suicidal
Resident

6

---

by David K. Conn and Alanna Kaye

*"The thought of suicide is a great consolation: by means of
it one gets successfully through many a bad night"*
— Nietszche.

This chapter will focus on the assessment and management of the suicidal resident. The term suicide is generally used to refer to the act of taking one's own life deliberately and intentionally. Self-destructive behavior is a very complex phenomenon, however, and several distinctions must be made:

- A completed suicide refers to a death resulting from deliberately self-inflicted causes.
- A suicide attempt refers to self-inflicted injury that does not result in death. Because in many suicide attempts there is no intention to cause death, but rather a desire to communicate to others feelings such as despair or anger, the term self-harm is preferred by many over the term suicide attempt.

109

Suicidal behavior may manifest itself as an acute violent act, but it can also take more chronic and passive forms. Reckless behavior, refusal to adhere to prescribed diets and medications or to continue life-sustaining treatments such as dialysis are examples of less active forms of self-destructive behavior. We will initially review active suicidal behavior and conclude with a discussion of more chronic passive suicidal behavior which is not infrequent in the long-term care setting.

HOW COMMON IS SUICIDAL BEHAVIOR IN THE ELDERLY?

The elderly have the highest completed suicide rates of any age group. For example, in the United States this group comprises approximately 11% of the population and accounts for 17% of all reported suicides. Moreover, suicide may be under-reported in the elderly, as the cause of death can be attributed to medical illness more easily than in the young. The high suicide rate in the elderly is predominantly due to extremely high rates among white elderly males. Despite the high rate of completed suicide, suicide attempts occur less often than in the younger population. This points to the fact that suicidal acts among the elderly are more likely to be lethal.

SUICIDE IN THE LONG-TERM CARE SETTING

The rate of suicide in nursing homes and other long-term care facilities has not been well investigated. A 2-year study of all completed suicides in Los Angeles county by Litman and Farberow did not reveal the rate of suicide in institutions to be much higher than that in the community [1]. Out of a total of over 2,000 suicides 20 occurred in "nursing convalescent units." The mean age of these patients was 76 years. The primary medical diagnoses included diabetes, cardiac disorders, cancer, multiple sclerosis, and atherosclerosis. Nursing staff had noted severe depressions in most of these suicidal patients and the majority of the patients had communicated something about their suicidal intention. Death was most likely to occur from the ingestion of pills that had been saved up or smuggled in or from self-inflicted lacerations. During the survey some informants raised the philosophical/ethical problem of why there should be any sanction against suicide in patients who were old, ill with incurable diseases, suffering from loneliness and abandonment, and conscious of being a drain on the resources of their families. It was noted that many of these patients had been chronically suicidal. Nevertheless, despite the fact that nearly all patients in such settings share to some extent the pattern of chronic illness and isolation, suicide was in fact quite rare. The authors suggested that the patients who committed suicide were characterized by a special inability to adjust to the nursing home environment.

THEORIES OF SUICIDAL BEHAVIOR

Sociocultural Theories

Durkheim's work, published in 1897, is still relevant today and suggests that the nature and extent of one's involvement in society is important in determining the vulnerability to suicide [2]. He used the term "egoistic suicide" to describe suicide in individuals who lacked a sense of belonging and were not well integrated into the society. These ideas clearly have relevance in the nursing home setting because many individuals feel abandoned by and removed from society when they are placed in an institution. This emphasizes the need to create a community atmosphere in the long-term care setting in order to counter the social withdrawal and isolation of residents.

Sociocultural theories also emphasize the importance of a rapidly changing society as a result of technological advances, urbanization, and "Westernization." Durkheim referred to suicide resulting from crises in the collective societal order as "anomic suicide." Suicide rates tend to be highest in urban industrialized countries where a negative stereotypical view of the elderly ("ageism") is prevalent, and where youth, beauty, productivity, progress, speed, and independence are highly valued.

Psychological Theories

Suicide often follows an "acute suicidal crisis," characterized by a period of hopelessness. The suicidal act is at times regarded as a form of communication to another person (a cry for help, an act of aggression or both).

Freud viewed suicide as aggression turned against the self, rather than expressed externally towards a person with whom the victim has a close but ambivalent relationship [3]. It may be precipitated by loss and feelings of abandonment and rejection associated with the loss. Again, this is clearly relevant in the nursing home resident. Bibring and Seligman emphasize the role of helplessness [4,5]. Feelings of helplessness are common in the elderly, especially the depressed elderly and result from the belief of individuals that they cannot control aspects of their lives.

Miller [6] notes that lying dormant within everyone is an extremely personal equation that determines the point at which the quality of one's life would be so poor that one would no longer wish to live. He termed this point the "line of unbearability" and we are not normally aware of it until we are actually confronted by an intolerable situation. At that time those who have the ability to maintain some hope will cry out for help, whereas those who are completely hopeless will attempt to kill themselves.

Biological Theories

Depression is very common but not universal in suicidal people. Depressed individuals typically perceive themselves as useless, worthless and may have profound feelings of low self-esteem and self-hatred. Suicide is seen as a preferred solution and an honorable way out. A number of studies have identified an underlying abnormality of neurotransmitter function in suicidal patients.

The Relationship between Medical Illness and Suicide

A high percentage of patients who have committed suicide also have active medical illnesses. Disorders that have been found to have a high association with suicide include pulmonary disease associated with severe shortness of breath, rheumatoid arthritis, chronic renal failure being treated with dialysis and peptic ulcer. In patients with cancer or incurable diseases there are several critical periods particularly while the diagnosis and prognosis are still being determined and during the phase when the true nature of the condition becomes apparent.

ASSESSMENT

How is Suicidal Potential Identified?

One of the most valuable resources for determining suicide potential is the staff who work day to day with the resident. Their intuitive "knowledge" that something is wrong, in the experience of the authors, has proven to be an excellent guide to further assessment and management. Acting on staff's observations that a resident is "different" or causing "worry," a major depression and/or suicidal potential have often been discovered and managed. Without these perceptions of the staff, successful management would not be possible. Finally, since suicidal ideation may represent a response to psychosis or major depression, a complete assessment is indicated in order to identify any treatable psychiatric illness.

It is important for staff to document clearly all relevant information (see assessment checklist). Direct observations and quotes are particularly useful in determining suicide potential as there is less opportunity for misinterpretation of the data.

How Do I Know if a Resident is Suicidal?

It is not always clear when someone is contemplating suicide. In certain cases, if impulsive behavior or cognitive impairment is a factor, there may be no warning signs.

Behavioral, situational, or verbal cues may be encountered. Behavioral cues include putting affairs in order or giving away possessions, increasing isolation, and alcohol or drug abuse. Recent losses such as loss of health, independence, cognitive capacity, family, or friends are situational factors that can precipitate suicide. Responses to these life crises vary with previous coping styles and abilities as well as with the degree of available support systems. Grief and mourning, especially when support systems are diminished, may contribute to the development of suicidal ideation.

Today's elderly belong to a generation that emphasized survival, rigid gender roles, and conformity. Little importance was attached to psychological awareness and the value of communication. Thus, the ability to recognize psychological distress and to communicate it verbally may be limited in this population. Spontaneous, direct expression of suicidal intent is less frequently encountered than are indirect veiled references. It is therefore crucial for staff working with the elderly to be aware of this factor during interactions. Phrases such as, "There's nothing left for me," "I can't take it anymore," or saying, "good-bye" to a staff person when "good-night" would be more appropriate, may convey an underlying message of desperation, isolation, and a feeling of being trapped. Directing conversation toward expression of these feelings promotes a sense of caring and trust. The assessment of suicidal ideation can then be facilitated.

Some Residents Say They "Just Want to Die." Are They Suicidal?

Not necessarily. It is important to distinguish between active and passive suicidal ideation. Active suicidal thoughts are present in individuals who discuss or demonstrate specific plans and intent to end their lives. Motivation to take control of their current situation is evident. For example, a mobile man who has decided that life is not worth living states, "I can't live this way any more. I'm going to stand in the road to get hit by a car." Clearly, there are plans, intent, motivation, and an ability to actually make an attempt.

The intent behind passive thoughts is more difficult to determine. During an interaction, the resident may say, "I want to die." When this statement is pursued more fully, the resident may voice active suicidal thoughts. Frequently, a true wish to die may exist, but moral or religious beliefs preclude active steps to accomplish this goal. Residents who appear to have "given up" may be among these individuals (see section on Chronic or Passive Suicide). However, residents who reveal a wish to die may require a mechanism to express their feelings of despair, depression, hopelessness, or helplessness without any actual intent for self-harm.

If I Ask Residents Whether They Are Suicidal Would I Be Giving Them an Idea or Be Encouraging Them to Think these Thoughts?

Although this is a common concern, asking directly about suicidal thoughts does not increase the risk of suicidal ideation or behavior. Generally, if an individual has decided definitively to commit suicide, he will attempt to do so despite any and all attempts to intervene. For some individuals, the opportunity to talk about the depth of their psychic pain may decrease the likelihood of an attempt. The act of asking these specific and sensitive questions conveys caring and acceptance and gives the individual permission to speak, all of which are essential to decreasing the sense of isolation and pain associated with suicidal thoughts.

Asking specific questions about suicidal thought or intent can be difficult and may produce anxiety in the caregiver during assessment.

Phrases such as "Have you ever felt life was not worth living?" or "Have you been thinking about ending your life?" can soften the tone of discussion and convey acceptance of the topic, thereby opening the door to further exploration directed at issues such as: whether a plan of action has been considered; if so, what this might be; do they intend to follow through with their plan; when would this occur; do they feel there may be options other than suicide to deal with their current situation?

Through these questions the level of suicide risk can be determined. For example, a vague, guarded response such as "Who knows?" or a question such as "Why are you asking me?" may indicate a higher risk than a direct answer. Verbalizing observations e.g., "I notice this is a hard question for you to answer." can act as a catalyst for further discussion.

Invariably, our own thoughts, attitudes, and judgements about suicide play a part in the interview process. It is crucial, therefore, that the interviewer be aware of his/her own feelings in order to minimize the effect on the discussion. When someone expresses suicidal thoughts it raises a myriad of reactions within the listener that can include anger, fear, vulnerability, guilt, helplessness, and denial. These reactions may be reflected in the way interviewers phrase their questions. For example, discomfort with the issue is revealed in questions such as "Just a routine question, you're not thinking of suicide are you?" It is clear from this question that the interviewer wants the answer to be "No," could not tolerate an honest answer and is therefore, creating an unwitting block to an open discussion of suicidal thoughts. Confronting the issue in an accepting, honest and gentle manner creates a climate in which painful issues can be revealed and discussed.

How Do I Assess Potential Risk?

While all expressions of self-harm require active exploration and intervention, the likelihood of death by suicide may be somewhat lower in an institutional setting than in the community. This is due to the presence of staff and the decreased access by residents to a means of inflicting self-harm. Nevertheless, attempts are sometimes made.

Predicting risk in individual cases remains difficult. There are, however, certain factors that have been associated statistically with a greater potential for suicide. These factors are listed in Table 1 along with the behavioral cues already mentioned in previous sections.

Table 1
Assessment of Suicidal Behavior

I. Suicidal Intent

- Verbalizes suicidal thoughts
- Describes suicidal intent
- Can outline a concrete realistic plan
- Methods are available
- Physical ability to carry out threat

II. Behavior

- Gives guarded answers to questions
- Diverts interviewer off topic
- Increasing withdrawal
- Depressed affect
- Resolving depression
- Sudden interest/disinterest in religion

- Gives away possessions
- Puts affairs in order
- Drug/alcohol abuse

III. Risk Factors

- Male
- White
- Low self-esteem
- Family history of suicide
- Support systems decreased/nonexistent
- Decline in physical status
- Decline in cognitive status
- Impulsivity
- History of suicide, attempts or violence
- Recent loss or change in life

The first part of the assessment checklist reflects the extent to which the resident has developed a plan. For example, if a bedbound resident states that he is planning on ending his life by going to the roof of the building and jumping off, there is less of a possibility of completion than if he had stated he was going to starve himself to death. Thus, careful attention must be directed toward exploring the details of the plan.

The second and third parts of the checklist identify the behaviors and life situations which contribute to the likelihood of suicide. Potential risk tends to increase with the specificity of the plan, availability of means, greater physical illness, resolving depression (which adds an energy to complete the act), and impulsivity either as a characterological trait or resulting from brain damage.

MANAGEMENT

Several principles guide the care of the suicidal resident. Safety, dignity, and promoting the trust within the relationship are primary considerations when determining a plan of care. Listed below are general guidelines for management.

Remove any potentially dangerous objects, i.e., medications, sharps, glass, ropes, belts. This is usually done by two staff members conducting a room search. Explanations to the resident regarding concerns for his/her safety must be provided to promote a sense of trust and to reduce the risk of the resident perceiving the search as punitive. If possible, permission from the resident to perform the search should be obtained. Careful documentation in the chart of actions taken, and why, personnel present, and the whereabouts of the resident's property is important for legal reasons.

Close observation of the resident is important. Individuals at high risk require constant observation, while lower-risk residents can be maintained on frequent checks (every 15 to 30 minutes). Realistically, this may not always be possible. Adequate staffing is rarely available with current constraints in budgets. Other options may include utilizing resources such as volunteers, family members, program workers. Rotating the nursing team to maintain frequent checks may be possible. This would require the staff to take turns staying with the resident for specified lengths of time throughout the shift. If family members can afford the cost of a sitter, this may be a short-term adjunct to professional observation. There are, however, pitfalls to this option. Once the crisis has passed, discontinuing a sitter may be problematic since residents can become very attached to the sitter and enjoy the one-to-one contact. The decision to obtain constant care must be made after carefully weighing the risks and benefits.

Where the situation is acute, access to a psychiatrist and/or psychiatric nurse specialist may be helpful. If acute psychiatric illness is present, definitive treatment becomes necessary. There may be circumstances which necessitate transfer of a resident to an acute care facility for psychiatric assessment and treatment. It is these authors' experience, however, that the majority of cases can be managed on their own units. Access by the long-term care facility to psychiatric services has proven to be beneficial to staff and residents, providing both support and assistance in diagnosis and management, while the residents are maintained in their own environment. Maintaining continuity of care is especially important since relocation of a frail and/or demented individual can produce catastrophic reactions, increase fear, and possibly worsen the risk of suicide.

Working with the residents to structure their day can help to build contact, self-esteem, and trust, as well as decrease the sense of isolation. Predictable, consistent routines provide a sense of stability and are reassuring to those whose inner life is chaotic. Setting aside a few minutes each day to talk with the resident about concerns and fears, as well as achievements, assists in providing some of this structure and promotes the rapport.

The degree of risk and a clear management plan should be determined and documented. The efficacy of the management plan must be evaluated in an ongoing manner and adjusted to accommodate the resident's changing needs.

CASE ILLUSTRATIONS

The following case illustrations underscore a number of different factors that can contribute to suicide potential. It should be noted that in clinical practice and in our case histories these factors tend to overlap.

Case 1: Depression

Mr W, a 72-year-old married man, was admitted to a long-term care facility one year after suffering a stroke. He had residual left-sided hemiparesis and contracture of his left hip. Although he had some cognitive deficits in the areas of memory, word-finding, and judgement, as well as problems with impulsivity, he was well able to communicate his thoughts verbally and understand staff's responses to him. Staff requested assistance for his extreme combativeness, especially during care or feeding.

Examination revealed a large man, curled up in bed, moving about restlessly and complaining of pain in his left hip. He was able to respond to questions about his life before the stroke. He had been a truck driver and spoke with great pride of "never (having) had an accident." In his spare time, he went to taverns with his friends or went up north with his wife in their trailer. He described himself as somewhat "wild" in his earlier years. He then spoke poignantly of how the stroke had affected him and the many losses with which he grappled. Mr W was, at times, aware of his aggressive behavior stating that he became impatient during care at which time his awareness of his physical deficits and dependency on others was heightened. He described some decrease in appetite and difficulty falling asleep. He had little interest or enjoyment in anything. It was determined that Mr W was suffering from a major depression as a result of the stroke and his response to his many losses.

The management plan included investigation of his hip pain and antidepressants (trazodone) to address the depression and agitation. Nursing measures included approaching him from his left side, and using two staff members to do his care. This lessened the chances of being hurt when he would strike out with his right arm. Adjusting the times of his a.m. care to later in the morning, when he was less agitated, proved to be beneficial in decreasing some of the aggression. Whenever possible, the assistance of male staff was enlisted as Mr W seemed to relate better to men. The anger and aggression began to decrease. Three months later, however, the aggression escalated again, but this time Mr W began talking about ending his life. He wrapped the telephone cord around his neck, attempted to drink a bottle of mouthwash and later tried to climb out through the bottom of his bed in order to "fall and break my head or my hip and die."

Comment: What kind of management would be appropriate?

He was assessed by the psychiatrist, who increased the antidepressant and added a neuroleptic, thioridazine, to decrease the intensity of agitation. Although Mr W's statement of intent, his planning, and impulsivity placed him at a high level of risk, the chances of a completed suicide were lessened by his compromised mobility. Staff removed all objects from his room, used paper plates, plastic utensils, and remained with him while he ate. A system of frequent observations was instituted by rotating staff to check on his activities every half hour. Firm limit setting was adopted, as his insight and judgement were impaired. These external limits added structure and provided Mr

W with realistic feedback on the impact of his behavior on others.

Although Mr W's depression and behavioral difficulties have improved, the possibility of further self-harm remained. Staff continued their efforts to offer support to Mr W but his cognitive deficits and the importance of mobility and independence to his self-esteem impeded his ability to work through, and accept his devastating losses. As a result, continued use of the antidepressant and neuroleptic remained an important part of his management.

Case 2: Dementia

Mr A, an 80-year-old widower, was admitted to a nursing home as a result of declining physical health and difficulty managing at home. He had always been a deeply religious man who took great pleasure in teaching his students about the complexities of the Bible. His daughter reported to the staff that at one point prior to admission, her father had said he would kill himself if he ever had to live in a nursing home. The staff grew to like Mr A's quiet, gentle ways with everyone around him.

Three months after admission staff were making early morning rounds and noticed that Mr A's sheets were wet. Thinking that Mr A had been incontinent, staff began to change the sheets. To their amazement, the sheet was not wet from urine, but blood from a stabwound next to the right carotid artery. They found a pair of small, steel surgical-type scissors among the sheets. Appropriate steps were taken to care for him through the night and a psychiatric consultation was requested. During the interview, it was apparent that Mr A was grossly cognitively impaired. Although unaware of his whereabouts, the day, the month or the year, he was able to remember the stabbing but could not relate why it had occurred. Painfully slowed in his responses, he was able to relate his thoughts about aging via Bible stories and eventually was able to state that he had been incontinent of urine for the first time several days previously. Although Mr A's primary diagnosis was dementia, a major depression could not be ruled out. An antidepressant was started in an attempt to elevate his mood and activate him.

Mr A did not make any subsequent suicide attempts. Despite treatment with antidepressants and the staff's provision of support and contact, Mr A continued to withdraw as the dementia progressed. He died 5 months following the suicide attempt.

Comment: How can we understand Mr A's suicide attempt?

It is most likely that the insight into his increasing disabilities coupled with the decrease in impulse control resulting from his dementia precipitated Mr A's suicide attempt. His profound shame may have had some effect in preventing any further attempts. The caregiving team met for several weeks to resolve their own feelings arising from this episode. The questions "Were there warning signs?" or "Was this preventable?" arose and professional guilt was addressed in these sessions. In a supportive atmosphere, the staff became more comfortable with the knowledge that, at times, there may be no warning preceding the suicidal gesture.

Cases 3 and 4: Personality Disorder

Two cases will be discussed in this section to illustrate the different manifestations and management of characterologically difficult residents who may be suicidal.

Case 3

Mr X, an 85-year-old widowed man, was admitted to a nursing home as a result of increasing debilitation secondary to Parkinson disease. He was a man who had never formed close relationships but did marry and have one child. Both his wife and child were killed in concentration camps during the Holocaust. He had been interred in both German and Russian war camps and had attempted to hang himself during that period. A prominent editor of political newspapers, he had always been a very independent, strong-willed man who scorned emotional ties as a sign of weakness. He had a long history of alcoholism and occasional violence. He spoke of hunting the officer responsible for his wife's death and murdering him. He also admitted to three other suicide attempts. On one occasion he had evidently shot himself, narrowly missing his heart.

Despite taking pride in his intelligence, he had poor self-esteem. He frequently became angry and demeaning to the staff trying to care for him.

His frequent references to suicide, coupled with his history and continued alcohol consumption, led to psychiatric evaluation. Depression was ruled out at this time but the risk of suicide was apparent as he would often threaten to walk out into the snow in order to freeze to death. He experienced life as a burden and was aware of his progressing Parkinsonism and failing cognitive abilities. Mr X had no family supports or religious affiliation. He had always been fairly suspicious and guarded in nature but these feelings were greatly intensified by paranoia associated with his Parkinson disease. The staff had become the objects of his paranoid delusions and he would frequently lash out at them with his cane when he became angry.

The management plan attempted to address his sense of isolation and impulsivity as well as the emotions of those caring for him. The psychiatric nurse clinician met with him individually several times per week. Low doses of thioridazine were used to attempt to control the impulsivity, with careful monitoring due to his Parkinson disease. He would not stop drinking and found elaborate ways of obtaining alcohol until staff began to dispense modest amounts at the nursing station. Volunteers were used to provide contacts and would engage him in chess games and political discussions. Threats of suicide occurred episodically but his explosiveness and paranoia continued to increase. He became unrelenting in his pursuit of one particular staff member, not unlike his hunt for the Nazi officer. Mr X's accusatory, threatening manner evoked fear, hurt, and anger in the staff. The situation gradually escalated as staff and Mr X began to react to each other's intense emotions.

Comment: What issues were the staff struggling with?

Staff meetings were held to provide support and explore the reasons for some of Mr X's behavior. Staff reported a number of concerns, including a sense that this behavior was purposeful and the staff's bewilderment as to how they may have contributed to his wrath, discomfort with the chronic risk of suicide, the feelings of helplessness and inadequacy, and difficulties ensuring safety for Mr X, other residents, and the staff. The length of time needed to resolve these issues speaks to the complexity of the case and the intensity of emotions aroused.

As the months passed, Mr X never attempted suicide but succumbed gradually to the effects of end-stage Parkinson disease. Following Mr X's transfer to another floor for medical reasons, staff were able to obtain some distance from their experience of caring for Mr X and ultimately to view their role with some measure of satisfaction. They had been able to provide as much care as humanly possible under extremely stressful conditions. The perseverance of the staff and their ability to provide some continuity in his life likely played a role in Mr X never having carried out his threat to end his life.

Case 4

Mrs B, an 83-year-old widow, had lived in a nursing home since the death of her husband several years previously. She had a history of depressions which were treated with antidepressants. She had always been a very dependent woman, unable to tolerate being alone for any length of time. She frequently sought out the staff for reassurance that they liked and cared for her. Frequent weepy periods were precipitated by perceived insults and rejection by other residents. Although she had many friends in the community who visited her frequently, she often felt slighted and said that they did not include her often enough in their gatherings. Problems with room-mates were frequent as she found fault with everyone. On one occasion following a particularly vocal argument with a room-mate, she announced to the staff that she planned to kill herself and then became very guarded, refusing to answer when questioned about her plans. She simply stated she wanted to change rooms because she "couldn't live like this any more."

Comment: What did assessment reveal?

Clear evidence of a major depressive disorder was not found during psychiatric evaluation. Her agitation and her lack of awareness of how her behavior was affecting staff were more prominent. She was, in many ways, attempting to gratify her needs in the only way she knew how — to become helpless, weepy, and threaten self-harm. She was indeed very distressed and agitated over her current plight but settled with assurances that staff would help her. Suicide precautions were instituted. She refused, however, to remain on the floor for observation.

How could staff respond?

Contact was increased through regularly scheduled interview times. She gradually became less agitated, weepy, and clingy as she began to realize that staff would respond to her distress. In turn, the staff began to understand her need to feel special and that this need might be met by providing her with a single room in addition to the increased support and structure. Once this move was accomplished, Mrs B settled and made no further threats to end her life. Crucial to this case was the staff's ability to look beyond the obvious demands. Staff's ability to tolerate her clinginess and address her need to feel wanted and special, allowed Mrs B's relationships to evolve without anger and rejection.

Case 5: Terminal Illness

Mrs D, a 74-year-old widow, was admitted to the palliative care unit with a diagnosis of metastatic cancer. Over the course of the first week, staff became aware of her apparent inability to "connect" with anyone. One day, staff overheard her ask her son to bring in her sleeping pills from home as she was having difficulty falling asleep. She was also noted to have alluded to the fact that she wanted to die. The next day another staff member saw bottles of medication in her purse. These incidents led to a psychiatric assessment regarding the question of suicide. During the initial interview, Mrs D spoke openly about these incidents, denying intent to attempt suicide and dismissing the team's concerns about her as "unnecessary." She gave an impression of politely complying with the interview in order to finish with us as soon as possible and graciously rejected any offers of support. She did, however, make a promise not to attempt to end her life. She was able to talk about how the cancer had "taken over" her life and what this meant to her. A fiercely independent woman, she could not easily accept anyone or anything else having control over her. The implications of hospitalization were clearly troublesome to her. Having some control over when and how she would die seemed to be connected to her need for independence.

Comment: How did the team approach this dilemma?

Despite assurances from her that she would not end her life, the unit team's discomfort remained very high. They had difficulty resolving the ethical issues of autonomy versus paternalism inherent in the act of removing the bedside medications (see Chapter 14). The team also felt that if they did take them, she might perceive this act as a breach of trust which would then impede any chance of making a therapeutic connection with her. The psychiatric team also struggled with these questions and met with Mrs D daily for 4 days. On the fourth day, a decision was made to remove the medications. The goal of this decision was to communicate that her distress was heard and taken seriously. In an attempt to promote her relationship with the unit staff, the psychiatric team decided to do the search. Persistent, gentle persuasion finally yielded permission from Mrs D to search her belongings with her assistance and all potentially harmful objects were removed. This act seemed to be a catalyst for Mrs D to then "connect" with many of the staff members. She was able to subsequently work through and resolve important issues with her children before her death 6 weeks later.

STAFF CONSIDERATIONS

Dealing with suicidal residents in a long-term care facility is a great challenge for care-givers. As the 8-year-old son of one of the authors stated, "Suicide is not a nice thing for anybody." Our own emotional responses can be varied and intense. Anxiety, fear, anger, and guilt are commonly experienced. Medicolegal, moral, religious, and ethical issues frequently surface. Emotions within caregiving teams may manifest themselves at the bedside as anger, over-solicitousness, protectiveness, or avoidance of the resident. Realistically, there are limits to what can be done to prevent suicide and it may occur regardless of precautions. Sometimes there are no warning signs at all. These factors contribute to the caregivers' sense of helplessness and frustration.

Frequent supportive meetings are important not only for staff to plan care, but to air thoughts and feelings about the situation. Creating a climate in which staff's opinions are accepted and valued is an integral component to the supportive nature of those meetings. These sessions facilitate open and honest discussion and give rise to creative solutions to circumvent problems associated with budget restraints and limited resources. It is important to balance the focus of these meetings so that positive achievements are recognized and intense emotions are dealt with as well. As staff work through these complex issues, a greater comfort and level of confidence are achieved and transmitted to residents. Thus, the key to effective management of suicidal residents involves the support of both staff and residents.

CHRONIC OR PASSIVE SUICIDE

The concept of suicide can be extended to include individuals who undertake passive measures to shorten their lives. Chronic suicide has been referred to as "systematic self-neglect, whether intentional or unintentional, which in extreme cases can lead to death" [7]. This includes such behaviors as refusing to eat, refusing to take medications, drinking excessively, delaying or refusing treatment of medical conditions, and taking unnecessary risks. Such patients should be carefully assessed from a psychiatric standpoint to consider the possibility of an associated depression or other psychiatric disorder. These cases often present difficult ethical and medicolegal dilemmas.

Suicidal Behavior in the Terminally Ill

The term "rational" suicide has been used to describe the behavior of individuals who make a personal decision to end their lives, in the absence of mental disease and often in association with terminal or chronic medical illness. There is increasing recognition that for an individual with severe chronic pain, that is untreatable and unbearable, or for individuals with terminal illness the decision to end their lives can be considered rational. Discussion around this issue dates back to the Greeks but its acceptance runs contrary to traditional Judeo-Christian thinking.

A recent review of six cases of terminally ill suicidal patients showed that their suicidal behavior was associated with depression that appeared to respond to treatment [8]. The authors suggested that suicidal behavior in this population should be evaluated and treated as it would be in physically healthy patients and should not be viewed as an inevitable result of serious physical disease. Nevertheless, some health professionals believe that suicide is a reasonable alternative for the terminally ill. One study of 32 cases of patients with cancer in a Veteran's Administration hospital who committed suicide revealed a particularly high suicidal potential among elderly men with throat cancer, younger men with Hodgkin's disease or Leukemia, or persons of any age with cancer associated with heightened stress, severe anxiety, or low tolerance for pain [9].

Self-Injurious Behavior in the Institutationalized Elderly

Passive suicidal behavior in the institutionalized elderly was studied by Mishara and Kastenbaum [10]. They found that self-injurious behaviors occurred at least once in 43% of men and 21% of women during a 1-week observation period. Their definition of self-injurious behavior was rather broad, however, and included behavior such as falling out of wheelchairs, injury from careless cigarette smoking, scalding oneself with hot water, eating foreign objects, injury from fighting or pushing, injury from being tripped over, striking solid objects, refusing medication, and refusing to eat. In a controlled study of the introduction of milieu techniques, they showed a decrease in such behaviors through the use of both a token economy program that rewarded individuals for engaging in desirable behaviors and an enrichment program involving increased activities, social stimulation, and increased opportunity to make decisions regarding their own care.

Case 6: "Rational" Passive, Suicide

Mrs E, a 72-year-old widow, was referred for psychiatric consultation because she had threatened to discontinue her peritoneal renal dialysis. She was on a continuing care floor of a geriatric hospital having developed acute renal failure at the time of moving into a residential setting 6 months earlier. She travelled by taxi to the general hospital about 5 miles away for dialysis 3 times per week, which she found to be an exhausting process. Shortly after her own illness her husband was discovered to have metastatic carcinoma and died 3 months later. Psychiatric consultation was requested some weeks after his death because Mrs E said that she was seriously

*considering discontinuing her dialysis. She also made it clear
that if her already failing vision worsened she would certainly
opt to discontinue her dialysis.*

*Mrs E had no children although she had a niece and several
nephews with whom she was close. At the time of initial
evaluation she was actively grieving her husband's death. She
appeared fatigued and unable to experience any pleasure. She
found dialysis to be an uncomfortable and exhausting procedure. She was clearly depressed about her situation, although
it was unclear whether she was indeed suffering from a "clinical depression." Because a major depression could not be
ruled out, an antidepressant was started but despite adequate
dosage, the medication appeared to have no impact on her
state of mind. Mrs E was asked to postpone her decision with
regard to dialysis because of the fact that she was actively
grieving for her husband. Although she agreed to this, she
began to talk with increasing determination about discontinuing the dialysis. The attending team discussed the situation and
had mixed feelings about her decision. Although the issue of
her competence to make this decision was raised because she
showed signs of cognitive impairment, it was concluded that
she was competent to make the decision.*

*Several weeks later she made it clear to the attending physician
and team that she would not go to the general hospital the
following day for her dialysis. To everyone's consternation her
condition deteriorated that same day and she slipped into a
semicomatose state. Medical examinations showed signs of
mild congestive heart failure but did not reveal a cause for her
loss of consciousness. She died peacefully that same evening.*

Comment: Did Mrs E will herself to die?

It has been suggested that individuals may have a degree of
control over the timing of their deaths, and there is some
literature to suggest that severe emotional reactions can
precipitate cardiac arrhythmia and death (e.g., voodoo
deaths). In this case, Mrs E's apparent decision that she was
going to die and the decline in her condition, which occurred
at exactly the time that she had made her decision, seemed
to be more than a mere coincidence.

Should she have been treated more vigorously for depression?

It was not clear that she was suffering from a major depression. The use of the antidepressant in this case was an attempt to rule out a clinical depression and also to reassure staff that everything possible was being done. When depression is suspected there is always a question of how vigorous the treatment should be. In this case pursuing aggressive measures such as ECT made no clinical sense.

Was Mrs E competent to make the decision?

Mrs E was at times somewhat vague and confused with regard to details. When it came to a discussion around her dialysis and her overall view of her life, however, she was consistent and able to give a clear explanation of her feelings. She believed she had lived an active and full life and that the quality of her life at present was virtually zero. Following her husband's death she believed her major role in life was over. In spite of feeling strongly about her relatives she did not feel the same kind of obligation towards them as some parents might feel towards their children. The determination of competence is often difficult (see Chapter 14) but in this case there was little doubt that she was competent to make this decision.

Was the team's attitude towards this issue important to Mrs E?

Mrs E seemed acutely aware of the fact that her decision was controversial. She asked on a number of occasions for team members, to whom she had become attached, to understand her position and to support her. It seemed important to her for the team members to accept her decision and recognize the courage that had been required to make it.

How does the team deal with its feelings?

Because of the differences among team members with regard to questions of life and death there will be varying degrees of disagreement that may engender heated debate and even hostility. It is important that team members have discussions among themselves both in small groups and as a whole team. All members of the team should get an opportunity to express their beliefs. It may be helpful to have a consultant from outside of the team to review the situation and discuss it in a group forum. It is important that medicolegal issues be clarified as they can increase the level of anxiety among team members.

KEY POINTS

- Team members should be vigilant with regard to the potential occurrence of suicidal behaviors.

- Where the potential for suicide is considered to be high, active interventions should be made to minimize the risk and identify and treat any associated psychiatric illness.

- It should be recognized that it is not possible to eliminate all self-destructive behaviors, and that not all suicides are preventable.

- There is increasing awareness of the possibility of "rational" suicide and of the possibility that in some situations, especially in terminal illness or chronic illness with very poor quality of life, decisions by competent patients to refuse treatment or nutrition may have to be respected. Ruling out depression in these instances is a therapeutic priority.

REFERENCES

1. Litman, R.E., Farberow, N.L. (1970). Suicide prevention in hospitals. In E.S. Shneidman, N.L. Farberow, R.E. Litman, (Eds.). *The Psychology of Suicide*. New York: Science House.
2. Durkheim, E. (1951). *Suicide*. New York: Free Press (originally published in 1897).
3. Freud, S. (1955). Mourning and melancholia. In J. Strachey (Ed.). *The standard edition of the complete works of Sigmund Freud*. London: Hogarth Press (originally published in 1917).
4. Bibring, E. (1953). The mechanism of depression. In P. Greenacres (Ed.), *Affective Disorders*. New York: International Universities Press.

5. Seligman, M.E.P. (1975). *Helplessness.* San Francisco: W. H. Freeman.
6. Miller, M. (1979). *Suicide after sixty: The final alternative.* New York: Springer.
7. Butler, R.N. (1989). Are your patients getting away with "Chronic suicide"? *Geriatrics* 44:15
8. Leibenluft, E., Goldberg, R.L., (1988) The suicidal, terminally ill patient with depression. *Psychosomatics*, 29:379-386.
9. Farberow, N.L., Shneidman, E.S., Leonard, C.V. (1970). Suicide among patients with malignant neoplasms. In E.S. Shneidman, N.L. Farberow, R.E. Litman, (Eds.). *The psychology of suicide.* New York: Science House.
10. Mishara, B.L., Kastenbaum, R. (1973). Self-injurious behavior and environmental change in the institutionalized elderly. *Int. J. Aging and Human Development,* 4:133-145.

SUGGESTED READING

1. Osgood, N. (1985). *Suicide in the elderly.* Rockville, Maryland: Aspen Publication.

   Useful textbook covering theoretical origins and management of suicide in the elderly.

2. Boyer, J.L., Guthrie L. (1985). Assessment and treatment of the suicidal patient. In E.E. Bechham & W.R. Leber, (Eds.). *Handbook of Depression.* Homewood, IL: Dorsey Books.

   Good overview of assessment and treatment approaches.

CHAPTER

The Suspicious
Resident

7

by Barbara Schogt

All people make assumptions about the extent to which they can trust those around them. These assumptions usually have some basis in fact and behavior is influenced by prior experience and by knowing how others have fared under similar circumstances. Thus, people decide when and where it is safe to leave the car unlocked, how much personal information to disclose to a new friend, and on whom to count in times of crisis.

Some degree of suspiciousness is necessary in any society. Individuals who are too trusting will encounter problems. At the other end of the spectrum, however, excessive mistrust also results in a wide range of difficulties both for suspicious individuals and those with whom they interact.

Excessively suspicious individuals perceive the world as a very hostile place, populated with people who are selfish, uncaring, and possibly motivated to do harm to others. When suspicious people encounter misfortune or make mistakes, they tend to blame others. They are extremely sensitive to real and imagined slights, criticisms, and injustices. In its most extreme form, suspiciousness reaches psychotic proportions. The individual loses touch with reality and begins to believe in, and act upon, imaginary ideas called delusions (see Chapter 2, The Mental Status Examination). The delusions can take many forms but common themes are those of being persecuted, harmed, or robbed.

It is not uncommon for suspicious people to feel that they have been singled out as objects of persecution because they are important and special. Grandiosity is thus closely related to suspiciousness and the two symptoms are often encountered together.

Paranoia is often used interchangeably with suspiciousness and persecutory ideation. The term which comes from the Greek and means "beside the mind," was originally used to describe any delusional state. In the current American classification of psychiatric disorders, the DSM-IIIR, there is an effort to overcome the confusion associated with the term. The word paranoid is used only in reference to a specific group of disorders characterized by delusions that may be, but are not necessarily, persecutory. To avoid ambiguity, paranoia will not be used as a synonym for suspiciousness in this chapter.

In order to better understand these individuals, it is useful to trace the development of their suspiciousness from a psychological perspective. A synthesis of elements from prevailing models suggests that some vulnerable individuals are unable to tolerate their need for others. Fearing rejection, they develop an attitude of hostility to protect themselves from feeling needy and inadequate so that "I love you." and "I need you." become "You hate me." Suspicious individuals perceive the anger as coming not from within themselves, but from those around them. Grandiosity and feeling special further protect such individuals from an intolerable awareness of their underlying feelings, needs, and vulnerabilities. This psychological process occurs at an unconscious level beyond the person's awareness and control. The resulting symptoms serve a protective function. This point will be discussed again later as it has important implications for management.

SUSPICIOUSNESS IN LONG-TERM CARE SETTINGS

There are several reasons why a chapter of this book is devoted to the problem of suspiciousness:

Suspiciousness is Common in the Elderly

In a community survey of almost 1,000 elderly done in 1984, 4% were found to have persecutory ideation [1]. In this survey, sensory deficits and cognitive impairment were found to be associated with an increased risk of suspiciousness. Impairments such as these make it more difficult for people to comprehend what is happening around them and result in misperceptions that can lead to persecutory ideation.

Rates of cognitive impairment and hearing loss are extremely high among institutionalized elderly. It is therefore reasonable to assume that suspiciousness will occur at least as frequently in long-term care settings as it does in the community.

Residential Settings Can Bring out Suspiciousness

Living within the highly structured community of the long-term care facility requires a considerable capacity to adapt to new circumstances, develop relationships, and cooperate with others.

Many very suspicious and even psychotic people live in the community and lead very isolated existences. Symptoms may not come to light until such individuals are forced into closer contact with people. Only under the stress of institutionalization will their inability to trust and failure to adapt emerge as problematic to others. For suspicious individuals, the move may represent a realization of their fears of being assaulted and imprisoned by strangers.

Others, who may not have been suspicious in the past, are limited in their capacity to adapt by sensory and cognitive difficulties. These individuals may also decompensate under the stress of moving from their familiar environment into a residential setting. Suspiciousness is a common response in these situations.

Suspiciousness Often Indicates the Presence of a Psychiatric Disorder

Suspiciousness, like fever, is a symptom and not an illness. Its presence indicates a need for a full assessment in order to establish an underlying diagnosis. There is a wide range of psychiatric disorders in the elderly in which suspiciousness may be one of the symptoms (see Table 1). Some of these disorders are covered in greater detail in other chapters of this book (see Chapters 3, 4, 5, and 8). A brief description of how suspiciousness manifests itself in different syndromes is given here, since understanding and managing the symptom of suspiciousness will differ depending on the underlying diagnosis.

Table 1
Disorders in which suspiciousness can occur

- Dementia
- Delirium
- Organic delusional syndrome
- Schizophrenia of late onset (paraphrenia)
- Delusional (paranoid) disorder
- Mood disorder
- Paranoid personality disorder
- Suspiciousness in the absence of a psychiatric disorder

Dementia

It is not unusual for individuals in the early and middle stages of dementia to accuse others of causing or contributing to the chaos that they cannot account for in any other way. They may blame others for stealing the things they misplace or for purposefully tricking and shaming them. The accusations can be very painful for family, friends, room-mates, and staff as they struggle to cope with the gradual loss of the person they once knew. The suspicions and persecutory delusions in dementia are usually quite simple and are an attempt by the resident to make sense of an increasingly incomprehensible world.

Delirium

Because delirium affects attention, level of consciousness, thinking and perception, delirious people perceive the world as if in a dream. The dream is usually a nightmare. The suspicions and delusions are often terrifying. They tend to be fleeting, poorly organized, and associated with perceptual disturbances such as illusions and hallucinations (see Chapter 2, The Mental Status Examination).

Organic delusional syndrome

In this disorder, delusions, usually persecutory, are the predominant finding. The global cognitive impairment seen in dementia and delirium is absent. The disorder is due to a specific organic factor such as medication or a brain lesion. In the elderly population, this disorder is sometimes seen in the context of Parkinson disease or after strokes. The delusions are variable in nature, ranging from simple ideas to highly organized, complex delusional systems.

Schizophrenia of late onset (Paraphrenia)

Also known as paraphrenia, the syndrome of late-onset schizophrenia is similar to schizophrenia that starts in early adulthood. Individuals who develop the disorder may share a genetic predisposition with those who suffer from early-onset schizophrenia. Other risk factors include being female and never married, living alone, and having sensory impairment.

The disorder is characterized by an absence of obvious cognitive impairment and elaborate delusions that are often associated with hallucinations, usually auditory. The illness may be associated with deterioration in many aspects of living including self-care and social functioning.

Individuals with this disorder tend to lead solitary lives, although they may emerge to report "evidence" of persecution or harassment to police and other local authorities. They are not usually seen in an institutional setting unless physical illness or the onset of cognitive impairment forces them to give up their independence.

Delusional (paranoid) disorder

This relatively uncommon disorder is characterized by the presence of a persistent, often well-organized delusion. Although most often persecutory, various delusional themes can occur. The elderly sometimes develop delusional jealousy becoming convinced, without due cause, that their spouses are unfaithful. The onset of the disorder may coincide with a loss of sexual functioning resulting, for example, from prostate surgery. In the somatic type of delusional disorder, individuals believe that they emit a foul odor or are infested with vermin.

Hallucinations are not prominent in delusional disorder and, unlike in schizophrenia, there is little or no impairment in areas of the individual's life not involved in the delusion. The symptoms may be similar to those in the organic delusional disorder but no organic etiology can be identified.

Mood disorder

Persecutory delusions can occur in both depression and mania. When they do, the suspicions are usually consistent with the predominant mood. Severely depressed individuals can develop a conviction that they are being punished and persecuted or that their imagined poverty results from their having led bad, sinful lives. The irritability and the grandiose themes seen in mania may be associated with suspicions that others are envious and wish to do them harm.

The suspiciousness almost always resolves with treatment of the underlying mood disorder but may be hard to manage in the acute phase.

Paranoid personality disorder

People with this problem have a life-long history of difficulty with trust and intimacy. They tend to be aloof, suspicious loners who are quick to take offence and bear grudges. In old age, they become increasingly reclusive and eccentric. They are vulnerable to psychosis when under stress, and have great difficulty adapting to an institutional setting.

Suspiciousness in the absence of a psychiatric disorder

The possibility that suspiciousness may be justified should be explored before concluding that it is evidence of illness. Stealing does occur in institutional settings from time to time and life in a small community can foster intrigue, the formation of cliques and the subsequent isolation or even persecution of certain individuals.

Moreover, behavior that is seen as excessively suspicious in one culture may be normal or prudent in another. Sometimes the safest place to store money may well be under the mattress and there are societies in which officials cannot be trusted to tell the truth. As already noted, (see Chapter 2, The Mental Status Examination), it is important to keep an open mind when evaluating the ideas and behaviors of others, particularly when their life experiences are significantly divergent from those of the predominant cultural group.

Suspiciousness Can Give Rise to Serious Management Problems

Although reclusive behavior is not necessarily problematic, suspiciousness contributes to many serious difficulties within institutional settings. Failure to comply with investigation and management of medical disorders, and to accept help with self-care or activities of daily living can result in significant risk to suspicious individuals.

THE FAR SIDE, COPYRIGHT 1985. UNIVERSAL PRESS SYNDICATE.
Reprinted with permission.

The potential for violence must always be kept in mind. It is natural for people to respond to perceived attack with defensive behavior or even counterattack. Suspicious individuals may lash out against those whom they suspect of wanting to harm them. From their perspective, they are acting in self-defense and the attacks are justified. The violence may be random or directed at specific persons involved in the delusions. Verbal behavior can include threats of violence and highly personal comments regarding the physical characteristics, sexuality, status or racial background of others. Suspicious people can be physically violent, especially if they are agitated and psychotic (i.e., suffering from delusions and hallucinations).

MANAGEMENT OF SUSPICIOUSNESS: GENERAL PRINCIPLES

There are some general principles that can be applied to the management of suspicious individuals. The approaches outlined focus on managing suspiciousness as a symptom. A comprehensive approach to the suspicious resident must also involve an attempt to identify and treat any underlying medical and psychiatric problems. The overall management plan should be based on the history, mental status, physical examination, and appropriate laboratory investigations. Management strategies are divided into environmental, psychosocial, and biological.

Environmental Strategies

Optimizing the level of stimulation

Modifying the environment in order to minimize the potential for misinterpretation by the suspicious resident is particularly important when dealing with disorders such as delirium and dementia that affect the capacity to integrate sensory information.

Whenever possible, agitated individuals should be brought to a quiet area where sensory stimuli are kept to a minimum. The number of people in the room with the resident at any one time may have to be restricted. Adequate, but not glaring, lighting can decrease the risk of visual illusions. Abrupt movements and sudden loud noises such as those from telephones, buzzers, intercoms, and slamming doors can be very alarming to agitated suspicious residents.

Removing dangerous objects

In other situations, environmental modifications are necessary to reduce the risk of violence. This may involve removing objects that can be used as weapons such as glass, knives, vases, and small lamps. Canes can be used to trip and hit staff or other residents. Replacing the cane temporarily with a walker that the resident cannot lift can be an effective safety measure. Room searches are indicated when residents say they are hiding weapons or when staff have reason to believe that there may be danger. The question of room searches is discussed further in Chapter 6, The Suicidal Resident. Whenever such interventions are made, staff should take time to prepare the resident, stressing that the aim is to promote safety and not to be punitive.

Reducing contact between the resident and individuals at risk

When the resident's delusions involve one particular person, placing that person at risk, it is wise to limit contact between the resident and that individual as much as possible. Changes in room-mates and staff assignments are sometimes warranted. Unfortunately, there is a possibility that the delusions will extend to incorporate the new room-mates and staff.

Physical restraint

Under extreme circumstances, it may be necessary to use physical restraint in order to isolate a suspicious resident. This is justifiable from an ethical perspective only in crisis situations, when there is an imminent risk of violence by the resident to self or others. In addition to weighing ethical considerations, staff should be familiar with the legislation in their jurisdiction. Physical restraint should be undertaken with adequate personnel under the guidance of one staff member assigned to coordinate the procedure.

Ideally an institutional protocol should be in place. (See Chapter 14, Legal and Ethical Dimensions). Frequent if not constant observation of the restrained individual is recommended along with detailed documentation in the chart of the reasons for and the consequences of the intervention. Physical restraint is a temporary crisis measure that is kept in place only until a more effective management strategy can be implemented.

Sometimes psychotic individuals respond favorably to being restrained since the imposition of external controls can be reassuring when internal controls have been lost. In many other cases, however, the restraints serve as further proof for suspicious individuals that others are out to harm them. Moreover, seeing an agitated person being placed in restraints can be extremely frightening for other residents.

Barricades

Suspicious residents occasionally barricade themselves in their rooms and cannot be persuaded to come out by staff or family. Although such residents may allow medications and food to be passed to them, they cannot be adequately supervised. Moreover, their deteriorating hygiene can pose a public health risk to an entire unit. If the risks become too great, forceful intervention is necessary. Because removal of the barricade can be physically difficult and will certainly be frightening to residents who already perceive themselves as being under siege, no action should be taken without careful planning and adequate staff resources.

Psychosocial Strategies

There are a number of general guidelines that can be followed when interacting with suspicious residents.

Maintain a natural manner with emphasis on consistency

Because suspiciousness and hostility are often associated with fear, it is best to approach the resident in as natural a manner as possible. If staff display their own fear and uncertainty, either by withdrawing support or through an overly solicitous, unnaturally cheerful approach, the resident will likely feel even more mistrustful and isolated. However, by maintaining a calm, consistent approach during frequent but relatively brief contacts, staff may be able to create an atmosphere where trust can begin to develop. When disruptions in the regular schedule are inevitable, the suspicious resident will benefit from an explanation that is not overly lengthy or apologetic. Contracting with suspicious residents around specific issues is a useful technique, but before taking this approach, staff must be certain that they will be able to hold up their end of the bargain.

Developing a profile of behavior

As caregivers learn to recognize the signs that indicate that a particular resident is feeling threatened, they can gauge how much contact the resident can tolerate and when it is necessary to withdraw. Documenting the antecedents to episodes of agitation and suspiciousness and the outcomes of various interventions can lead to the development of a behavior management approach that can be used even by staff less familiar with the resident (see Chapter 10, Behavioral Strategies).

Maintaining a safe distance

Many suspicious individuals need more space around themselves than the average person to maintain a sense of comfort. Intrusions into this space can result in agitation and even violence. Whenever there is any potential for violence, it may be unsafe for the caregiver to come between the suspicious resident and the door, as this causes the resident to feel trapped. Ideally both staff and resident should have free access to an exit.

The use of touch can be a powerful and often very positive intervention when it is applied judiciously. Suspicious people may experience it as an attack, however, and respond accordingly, so that caution should be exercised around the use of touch in this population.

When examining the resident or providing physical care, reassure the resident with a brief explanation of each step before performing the action. At times, some suspicious residents will refuse all care. This can result in potentially life-threatening situations and force caregivers to make difficult clinical decisions. Ethical and legal considerations, the resident's competence to make informed decisions, the opinions of relatives and guardians, and the need for transfer to an acute care facility are factors that need to be addressed as part of the decision-making process.

Verbal strategies

Any communication that takes place in the presence of suspicious residents not involving them as participants can add fuel to the fires of mistrust. Whispering and gesturing between staff should be avoided. When addressing the resident directly, every effort should be made to communicate in a clear, unambiguous manner. Consistent use of the pronouns "I" and "you" as opposed to "we" helps maintain a clear boundary between the speaker and the suspicious person.

Discussing suspicions

When residents discuss their suspicions and delusional beliefs, it can be difficult to maintain an attitude of sympathetic listening. Arguing with suspicious individuals about their beliefs is not only futile, but it can increase their feelings of isolation, inadequacy, and mistrust, and destroy any basis for a positive alliance. However, taking sides with residents against the world by supporting their delusional perspective undermines their already tenuous hold on reality and can strengthen their beliefs. Sometimes it is possible to listen without making more than a few neutral comments and then to redirect the conversation to another topic. When residents demand a response from staff about their suspicions, distraction is not always possible or appropriate. At such times, an honest, non-evasive response is best. For example, one might say, "You have described the way you see the situation and I understand things are very difficult for you at the moment. I don't share your view, but maybe you and I can still work on these problems together."

Giving feedback to the resident

When suspicious residents have behaved in a hostile or violent manner, it is often appropriate to inform them that the behavior affects others. Feedback is best given in the context of a quiet conversation, after the behavior has stopped. The time lag allows the caregiver to reach a clinical decision regarding the extent to which the resident is able to take responsibility for the behavior and the risk that the feedback will become punitive is reduced.

Focusing on strengths

Residents may continue to function well in areas not involved in their suspicious beliefs. Whenever possible, areas of strength should be encouraged. This distracts residents from their preoccupation and provides an opportunity for building self-esteem and interacting with others in a more positive manner.

Supporting those around the resident

Since being attacked leaves people feeling angry, frightened, and vulnerable, providing support to those who come into contact with the suspicious resident is extremely important. Staff should be encouraged to share their experiences with each other informally or in sessions scheduled for this purpose. This can happen only if caregivers feel confident that they are being supported at all levels within the institution, even when the resident's accusations involve politically sensitive issues.

Family members and other residents will also need an opportunity to voice their fears and may benefit from education designed to help them understand and respond to the suspicious person.

Biological Strategies

Identifying and treating underlying disorders

The medical and/or psychiatric disorders that are identified in association with the suspiciousness should be treated where possible. Certain conditions such as delirium or mood disorder may be fully reversible and their treatment will result in the resolution of the suspiciousness. Unfortunately, in other situations, little can be done to reverse or even halt the progression of the underlying disease. It is still possible, however, to provide relief from anxiety and discomfort and thereby achieve a significant amelioration of the suspiciousness.

Identifying and reducing sensory impairment

Identification and treatment of visual and hearing impairments are important in reducing the risk that the suspicious resident will misinterpret sensory cues.

Using medications to manage suspiciousness

The use of medication is an option in managing suspiciousness. The potential benefits of using medication must always be weighed against the risks of producing side effects and toxicity, especially when the medication is being used for symptom control rather than as a definitive treatment for the underlying condition. Moreover, not all forms of suspiciousness respond to medication. Once a medication has been started, its effects should be monitored and the ongoing need for its use reassessed at regular intervals (see also Chapter 9, Psychopharmacology).

Neuroleptics (antipsychotic medications) can be very effective when psychotic symptoms are present. Not only do they reduce agitation, but they also have a specific antipsychotic effect. This is true whether the psychosis originates from a medical condition, as in delirium, or from a psychiatric disorder. Generally, the reduction in agitation is seen well before the persecutory delusions disappear. In some cases the delusions never go away but they do become less troublesome to the resident. The presence of delusions does not automatically indicate a need for treatment. Long-standing delusions and those that do not result in distress are often best left alone.

In the absence of psychosis, neuroleptics are rarely indicated in the treatment of suspiciousness. Anxious, suspicious residents sometimes respond favorably to a brief course of an intermediate-acting benzodiazepine such as lorazepam or oxazepam. In other cases, however, the anxiolytic and sedative effects of these medications undermine the resident's sense of being able to guard against danger and may actually increase the level of agitation. Thus, before initiating benzodiazepines, the physician must decide how important it is to a particular resident to be able to remain alert and vigilant.

Suspicious people often agree to take medication if it is presented as something that might help reduce their agitation and suffering. The medication should be administered in such a way that the resident can see and count the pills. The resident should also be informed about changes in dosages, times and the form in which the medication is dispensed. Sometimes residents will only agree to take medication from certain trusted staff or family members. When residents refuse medication, the same considerations must be applied as when other aspects of care are refused.

CASE ILLUSTRATIONS

Case 1: Tolerating Risks

Miss G is an 85-year-old single woman who was admitted to a nursing home when she was evicted from her apartment for failing to pay her rent. The apartment was badly neglected and filled with hoarded objects and old newspapers. A distant cousin described Miss G as a lifelong loner who had become increasingly eccentric and reclusive since retiring 20 years earlier.

On admission, Miss G was found to be unkempt and malnourished. She refused to participate in any aspect of the assessment and accused staff of meddling in her affairs. She insisted that she was vacationing in a hotel and would soon return home. Offers of assistance with self-care were politely but firmly refused. She walked unsteadily, refusing to use aids, and did not participate in social activities. When challenged, Miss G became extremely angry, lashing out at staff verbally and physically.

Comment

Miss G has a long-standing pattern of suspicious behavior. In addition, she may have acute nutritional, medical, and/or psychiatric disorders, but without a full assessment, any hypothesis remains tentative. She is clearly least distressed when left to her own devices and is having difficulty adapting to her new environment. Her pride and suspiciousness are interfering with her judgment, and her competence to make informed decisions is in doubt. The potential that she will harm others, especially if they cross her, is significant.

Are there ways of facilitating Miss G's adjustment?

Allowing Miss G as much independence as possible while attempting to maximize her safety is all that can be done. In order to preserve her dignity, Miss G's insistence that she is "on vacation" should not be challenged. Encouraging her to join group activities would likely be very threatening to her and contrary to her lifelong pattern of keeping people at a distance.

Miss G may gradually develop some degree of trust that those around her will not violate her privacy and dignity, and then begin to accept occasional assistance with certain aspects of self-care. If possible, the cousin could be involved in this process. It is unlikely that Miss G will ever engage fully with those around her or accept care easily.

Does it make sense to contract with Miss G?

Yes. Allowing Miss G to participate in decisions around bathing and other aspects of self-care will increase her sense of control and enlist her as an ally rather than an adversary. For example, it may be possible to arrange a regular bathing time by allowing Miss G to choose her preferred time from a number of options, and then placing copies of the agreed upon schedule in her room and at the nursing station.

How do staff decide when to intervene?

This is an extremely difficult decision to make at both the ethical and clinical levels. Although Miss G is clearly at risk, it is likely that this risk was much greater when she was still alone in her apartment. Caregivers may have to learn to tolerate their own anxiety as Miss G teeters down the hall, because there is no safer alternative. Careful documentation of the situation and discussion with the cousin are recommended.

Should Miss G develop a medical emergency or suffer a fracture, interventions will be necessary. She may be more willing to accept care around a clearly identifiable and symptomatic illness but if not, temporary restraint may be necessary. Her relative should be kept informed as the situation unfolds.

Is there a role for medication in this case?

Even if she agreed to take them, psychotropic medications will most likely have no effect on Miss G's chronic suspiciousness and may result in troublesome side effects.

Case 2: A Case of Missing Underwear

Mr N is a moderately demented 77-year-old widower who has lived in the institution for some years. Although forgetful, he is generally cheerful and appears to enjoy social activities. His vision is failing. Mr N frequently misplaces personal belongings. Whenever this happens, he becomes very distressed and agitated. Lately, he has started to accuse others of stealing the objects. At first, the accusations were not directed at specific people, but this morning, he threatened to hit his room-mate for stealing his underwear. Responding to this situation, the staff located the garment under his bed.

Comment

Mr N's failing vision and memory have left him floundering and unable to hold onto either his thoughts or his belongings. Accusing others of stealing protects him from an awareness of this painful reality.

What can be done to deal with the consequences of the morning's events?

If Mr N's memory remains sufficiently intact that he is able to recall the morning's events and able to acknowledge what happened, he could be confronted gently with the seriousness of the threat and its effects on his room-mate. Mr N should be encouraged to report any missing articles to staff, and this message will have to be reinforced over the coming days. The key to Mr N's cupboard could be put on a cord so that he can wear it around his neck at all times. Staff should check whether the lighting in Mr N's room is adequate, and perhaps encourage a trusted family member to come in and help sort through his belongings with him.

At the same time, Mr N's room-mate should be reassured that steps are being taken to prevent further incidents and that if Mr N does threaten him again, he should get out of the way immediately and report to staff.

What can be done when Mr N comes to the desk two days later shouting that his room-mate has stolen his glasses?

Rather than confronting Mr N with the likelihood that he has misplaced the glasses, the caregiver should calmly offer assistance in retrieving them. If they cannot be found, Mr N could be reassured that everything will be done to locate them. This may be sufficient to reduce Mr N's agitation and if so, it may then be possible to distract him by changing the topic or involving him in an activity. However, if Mr N continues to rail against his room-mate, it will be necessary to remind him that threats and violence are unacceptable. If he is unable to calm down, Mr N may have to be moved to another room temporarily.

What can be done if the relationship between Mr N and his room-mate continues to deteriorate?

If violence is an ongoing risk or has actually occurred, a permanent separation may have to be arranged. Although Mr N may begin to accuse his new room-mate of stealing, this is by no means an inevitable outcome of such a move. Moreover, as Mr N's dementia progresses, he will likely become less aware of and distressed by his losses.

Case 3: A Case of a Little Contact Going a Long Way

Mrs W is an 89-year-old widow who has lived in the institution for 10 years. She has Parkinson disease for which she takes

several medications. For the last 6 years, she has been con-
vinced that a group of unknown assailants comes into her room
every night, ties her to her bed and begins to inject noxious
chemicals into her body. She points to her varicose veins as
"proof" that this is taking place.

The onset of the delusions coincided with the death of her sister
and the initiation of medication for Parkinson disease. Her
delusions and the distress associated with them become much
more pronounced when there is a crisis in her life. There has been
a dramatic rise in symptoms recently. Staff have finally been able
to link these symptoms to the upcoming departure of a caregiver
who was in the habit of occasionally spending a few minutes with
Mrs W, listening to her talk about the horrible nights.

Comment

Mrs W's delusions are elaborate, stable and well circum-
scribed. The medication used to treat Parkinson disease can
cause psychotic symptoms as a side effect and may be an
etiologic factor. Psychosocial variables clearly affect the intensity of the delusions and the level of Mrs W's distress.

What can be done to alleviate Mrs W's distress?

The departing caregiver has been providing Mrs W with psychotherapy, albeit informally. It would be helpful if this person
could meet a few more times with Mrs W in order to say
good-bye. The recognition by the staff of the importance of this
loss for Mrs W will allow the latter to begin the process of
mourning that may also enable her to talk about her sister.

Since Mrs W has derived so much benefit from this contact, it
would be useful to reinstate some form of ongoing psychotherapy. Whoever provides Mr W with this contact should have a
capacity to listen and be able to make a commitment to see her
on a consistent basis.

Would neuroleptics be useful?

The delusions from which Mrs W suffers might respond to a
neuroleptic, but any neuroleptic would also have the effect of

worsening the Parkinson disease. Before considering a neu-roleptic, the anti-parkinsonian medication should be reassessed and reduced if possible. Moreover, if Mrs W responds to psychotherapy with a significant decrease in her distress, it may not be necessary to use medication to treat the delusions.

The use of neuroleptics should be limited as much as possible, unless the consequences of the psychosis become more serious and disabling than those of the Parkinson disease.

Might Mrs W be suffering from a depression?

A careful inquiry into this question might reveal the presence of a depression. A trial of an antidepressant might be consid-ered as an adjunct to the psychotherapy. Mrs W would have to be monitored closely to ensure that the medication was not worsening her psychosis.

Case 4: A Case of Dangerous Loyalties

Mr and Mrs A moved into the institution when Mrs A became too demented to manage her household any longer. They share a room. Mrs A is diabetic, while Mr A is in excellent health apart from mild cognitive impairment.

Several months after admission, Mr A, who spent all his time with his wife, began to accuse male staff of raping her. He barricaded himself into the room with Mrs A and refused staff any access to either of them. Although he allowed meals to be left at the door, Mr A would not let staff in to give Mrs A the oral hypoglycemic medication that controlled her diabetes.

Comment

Mr A has decompensated under the stresses of his wife's ongoing decline, the move to the institution and his own failing cognitive capacity. His behavior is placing both himself, and especially his wife, at risk. The potential that he might attack anyone who tries to intervene is considerable.

What can be done to break the deadlock?

It may be possible for female staff to engage Mr A in a conversation, find out what he fears might be the consequence of letting someone in, and reassure him if possible. Mr A might respond to the suggestion that he will be better able to look after his wife if he gets some rest and that there are others willing to share with him the task of watching over her and ensuring her safety. Another approach would be to discuss Mrs A's need for medication and to enlist Mr A's help by asking him to be present when the medication is being given.

If these strategies do not work, and the risk to Mrs A is considered high enough, staff may have to force their way into the room and be prepared to restrain Mr A if necessary. It is possible that Mr A has been so frightened, that he may begin to calm down as soon as he senses that others are taking control. If not, sedation with a neuroleptic is an option, although if Mr A refused to take the medication, legal and ethical considerations may necessitate a temporary transfer to an acute care facility.

Can anything be done to prevent further crises?

It may help to give Mr A feedback regarding the risk at which he placed his wife, even though he was clearly trying to protect her. If Mr A can be convinced to share the task of looking after his wife, he could begin to participate in activities that could distract him and provide him with the opportunity to establish some positive contacts. Gradually he may be encouraged to express his confusion and grief.

If Mr A does not respond to this approach, he may have to be moved to a separate room to ensure his wife's safety. His access to his wife's room would have to be carefully planned, negotiated and monitored. As the conditions of both Mr and Mrs A deteriorate, new difficulties will arise.

Is there an ongoing role of medication?

It is possible that Mr A might respond to a small regular dose of a neuroleptic until the effects of this crisis have abated, at which point the need for the medication would have to be reassessed. He might be more amenable to taking something if it is explained to him that the medication will help calm him and thereby give him more strength to cope with his difficult situation.

KEY POINTS

- Suspiciousness occurs on a "trust" continuum from excessive trust to psychotic mistrust.

- Suspiciousness is common among the elderly, especially in long-term care settings. Risk factors include cognitive and sensory impairment.

- Suspiciousness is a symptom, NOT a diagnosis or illness. It can occur as a symptom in a wide range of psychiatric and medical disorders.

- Environmental, psychosocial, and biological strategies are used to manage suspiciousness.

- A comprehensive approach to identifying and managing the underlying illness should always take place in conjunction with efforts to achieve symptom control.

REFERENCES

1. Christenson, R., Blazer, D. (1984). Epidemiology of persecutory ideation in an elderly population in the community. *American Journal of Psychiatry*, 147(9):1088-1091.

SUGGESTED READING

1. Burnside, I.M. (1981). Paranoid behavior in the elderly. In I.M. Burnside, (Ed.). *Nursing and the aged*, pp. 157-165. New York: McGraw Hill.

Humanistic overview of responding to and managing suspicious residents.

2. Silver, I.L. (1986). Paranoid disorders in old age. *Geriatric Medicine*, 2:81-84.

This paper is an excellent summary of the different paranoid disorders in old age.

3. Verwoerdt, A. (1987). Psychodynamics of paranoid phenomena in the aged. In J. Sadavoy & M. Leszcz, (Eds.). *Treating the elderly with psychotherapy*, pp. 67-93. Madison: International Universities Press, Inc.

An interesting look at paranoid phenomena from a psychodynamic perspective, that can increase the ability to understand this population.

CHAPTER

The Resident with Personality Disorder

8

by Anne Robinson and Barbara Schogt

As described in the Diagnostic and Statistical Manual of Mental Disorders (DSM-III) "personality traits are enduring patterns of perceiving, relating to, and thinking about the environment and oneself, and are exhibited in a wide range of important social and personal contexts" [1]. These traits are what give people their unique "character" or "personality." When personality traits are so inflexible and maladaptive that they cause significant functional impairment or subjective distress, they constitute a personality disorder. The manifestations of personality disorders are often recognizable by adolescence or even earlier, and continue throughout adult life into old age. This chapter will focus on the problems that arise when elderly individuals with personality disorders enter long-term care settings.

CLASSIFICATION

In the DSM-III, personality disorders are separated from other psychiatric disorders [1]. Clinicians who use this diagnostic system indicate first whether an individual has a nonpersonality diagnosis such as depression or schizophrenia, and then, on a separate axis, whether there is a personality disorder.

This separation of personality disorders from other diagnostic categories has several purposes. It encourages clinicians to remember the importance of character as it contributes to and interacts with other diagnoses. It also emphasizes that personality disorders can coexist with any other mental disorder. Furthermore, it is a reminder of how difficult it can be to diagnose a personality disorder in the presence of an acute episode of another mental disorder.

Many features characteristic of personality disorders may also be seen when people are ill with an episode of, for example, mania or schizophrenia. The diagnosis of personality disorder should be made only when "the characteristic features are typical of the person's long-term functioning and are not limited to discrete episodes of illness" [1].

As listed in the DSM-IIIR, personality disorders represent a fairly heterogeneous group of problems that have as common features a long-term style of behavior and impaired functioning or subjective distress [2]. To facilitate diagnosis, personality disorders have been grouped into three clusters.

Individuals in the first cluster, which includes paranoid, schizoid, and schizotypal personality disorders, often appear odd or eccentric to others. Dramatic, emotional, and erratic behavior is characteristic of people with histrionic, narcissistic, antisocial, and borderline personality disorders. People with avoidant, dependent, obsessive-compulsive, and passive-aggressive personality disorders often appear anxious or fearful. There can be considerable overlap between different personality disorders, especially within one of the clusters and individuals can be diagnosed as having more than one personality disorder.

A brief description of the different personality disorders is given in Table 1. Full diagnostic criteria for each of these disorders are listed in the DSM-IIIR [2].

Table 1
Personality Disorders

Cluster A:

Paranoid Personality Disorder

These individuals have a pervasive tendency to interpret the actions of others as deliberately demeaning or threatening. They do not trust other people and are reluctant to confide in them. They are easily slighted and bear grudges.

Schizoid Personality Disorder

These individuals have a pervasive pattern of indifference to social relationships and a restricted range of emotional experience and expression. They have no close friends, are cold and aloof, do not appear to have strong emotions and almost always choose solitary activities.

Schizotypal Personality Disorder

These individuals have a pervasive pattern of deficits in interpersonal relatedness. They have peculiar ideas, beliefs and experiences such as clairvoyance, telepathy and sixth-sense experiences. They may display odd or eccentric behaviour, speech or appearance.

Cluster B:

Antisocial Personality Disorder

Criteria for this disorder are more stringent than for other personality disorders. Individuals show evidence of a conduct disorder in childhood as indicated by a history of such things as truancy, running away, fighting, cruelty to animals, lying, stealing, etc. As adults they fail to conform to social norms, fail to honour obligations, are reckless and lack remorse. They are unable to sustain consistent work behaviour or function as a responsible parent.

Personality Disorders (continued)

Borderline Personality Disorder

These individuals show a pervasive pattern of instability of mood, interpersonal relationships and self-image. Their relationships are intense and alternate between extremes of overidealization and devaluation. They are impulsive and prone to inappropriate, intense displays of anger. Suicidal threats, gestures and self-mutilating behaviour may occur.

Histrionic Personality Disorder

These individuals have a pervasive pattern of excessive emotionality and attention-seeking. They constantly demand reassurance, approval or praise. They may be inappropriately sexually seductive and exaggerated in their expression of emotion, while at the same time being self-centred and shallow.

Narcissistic Personality Disorder

These individuals show a pervasive pattern of grandiosity (in fantasy or behaviour), lack of empathy and hypersensitivity to the evaluation of others. They react to criticism with feelings of rage, shame or humiliation (even if not expressed). They exploit others to achieve their own ends, believe themselves to be unique, special and entitled and are preoccupied with feelings of envy.

Cluster C:

Avoidant Personality Disorder

These people show a pervasive pattern of social discomfort, fear of negative evaluation, and timidity. They are easily hurt by criticism and have no close friends. They avoid involvement with others unless they are certain of being liked and fear being anxious or embarrassed in front of people.

Personality Disorders (continued)

Dependent Personality Disorder

These individuals have a pervasive pattern of dependent and submissive behaviour. They are unable to make everyday decisions or initiate activities on their own. They allow others to make their important decisions and agree with people even when they believe them to be wrong, because they fear being rejected or abandoned. They go to great lengths to avoid being alone.

Obsessive Compulsive Disorder

These individuals show a pervasive pattern of perfectionism and inflexibility. Their perfectionism interferes with task completion and they are overly preoccupied with details, rules and schedules. They are excessively devoted to work, indecisive, overly conscientious and restricted in the expression of affect. They want others to submit to exactly their way of doing things and may be unable to delegate.

Passive Aggressive Personality Disorder

These people show a pervasive pattern of passive resistance to demands for adequate social and occupational performance. They procrastinate, become sulky or argumentative when asked to do things, seem to work deliberately slowly and believe themselves to be doing a much better job than others think they are doing. They may be unreasonably critical of or scorn people in positions of authority.

Adapted from DSM-IIIR, American Psychiatric Association, 1987.

THE DEVELOPMENT OF A PERSONALITY DISORDER

The question of how personality disorders arise has yet to be resolved. It has become clear, however, that early childhood deprivation, abuse, and neglect contribute to their emergence. In order for individuals to develop a stable sense of themselves and the capacity to form healthy relationships, they need to grow up in a reasonably predicable environment that provides some degree of consistency and is sensitive to emotional needs. Theoretical models supported by extensive clinical experience with children and adults suggest that people's sense of self, their capacity to trust others and cope with conflicting emotions, and their ability to see others as truly separate from themselves develop in infancy and early childhood. In the first years of life, a child's perspective of itself in the world goes through many changes as its physical and cognitive capacities grow. During this period, emotional sophistication also increases rapidly. Growth is fostered by the countless interactions between child and caregiver that allow the child to gradually assimilate new information and change its views to accommodate this information.

A child whose needs are usually met feels cared for and perceives the world as a fairly predictable place. This leads to the development of trust and the capacity to identify, voice and cope with emotional needs. Later in life, such an individual can maintain a secure and stable sense of self even in the face of changing circumstances, loss and other stresses. However, if a child's needs are rarely responded to in an appropriate manner, or if the response is inconsistent and unpredictable, this child's view of the world will be quite different. Not only is such a child's environment a hostile place, but its inner world becomes equally frightening. Because external support is lacking, the child's emotional needs constantly threaten to overwhelm its capacity to deal with them. Unmet needs which cannot be voiced or understood become enemies that must be fought against. Such children develop different ways of defending against being overwhelmed by their hostile inner world.

These largely unconscious coping strategies constitute some of the symptoms of personality disorders. Later in life, the often rigid defensive structure that has developed leaves the individual ill-equipped to engage in satisfying relationships with others and very vulnerable to breakdown under stress. Early world views, once established, are hard to modify. Just as it is more difficult for adults than for children to learn a foreign language, a new emotional language is also not easily acquired later in life.

There are many different reasons why the environments in which people grow up fail to meet the criteria necessary for healthy development. These reasons range from a physical and/or emotional illness in caregivers to socioeconomic upheaval and war.

Apart from environmental variables, there may be constitutional factors that predispose to the development of a personality disorder. There have been attempts to identify a genetic vulnerability in some personality disorders and genetic links between other psychiatric disorders and certain personality disorders have been investigated. The notion that problems arise when an infant's temperament and particular needs do not "fit" well with what its environment can provide has also been explored. It is not possible to say, however, that there are any inherent factors that predispose to the development of a personality disorder. Also, the question of why an individual develops one particular set of defensive personality traits, as opposed to any other, remains unanswered.

THE IMPACT OF AGING

Aging is associated with many changes, and change is particularly difficult for those with personality disorders. As people age, they generally incur an increasing number of losses. Deaths of loved ones, loss of important roles, physical deterioration, and, in the case of nursing home residents, institutionalization, all threaten a person's sense of self. To mourn these major losses without succumbing to hopelessness and despair requires strengths that many people with personality disorders do not possess. At the same time, the individual's usual means of defending against loss may be curtailed by ill health and changes in mobility and financial status. The socialite who warded off loneliness and pain by entertaining extravagantly may lose the capacity and means to do this. Flights from reality that involve, for example, drug abuse, sexual promiscuity or travelling become less feasible. As the aging body becomes a focus of concern, emotional distress may be expressed increasingly in somatic terms.

Redefining their role in relation to others is another challenge that the elderly face. This too involves letting go of cherished aspects of the self: what it meant, for example, to have been a boss, a teacher, a valued employee or manager of a large household. Aging individuals may have to turn increasingly to others in order to survive. Since individuals with personality disorders have problems in their interpersonal relationships, they often lack the kind of support network that would allow them to continue to function in the community. Even if such networks exist, these individuals may have conflicts around acknowledging their need for help. To do so would recall the failures of the early environment. Individuals with paranoid or schizoid tendencies may become reclusive, reject all assistance, and end up living in appalling conditions that sometimes lead to enforced institutionalization. At the other extreme, conflicts around dependency needs may result in people clinging helplessly to those around them, thereby rapidly exhausting their community resources. For these reasons, individuals with personality disorders are often less able than others to continue living in the community in the face of disability. As a result, they may be overrepresented in the nursing home population.

THE IMPACT OF INSTITUTIONALIZATION

Moving into a long-term care setting is an extremely stressful experience. For people with personality disorders, the difficulties of this process are compounded by their vulnerabilities. Institutionalization may echo early life history and provoke intense feelings of loneliness and abandonment. For people to be bombarded relentlessly by the sights, sounds and smells of aging and to be thus reminded of their own aging and mortality may be an intolerable assault on their sense of self. At the same time, they are put in a situation characterized by dependency on others and intense, frequent interpersonal contact that resembles family life.

Direct caregivers in particular provide intimate physical care to residents on a daily basis. This kind of care requires intrusions into privacy and is reminiscent of the nurturing care provided by a mother. For some residents, such care can arouse unconscious rage and disappointment at not receiving the kind of nurturing which they seek and to which they feel entitled. For others, caring may evoke feelings of shame, humiliation and mistrust or precipitate regression and helplessness. Thus the emotional demands of institutionalization may cause vulnerable residents to intensify their reliance on characteristic behavior patterns that give rise to various symptoms and interpersonal conflict with staff and other residents. Unaware of their own contribution to their problems, these residents will blame those on whom they are now most dependent — the care providers.

DIAGNOSING PERSONALITY DISORDERS

Because the symptoms are pervasive, chronic and less likely to be striking or bizarre than those of episodic psychiatric illnesses, personality disorders can be difficult to identify for those not used to dealing with this diagnostic category. There may be clues in the history. Childhood experience of abuse or severe disruptions in the continuity of parenting are often associated with problematic personality development. A history of difficulties in interpersonal relationships or an absence of connections to others are often present. Work histories can also provide useful information.

Sometimes it is possible to get a sense from relatives or others that the person is either odd or difficult to get along with. It must be kept in mind however, that such opinions are formed on the basis of many factors and that not all those judged by conventional norms as odd or eccentric suffer from personality disorders. As staff become familiar with a resident, certain persistent behavior patterns may become apparent. What initially presents as the resident's conflict with a particular room-mate may emerge as a pattern of failing to get along with any room-mate. Suspiciousness, inability to adapt to routines, excessive demands, rages and difficulty establishing social contacts may all be symptoms of a personality disorder.

A personality disorder can also become apparent through the ways in which a resident affects other people. The impact that individuals with a personality disorder have on their environment can be very powerful. Strong emotional responses evoked in staff can, if not examined, interfere with clinical judgment and create havoc in the treatment team. Experienced clinicians learn to monitor their own feelings towards the individuals they assess and work with. Strong, surprising or unusual reactions are important diagnostic clues. For example, while assessing a notoriously "difficult" resident who has alienated all those around him, a clinician may experience a feeling that he, and he alone can understand this particular resident. The clinician's response has been evoked by the resident's strong, but unconscious need to have the clinician behave as the all-powerful ally he craves. If the clinician acts on his urge to confront the staff about the way they have mistreated the resident, he will alienate them. Moreover, because nobody can fulfil the role of all-powerful ally forever, the clinician will soon feel burdened by his special relationship to the resident. Inevitably, at some point he will fail to meet the resident's unrealistic expectations of him and leave the resident feeling even more disillusioned and alone than before.

The process described in this example is splitting. Splitting is a central defence mechanism of the borderline personality disorder.

Individuals with this disorder cannot integrate good and bad aspects of themselves or others. Because the bad always threatens to overwhelm the good, they cannot tolerate seeing people as they really are, possessing both good and bad qualities. Instead they have to split the bad from the good and divide the world into people who are idealized in an unrealistic manner as all good (e.g., the clinician), and others who are all bad (e.g., the rest of the staff). When splitting is not recognized, staff can begin to act out the roles in which the resident has cast them. Not surprisingly, splitting can create chaos by pitting staff members against each other. The resident's care is compromised as staff fight among themselves.

Apart from splitting, there are many other ways in which the defenses of residents with personality disorders can affect staff functioning. When staff feel helpless or demeaned, experience that nothing they do for a resident is ever enough, or find themselves consistently doing things for a resident that he or she can do independently, then the question of whether there is a personality disorder should be asked.

Differential Diagnosis

Care must be taken to identify other psychiatric disorders whose symptoms may overlap with those of personality disorders. Depression, which, unlike a personality disorder often resolves with antidepressants, may also interfere with a resident's interpersonal relations and ability to adapt. Suspicious residents or those with odd behavior may have a psychotic disorder that could respond favorably to antipsychotic medication. Dementia may be associated with rigid behavior, attacks of rage, and other symptoms that can make it difficult to differentiate from a personality disorder without a careful history and cognitive assessment. Any of these other psychiatric disorders may coexist with a personality disorder leading to particularly difficult diagnostic and management challenges.

The Implications of the Diagnosis

Residents with personality disorders have been described in the professional literature as "difficult," "manipulative," "hateful," and "destructive." The feelings that these disturbed but vulnerable people evoke in those who work with them can cause staff to lose sight of the fact that their behaviors are not intentional. Although they may be defined as maladaptive by the institution's standards, the behaviors represent the resident's attempt to cope. Defenses like splitting are unconscious and beyond the individual's ability to control at will.

Once a personality disorder has been identified, its manifestations become easier to recognize. Although the risk exists that these diagnostic terms may be used in a pejorative fashion to vent frustration and anger, establishing a diagnosis can lead to greater understanding and the development of a sound approach to management.

MANAGEMENT

General Considerations

Although personality disorders represent a heterogeneous group of problems, certain general comments can be made regarding their management in long-term care settings. The development of a comprehensive treatment approach should always be based on an understanding of the resident's problems and limitations.

Personality disorders are life-long patterns of behavior that are deeply ingrained and exceedingly difficult to modify. To expect a resident who has been a loner all his life to adapt to an active schedule of group activities is not realistic. Those who have always been perfectionistic and governed by strict rules will not be able to "relax" or "let go" when their personal routines come into conflict with those of the institution. Someone who was never able to be sensitive to the feelings of others will not suddenly learn tolerance of and consideration for fellow residents. Residents who come with a history of having been impossible for their families will likely be impossible for staff. Unrealistic expectations can result in feelings of alienation and abandonment on the part of the resident, and feelings of anger, frustration, and helplessness on the part of the staff. Despite the difficulties, however, it is possible to develop a treatment plan that can be beneficial to all involved. A workable set of goals strives to minimize tension and chaos by finding ways for the resident to coexist optimally with others in the institution. Several important aspects of management will be described in the following sections.

Clarity, Consistency, and Communication

One aspect of developing a management approach involves identifying problem areas and developing strategies to deal with them as described in Chapter 10, Behavior Management. Clarity is essential when working with this population. Only if the treatment goals are clearly articulated and documented will staff have an opportunity to evaluate various approaches without losing their sense of direction.

Although staff must be flexible in acknowledging a resident's problems and defining their expectations, once a particular treatment direction has been chosen, consistency is important. For example, a decision may be made to respond to a particular resident's need for control by allowing her some choice around certain aspects of daily care. Unless the areas of choice are clearly specified and consistently communicated to the resident, a battle for control may develop around other issues such as medications and smoking.

There must be extensive communication among staff in order for a management plan to be applied consistently. This involves charting plans, communicating approaches to consultants who are not familiar with the situation, and reporting between shifts. Particularly in cases where the potential for splitting is high, staff meetings may have to be scheduled and communication must extend to all those involved, including family and administrative staff. The management plan needs to be communicated to the resident who may become a willing ally if he or she perceives the plan as a means of achieving desirable common goals. Even when such an alliance is not possible, clear and consistent communication to the resident of staff intentions is essential.

Staff Support

Working with this population is stressful. Because of the difficulty residents have in establishing and sustaining a therapeutic relationship, they fail to confirm for staff that their work is valued. In order to derive satisfaction from their role, most caregivers need to feel that residents consider them compassionate, caring and helpful. Instead, these residents demean, accuse, demand, and seem oblivious to the efforts of the staff. Those providing direct physical care have to cope with these reactions to their work repeatedly, often on a daily basis. Nondirect caregivers may become the recipients of a litany of complaints about the direct caregivers. This can lead to divisiveness among staff as the team is split along professional lines. Typically, nursing staff are pitted against physicians, social workers, and administrative staff. Staff meetings, by providing an opportunity for interdisciplinary communications, can foster greater understanding of what effect the resident's way of relating to the environment is having on care and care providers.

Understanding the Role of Psychoactive Medications

In the face of the stress of caring for these residents, it can be tempting to seek "magical" solutions for complex problems. Physicians may feel pressure to "do something" in response to a sense of helplessness, urgency or angry frustration in themselves or the staff. A prescription for a psychoactive medication, however, rarely resolves the problems and may complicate the situation. Apart from producing side effects and possibly leading to addiction, the medication may become a powerful symbol to the resident. The meaning that medication carries will vary with the individual. For some, the medication represents a sign of caring, but for others it may be interpreted as evidence they are being dismissed as "mental cases." Medication may also be seen as a tool by which staff usurp control.

There are, nevertheless, situations where the use of medications can be helpful. Whenever another psychiatric disorder is superimposed on a personality disorder, the acute illness must be treated in the usual manner, even as staff keep in mind that taking medication is an aspect of relating to others and can become a focus of conflict. Less commonly, the symptoms of the personality disorder itself may be an indication for using medication. Extreme anxiety, agitation, or occasionally even psychotic symptoms can be precipitated by stressful events. A brief course of anxiolytic or antipsychotic medication can help to reduce these symptoms and restore a sense of control to the resident.

The Use of Psychotherapy

Where resources permit, the use of formal psychotherapy can be considered. Experience and skill are necessary in deciding when psychotherapy may be a helpful part of the management plan, and if so, what kind of psychotherapy is indicated. When used inappropriately, psychotherapy can exacerbate an already difficult situation by promoting regression and uncovering needs and longings that cannot be met.

CASE ILLUSTRATIONS

Case 1

Mrs A, a gaunt 80-year-old resident with congestive obstructive pulmonary disease, led a chaotic life characterized by

*interpersonal difficulties and disappointment in those around
her. Unhappy and critical of the amount of care and attention
her two daughters are able to provide, she berates and de-
means them for not visiting or caring enough.*

*Although her younger daughter is confined to a wheelchair
and visits when she can, Mrs A is unable to appreciate her
daughter's efforts or empathize with her daughter's problems.
Her relationship with her elder daughter seems characterized
by demands that her daughter intervene and insist that the
administrators of the institution accede to Mrs A's wishes.*

*The daughters describe their mother as having given up their
care to their grandmother, in order that she might accompany
her husband in his work travels. They describe the marital
relationship as having been chaotic. Infidelity eventually led
to separation. During this time, Mrs A threatened suicide and
took an overdose of medication.*

*Mrs A idealized both her husband and the relationship de-
scribing it as "special, like no other marriage; he adored me."
Needing to work, but unable to maintain a steady job because
of her explosive reaction to any criticism, Mrs A barely made
a living. Although clever and articulate, she eventually alienated those around her by demanding their undivided attention
and blaming them when things went wrong. Angry and alone,
demanding more than the family could provide, she was admitted into a long-term care facility.*

*Her pattern of relating is duplicated in her relationship with
staff. She frequently hurls insults at them and comments in a
demeaning and derogatory fashion on appearance, race, and
ethnic background. No staff member escapes her anger. She
often refuses to be bathed, forgetting that she had agreed to a
particular schedule earlier. She accuses staff of preferring
other residents over her. She calls staff frequently and attempts
to keep them in her room with numerous requests for assistance. She accuses staff of taking her belongings when she has
misplaced them, but will not allow them to tidy her room. She
pits staff against one another, alternating praise with criticism. Staff are never sure where they stand with her, and no
one wants to be assigned to provide her care.*

Comment

Mrs A's manner of relating to others, her affective instability and her history of self-harm are typical of borderline personality disorder. Familiarity with Mrs A's history helps caregivers understand that her behavior is not new or purposefully directed at them, and that they did not provoke her responses because they are inept. At this point, staff need assistance in containing and responding to Mrs A's behavior. The following can be considered:

1. Providing consistent caregivers as opposed to rotating assignments involving the whole team, will give Mrs A the opportunity to begin to develop a relationship with a few of the staff. Because Mrs A is so difficult to work with, thought and discussion must take place within the team before the new approach is implemented.

2. The plan of care should be structured so that all staff can agree upon it and will follow it in a consistent manner. Posting a copy of the care plan in Mrs A's room, and having a copy readily available in the nursing station will ensure that it will be used on a daily basis and provide staff with the structure they need when caring for Mrs A. If it is presented to Mrs A in a constructive rather than a punitive manner, the care plan may be very reassuring to her, and serve as a concrete sign that she is not being abandoned.

3. As part of the care plan, the verbal abuse may be targeted for behavior management using the techniques described in Chapter 10. Based on their assessment of the behavior, whenever Mrs A yells, screams, insults, and makes racial remarks towards staff, she is told that they will leave the room until she is in control, at which time they will return to continue her care.

4. To help reduce the tendency for splitting, whenever Mrs A attempts to talk about one staff member to another, she is gently told to redirect her remarks to the caregiver she is discussing. If she continues, the staff member leaves the room until she stops.

5. Administration should be informed of the plan of care and asked to support it by redirecting complaints back to the unit providing the care. Meetings between Mrs A's family and

administration should always include a representative from the team providing the care.

6. The daughters can be assisted in setting appropriate limits on their contact with Mrs A and by involving them as part of the team effort to cope with Mrs A's needs.

Case 2

Mrs B, a beautiful 85-year-old woman, is described by her daughter as always needing to be the most important person in the family. She remembers how both she and her father struggled to prove to Mrs B how much they loved her. The daughter also tells staff that her mother was unable to be genuinely interested in her grandchildren, seeing them as competition for her daughter's time and attention.

Living in a long-term care facility where she is one of many residents is difficult for Mrs B. She is easily offended and reacts to perceived insults vigorously by screaming or refusing to do what is asked of her. She demands instant gratification of her needs, constant flattery, and insists she is not "like those others with no brains," but is "of a superior class." She places great emphasis on her beauty and has a portrait of herself on her bedroom wall to which she constantly refers. She is unable to tolerate the notion of looking any older and refuses to look in the mirror or believe that "the old woman" is herself.

Mrs B has cognitive deficits and is often unaware that her clothes are soiled and that she needs bathing. She sometimes resists care, hitting out at staff and hurling insults at them. At other times, she flatters staff and cooperates with them. This unpredictability in Mrs B's level of cooperation makes staff feel that her behavior is purposeful and that she is a nasty, self-centered old woman.

Comments

Mrs B's sensitivity to criticism, her need to be special, her sense of entitlement and her disregard for others characterize her as having a narcissistic personality disorder. It is difficult for staff to understand that her behavior is not purposeful but a function of her dementing process superimposed on a personality that feels entitled to be treated as a special person. Knowledge of Mrs B's history, however, helps staff to understand that she always needed to come first. Management is based on the understanding that underlying her need to emphasize her superiority and beauty is a deep-seated fear of worthlessness.

1. Given Mrs B's vulnerability in the face of multiple assaults on her fragile sense of self, staff can help her by supporting her defenses. This could involve encouraging her to talk about her past accomplishments or discussing her clothes, her picture and other areas of interest that give her pleasure. Pushing Mrs B in the direction of facing truths about her aging and decline would overwhelm her already tenuous ability to hold onto a positive image of herself. What might be construed in a less vulnerable individual as coming to terms with painful realities, would in Mrs B's case likely lead to despair, anger, and an exacerbation in interpersonal difficulties.

2. Understanding that Mrs B's feelings about herself, and her ability to accept the care she needs, fluctuate with her self-esteem, will prepare staff for Mrs B's unpredictability. In this case, the unpredictability is also a function of cognitive difficulties. Staff must remain consistent in their approach to what was agreed upon. In order to maintain consistency, the management plan should anticipate conflicts by, for example, spelling out how staff can respond in case Mrs B refuses a certain aspect of care. As in the previous case, certain behaviors may be targeted for modification. For example, allowing Mrs B to insult caregivers is not helpful, and staff might decide on a plan in which Mrs B is told that staff will leave and return when she is less agitated.

3. As in Mrs A's case, Mrs B will benefit from continuity and consistency in caregivers. Gradually she may begin to build relationships in which she can feel safe with a few of the staff. Through such relationships, staff may begin to understand Mrs B a little better. For example, Mrs B's consistent battle over bathing might be reassessed when it becomes known that she never liked to be touched and that she never bathed except in absolute privacy. Using this knowledge, bubble bath and perfumed soap could be added to the bathing routine. Staff could

make sure to turn their backs as much as safety will allow. Although with these changes Mrs B's aggression may decrease, it would be unrealistic to expect it to go away.

Case 3

Mrs C, an 82-year-old widowed woman, currently lives in the long-term facility that a decade earlier, she had visited every day for 4 years, until her husband died. Although at the time her children and others encouraged her to take time for herself, she was unable to do so. She felt she would be criticized for being a bad wife and said that her husband cried whenever she raised the issue of not coming in the next day. Unable to tolerate being alone, she constantly called her married children to be with her and to make decisions for her.

Mrs C was admitted to residential care after she broke her hip. Although competent, she gave her daughter financial power of attorney, feeling she did not want to make decisions about selling her home or managing her money. Since admission, Mrs C has been disappointed that staff encourage her to be independent in activities of daily living. She experiences this as staff "not caring" about her or, "being lazy."

She has a long history of depression. She describes herself as having had a very hard life and says that she, "never had a happy day." Without the presence of relatives or other people, she feels completely alone and gets what she describes as, "very nervous." She often mistakenly refers to her daughter as "my mother."

Whenever Mrs C's daughter is away she becomes increasingly irritable, anxious and somatic. Her mood is more depressive and she is more critical of the care being provided. At these time she wonders aloud if she should be admitted to hospital.

She has some problems with recent memory and worries about becoming like the others who have "lost their minds." She is aware of her need for others and says that, "being between people helps." She goes to craft class and recreation programs and likes to knit when alone.

No amount of family contact diminishes her wish to be with them or her feeling that she is neglected by them. No matter what they do, it is not enough and she is left feeling alone and unhappy. This way of relating to others is replicated in her relationship with the staff. She is disappointed in the direct caregivers whom she perceives as not doing enough for her. Yet she does not tell them this directly, feeling that they will reject her if she does. Instead she becomes unhappy and irritable, expressing her distress in the form of physical symptoms.

Comments

Mrs C has a dependent personality disorder. Her behavior is characterized by dependency, submissiveness and an inability to make important decisions on her own. Her attachments to others have a clinging, helpless quality and she is unable to tolerate being alone. Helping Mrs C involves the following:

1. An assessment of Mrs C's needs would identify clearly those areas in which she needs assistance. At the same time, functions that she can carry out independently will become apparent. Care can then be planned to ensure that Mrs C receives help where she needs it. By coming to Mrs C's assistance before she asks for help, staff can begin to build for Mrs C a sense that her needs are being taken seriously and attended to promptly.

2. Sharing the results of the needs assessment with Mrs C is an important aspect of this approach, because it establishes clearly those areas in which Mrs C will be expected to function independently. Whenever Mrs C requests help around one of these functions, staff can remind her gently of the assessment and assist her in finding ways to overcome the problem on her own.

3. Mrs C's tendency to somatize (i.e., to express her distress in the form of physical symptoms) can present a significant management challenge. Even though staff recognize that when Mrs C says "I feel weak, my head is spinning and I can't breathe," she is unconsciously voicing her fear of being alone, staff cannot dismiss these symptoms without investigating them. In giving her the concern and caring she craves through the investigation, staff unfortunately reinforce Mrs C's tendency to somatize. Particularly in the elderly such patterns can be

difficult to avoid. Investigations can however be done in a judicious and conservative manner once staff become more familiar with Mrs C's symptoms. Moreover, by linking crises such as her daughter's holidays with an escalation in Mrs C's physical symptoms, staff can anticipate problems. It may be possible to modify the approach during difficult periods by, for example, spending a little extra time with Mrs C and acknowledging her feelings about her daughter.

4. Mrs C's character structure and behavior may be difficult to differentiate from depression and may predispose her to developing clincial depression. A trial of antidepressant therapy may be considered, even in situations where depressive symptoms appear to be very long-standing.

KEY POINTS

- Personality disorders are pervasive, life-long patterns of perceiving, relating to, and thinking about others that cause significant functional impairment and/or subjective distress.

- Personality disorders can coexist with and complicate the diagnosis and management of other psychiatric disorders.

- The development of personality disorders has been linked to deficits in the childhood environment.

- Because of the rigid way in which people with personality disorders cope with living, they are very vulnerable to breaking down under stress. The losses, role changes, and dependency that come with aging are particularly difficult for this population to adapt to.

- The demands of institutional living cause ingrained behavior patterns to surface and because these residents are unaware of their contribution to their problems, they will blame caregivers for all that goes wrong.

- If the powerful impact of these behavior patterns on staff is not understood, it can interfere with clinical judgement, team functioning and the resident's care.

- Setting realistic treatment goals involves accepting the resident's limitations and working within these limitations to promote the optimal coexistence of the resident with others in the institution. Improving communication at various levels, applying behavior management strategies and occasionally using psychoactive medications and/or formal psychotherapy are important aspects of a comprehensive approach to management.

REFERENCES

1. *Diagnostic and statistical manual of mental disorders*. (1980). 3rd edition. Washington, DC: American Psychiatric Association.
2. *Diagnostic and statistical manual of mental disorders*. (1987). 3rd edition, revised. Washington, DC: American Psychiatric Association.

SUGGESTED READING

1. *Diagnostic and statistical manual of mental disorders*. (1987). 3rd edition, Revised. Washington, DC: American Psychiatric Association.

    Provides comprehensive listing of the criteria by which personality disorders can be diagnosed.

2. Groves, J.E. (1978). Taking care of the hateful patient. *New England Journal of Medicine*, 298:883-887.

3. Main, T.F. (1957). The ailment. *British Journal of Medical Psychology*, 33:128-145.

    These two classic papers provide excellent and readable discussions on the problem of the individual with a personality disorder within institutional settings, with special emphasis on patient-staff dynamics.

4. Sadavoy, J. (1987). Character disorders in the elderly: An overview. In J. Sadavoy & M. Leszcz (Eds), *Treating the elderly with psychotherapy*, pp 175-227, Madison: International Universities Press, Inc.

Provides a more in-depth look at personality disorders in the elderly, highlighting the problems seen in borderline and narcissistic personality disorders.

CHAPTER

Principles of   9
Geriatric Psychopharmacology

by Nathan Herrmann

The introduction of psychoactive medications in the 1950s and 1960s revolutionized the treatment of psychiatric illness. With the help of antidepressants and antipsychotic (neuroleptic) drugs the chronic inpatient population of mental hospitals declined dramatically. Consequently, the percentage of residents with psychiatric disturbances in nursing homes, rest homes, and homes for the aged increased markedly. Because of the scarcity of resources in many of these facilities, pharmacological management is often the only form of therapy these residents receive.

Despite the potential benefits for some residents, there is mounting data to suggest that psychoactive drugs are at times misused, occasionally abused, and often administered by individuals with limited knowledge of their indications and side effects [1].

When indicated, the use of psychoactive medications for treatment of depression, anxiety, or control of behavioral symptoms, should be viewed as only one component of a treatment plan made up of multiple modalities. Often, as in the case of residents with dementia, these medications should not be considered the treatment of first choice. The institutionalized elderly are a population at high risk for side effects, particularly in the presence of physical illness and multiple medical drug use. Safe and effective use of psychotropics requires careful observations and regular periodic reappraisal of effectiveness.

PRINCIPLES OF PHARMACOTHERAPY IN THE ELDERLY

The elderly experience many physiological changes which can alter the way drugs are metabolized. Some of the factors which affect drug handling in the elderly are listed in Table 1. As a result of these changes, many psychotropic medications will have prolonged effects and tend to accumulate more in the elderly than in younger individuals. The elderly are very susceptible to side effects; even so-called "therapeutic" doses of common psychotropic medications may lead to complications such as delirium or hypotension. All these factors highlight the need for careful administration of psychotropics with close monitoring.

Table 1
Factors Affecting Drug Metabolism in the Elderly

- Decreased lean body mass
- Increased body fat
- Decreased serum albumin
- Changes in absorption
- Changes in liver function
- Decreased kidney function
- Changes in drug receptor sensitivity
- Changes in amount of neurotransmitters

Prior to initiating pharmacotherapy, the clinician should establish the relative indications and contraindications of drug use in each resident. Indications should include a specific diagnosis as well as a number of target symptoms which can be used to monitor the efficacy of treatment. Target symptoms should be easily measurable and could include weight changes, hours of sleep, number of aggressive outbursts, frequency of shouting, participation in social activities, etc. Nursing staff and other members of the treatment team should be aware of these target symptoms and record changes in the chart. The relative contra-indications depend on individual characteristics which may place the resident at greater risk (e.g., those residents with pre-existing cardio-vascular or renal disease, or those residents on numerous medications maybe more susceptible to serious side effects).

If the potential benefits outweigh the risks, the clinician must then choose an appropriate medication. There are many psychotropic medications which are better tolerated than the older traditional medications such as amitriptyline and chlorpromazine. For the elderly the drugs of choice should 1. have fewer active metabolites, 2. accumulate in the body to a lesser extent, 3. have shorter action, and 4. be less prone to causing side effects such as hypotension and confusion. The drug should be started at very low dosages and increased slowly while monitoring for side-effects. The effective dosage of many psychotropic medications is usually lower than in younger populations, and the medications can often be given in single daily dosages.

Use of psychotropic medication should be reviewed on a regular basis. Because many conditions such as depression or agitation associated with dementia are episodic, long-term treatment with these medications, which are prone to causing side effects, is not necessarily indicated. Attempts to reduce and even discontinue the drugs should be a regular part of the resident's management.

TREATMENT OF DEPRESSION

Depression is a common form of psychiatric illness in nursing home residents which can have serious consequences if it is untreated (see Chapter 5). Appropriate pharmacological management of major affective disorders is often extremely effective at ameliorating depressive signs and symptoms. Although there are numerous medications available to treat major depression, the drugs used most commonly are the heterocyclic (also called tricyclic) antidepressants. Medications such as amitriptyline (Elavil) and imipramine (Tofranil) were first introduced more than three decades ago, and while many new medications have been marketed, no single drug has been shown to have consistently better efficacy than these two agents. In view of this fact, how is a medication chosen for a specific resident?

Personal and Family History

If a resident has experienced a depression in the past which was successfully treated with a specific drug, that same medication should be considered the agent of first choice. Occasionally, clinicians will carefully review a family history to determine if other family members have been successfully treated with certain types of antidepressants, and choose the same one for the resident.

Side Effect Profile

The elderly are extremely sensitive to the side effects of antidepressants; those medications with the fewest bothersome side effects will therefore be better tolerated. Occasionally, the presence of side effects can be a positive indication for choosing a particular agent (e.g. the depressed resident with severe insomnia may benefit from a drug that causes more sedation).

The most common troublesome side effects of the cyclic antidepressants are sedation, orthostatic hypotension, and anticholinergic effects.

Orthostatic hypotension is a drop in blood pressure that occurs when a resident rises from a chair or gets out of bed. It is easily measured by taking the resident's blood pressure while lying or sitting, asking the resident to stand, and after waiting 1 minute measuring the pressure again. A drop of systolic pressure greater than 10 mmHg associated with complaints of dizziness or lightheadedness is indicative of this side-effect. Residents with this problem should be advised to get out of bed slowly, and to then rise to a sitting position prior to standing up. The dizziness caused by orthostatic hypotension can be a serious problem in the elderly — leading to falls and possible fractures. Management usually involves reducing or discontinuing the medication. Because orthostatic hypotension is a common and potentially serious problem, all residents on antidepressants and antipsychotic medication should have regular monitoring of their blood pressures while lying and standing.

Anticholinergic side effects are a common problem caused by many antidepressants and antipsychotics (Table 2). The most frequent complaints include dry mouth, blurred vision, and constipation. Although these problems are not serious, they can be very bothersome; constipation can be extremely distressing to the elderly who often focus on bowel function.

The elderly are also more susceptible to the more serious anticholinergic side effects: confusion and delirium (see Chapter 4).

Table 2 Anticholinergic Side Effects
• Dry mouth • Blurred vision • Constipation • Tachycardia • Urinary retention • Sweating • Exacerbation of narrow angle glaucoma • Anticholinergic delirium (delirium, disorientation, confusion, cognitive impairment)

Heterocyclic Antidepressants

Table 3 groups some of the commonly used antidepressant medications according to their propensity to cause these side effects. Amitriptyline (Elavil) and imipramine (Tofranil) appear to cause side effects more frequently and clinically they are not well tolerated in the elderly. Unless there is a clear history of previous response to these medications, they

Table 3
Relative Frequency of Antidepressant Side Effects

Relative Frequency	Sedation	Orthostatic Hypotension	Anti-cholinergic Effects
Common	Amitriptyline	Imipramine	Amitriptyline
	Doxepin	Amitriptyline	Imipramine
	Trazodone	Doxepin	Doxepin
	Imipramine	Trazodone	Nortriptyline
	Nortriptyline	Fluoxetine	Desipramine
	Desipramine	Desipramine	Fluoxetine
Uncommon	Fluoxetine	Nortriptyline	Trazodone

should not be considered agents of first choice. Nortriptyline (Aventyl, Pamelor) conversely, has a relatively low frequency of side effects and tends to be well tolerated. Nortriptyline can be initiated at a dose of 10 mg h.s. and increased slowly to a dose of 50-100 mg h.s. The blood level of this medication can be checked, as several studies have shown that serum levels 50-150 ng/ml (150-500 nmol/L) are associated with therapeutic efficacy, while levels above or below this "therapeutic window" may be ineffective.

All antidepressants require several weeks until they are completely effective. Sleep and appetite may improve within the first 2 weeks of treatment, but it may take up to 6-8 weeks until there is complete objective and subjective improvement. It is, therefore, important to allow this amount of time to pass before switching to another medication.

Monoamine Oxidase Inhibitors

Two other classes of medication which have been used to treat depression in the elderly are the monoamine oxidase inhibitors (MAOIs) and psychostimulants. The commonly used MAOIs phenelzine (Nardil) and tranlycypromine (Parnate) are well tolerated and extremely useful for residents whose depression has not responded to other agents. The MAOIs have fewer anticholinergic and cardiac side effects, but can cause significant orthostatic hypotension and insomnia. The main concern with MAOIs, however, is the potential to cause a hypertensive crisis when taken with foods that contain the compound tyramine. Residents taking MAOIs must adhere to certain dietary and medication restrictions (Table 4).

Any resident on an MAOI who complains of an acute severe headache (usually at the back of the head), stiff neck, nausea or vomiting must have their blood pressure checked. If this is significantly elevated the physician should be notified immediately or the resident should be transferred to an emergency department for treatment and monitoring.

Psychostimulants

The psychostimulants methylphenidate (Ritalin) and dextroamphetamine (Dexedrine) are occasionally used as antidepressants in the elderly. Some studies have shown them to be particularly effective in patients who are elderly, medically ill, withdrawn, and apathetic. These medications are well tolerated and cause few side effects. Some resi-

Table 4
MAOI Dietary Restrictions

Foods to avoid:
- Aged or matured cheeses (e.g., Cheddar, Blue, Swiss)
- Aged or fermented meats and fish (e.g., pepperoni, corned beef, pickled herring)
- Meat and yeast extracts (e.g., Bovril, Marmite, Oxo)
- Broad bean pods

Medications to avoid:
- Cold medications
- Decongestants (including nasal sprays)
- Asthma medications
- Narcotic analgesics (especially meperidine [Demerol])
- Appetite suppressants and stimulants

N.B. Many other foods and drugs have been implicated in causing MAOI adverse reactions. For a list of these foods and drugs please refer to [2] and [3].

dents may experience insomnia or agitation, and occasionally delirium may be precipitated. They are given orally in two daily doses (the last dose given no later than the early afternoon to avoid insomnia). In contrast to the previous classes of antidepressants described, if no therapeutic effect is noticed within the 2 weeks, these medications should be discontinued.

Lithium Carbonate

Although it is not often considered to be an antidepressant, lithium does have antidepressant properties. It is also used to treat acute mania, as prophylaxis against manic and depressive episodes, and it can be added to an established course of antidepressants to improve efficacy. The administration and monitoring of lithium require special consideration in the elderly. With aging, renal functioning becomes progressively compromised; the dose of lithium, which is excreted solely by the kidneys will need to be markedly reduced. The elderly are also more sensitive to the side effects of lithium and therefore should be maintained at lower serum levels than younger populations. All patients on lithium therapy must have periodic measurements of blood levels of lithium, best examined 12 h after the last dose. The vast majority of elderly require 150-600 mg o.d. to attain 12-h serum levels of 0.4-0.7 mmol/L (a level considered safe/effective in this population).

Table 5 Side Effects of Lithium	
Gastrointestinal	**Central nervous system (CNS)**
Nausea Abdominal pain Diarrhea Vomiting Constipation Metallic taste	Fatigue Restlessness Stupor or coma Confusion Dizziness Blurred vision Slurred speech
Neuromuscular	**Endocrine**
Muscular weakness Tremor Abnormal involuntary movements	Hypothyroidism
Renal	**Other**
Reduced concentrating ability Polyurea (urinary frequency) Polydipsia (thirst)	ECG changes Skin rashes Exacerbation of psoriasis Weight gain Baldness

Lithium can cause numerous side effects, the most common being nausea, a fine tremor of the hands, urinary frequency, and thirst (see Table 5). Signs of lithium toxicity include coarse tremor, slurred speech, ataxia, confusion, and drowsiness. Lithium toxicity should be considered a medical emergency necessitating withholding of the drug and immediate measuring of the serum level. Although mild toxicity develops in some adults at levels between 1.5 and 2 mmol/L, the elderly may experience these same effects at levels as low as 1.0 mmol/L.

Besides regular monitoring of serum lithium levels, all residents taking lithium should have yearly checks of serum creatinine and urine osmolality for lithium-induced renal impairment and thyroid function tests for lithium-induced hypothyroidism.

TREATMENT OF PSYCHOSIS AND AGITATION

Psychiatric symptoms such as delusions and hallucinations, can occur in a variety of illnesses including major affective disorder, schizophrenia, paranoid disorders, delirium, and dementia. Neuroleptics are used to treat psychosis, as well as the agitation and aggression associated with dementing illnesses. The first neuroleptic introduced to North America in the early 1950s was chlorpromazine (Thorazine, Largactil). As with the antidepressants, although there are numerous neuroleptics marketed today, none have been shown to have superior efficacy when compared with chlorpromazine.

There are many studies that have demonstrated the effectiveness of neuroleptics in reducing and eliminating hallucinations and delusions in schizophrenia and affective disorders, but there has been little formal research on their usefulness in treating agitation and other behavioral disturbances associated with dementia. Despite this, the neuroleptics remain the most commonly prescribed drugs for treating these problems, and from a clinical standpoint careful, monitored trials of these medications can be helpful. Recent surveys have indicated that neuroleptics are prescribed very frequently in long-term care institutions, that they are not monitored closely, and that the staff is often unfamiliar with their significant and potentially serious side effects [1]. Because of these concerns and their questionable efficacy, neuroleptics should only be prescribed as part of a management plan that includes environmental, behavioral, and other psychosocial treatments.

Since all neuroleptics are equally effective, the choice of drug for an individual resident should be based on the medication's side-effect profile (see Table 6). The neuroleptics can be classified on the basis of their relative potency. In general the low potency neuroleptics (e.g., chlorpromazine and thioridazine [Mellaril]) produce the most sedation, hypotension and anticholinergic effects, while the high potency neuroleptics (e.g., haloperidol [Haldol] and trifluoperazine [Stelazine]) produce the greatest amounts of extrapyramidal symptoms (see Table 7). Regardless of the choice these medications must be prescribed in

Table 6
Neuroleptic Side Effects I

Anticholinergic effects*

Extrapyramidal symptoms
    Dystonias
    Parkinsonism
    Akathisia
    Tardive dyskinesia

Sedation
Hypotension
Weight gain
Retinopathy
Skin rash/pigmentation
Jaundice
Neuroleptic malignant syndrome (elevated temperature, muscular rigidity, increased creatine phosphokinase (CPK), tachycardia, altered consciousness)

*See Table 2

Table 7
Side Effects of Neuroleptics II

	Anti-cholinergic Effects	Sedation	Extra-pyramidal Effects
Low Potency (e.g., chlorpromazine, thioridazine)	+++	+++	+
Middle Potency (e.g., perphenazine, loxapine)	++	++	++
High Potency (e.g., haloperidol, trifluoperazine)	+	+	+++

very small doses as the elderly are exquisitely sensitive to side effects; small doses of thioridazine (10-25 mg h.s.) may cause excessive day-time sedation or confusion, while small doses of haloperidol (0.5-1.0 mg h.s.) may cause severe parkinsonism with stiffness and rigidity.

Neuroleptic extrapyramidal reactions include dystonias, parkinsonism, akathisia, and tardive dyskinesia. Dystonias, which occur relatively infrequently in the elderly, are dramatic, acute, sustained contractions of specific muscle groups. These distressing reactions occur within the first days of treatment and can involve the muscles of the neck, mouth, and eyes. Neuroleptic-induced parkinsonism is ex-

"That's what it says: one tablespoonful, 300 times a day."

HERMAN COPYRIGHT 1981 (Third Treasury). Jim Unger.
Reprinted with permission of Universal Press Syndicate.

tremely common in the elderly presenting with rigidity, slowed movements, tremor, shuffling gait, stooped posture, an inexpressive face, and drooling. Akathisia is motor restlessness in which the resident feels compelled to keep moving and pacing. Residents often complain about feeling anxious and being unable to sleep. In younger adults these symptoms are often treated with anticholinergic agents such as benzotropine (Cogentin), diphenhydramine (Benadryl) and trihexyphe-nidyl (Artane). Because the elderly and demented patients are so prone to developing confusion and delirium with anticholinergic medications, the use of these agents is not often recommended. When extrapyramidal symptoms are prominent, the neuroleptic should be reduced, or a drug from a different class should be tried.

The other serious extrapyramidal symptom is tardive dyskinesia. This syndrome appears gradually after prolonged use of neuroleptics (months to years) and can present with various abnormal, involuntary movements most often involving the tongue, mouth and face (e.g., tongue-writhing, lip-smacking, facial grimacing). The risk factors for developing tardive dyskinesia include length of drug exposure, increased age of the patient, female sex, and the presence of dementia. In a significant percentage of patients this movement disorder may last for years or be permanent even after the discontinuation of medication. Because tardive dyskinesia can be permanent and because there are no really effective treatments available, prevention is essential. For the institutionalized elderly at high risk for tardive dyskinesia, prevention involves: 1. avoiding the use of neuroleptics if possible, 2. reducing and discontinuing the medication as soon as possible following amelioration of symptomatology, and 3. examining each resident receiving a neuroleptic regularly to determine if there is any evidence of abnormal involuntary movements.

Neuroleptics are often not effective in managing the agitation associated with dementia so many other medications have been used. Drugs such as lithium, beta-blockers (propranolol, pindolol), carbamazepine, benzodiazepines, and some antidepressants (e.g., trazodone) have all been shown to be occasionally effective in the agitated demented resident who has not responded to neuroleptics. At the present time, however, these drugs should be considered only after the standard therapies described earlier have been used.

TREATMENT OF ANXIETY AND INSOMNIA

The most commonly used agents to treat anxiety and insomnia are the benzodiazepines. Prior to the introduction of the benzodiazepines in the 1960s the drugs of choice for these problems were the barbiturates, known for their tendency to produce addiction, severe withdrawal reactions, and extreme lethality in overdose. Compared with barbiturates, the benzodiazepines are more effective and far safer.

The benzodiazepines can be grouped on the basis of their relative half-lives, a measure of how quickly the drugs are metabolized. In the elderly the rate of benzodiazepine metabolism is significantly slower than in younger populations; diazepam (Valium) which has a half-life of approximately 24 h in a young adult may have a half-life of 90-120h in an 80-year-old. The longer the half-life, the more likely a drug will accumulate in the body, potentially leading to increased risk of side effects. The drugs of choice for institutionalized elderly will, therefore, be the short- or intermediate-acting benzodiazepines such as lorazepam (Ativan) and oxazepam (Serax).

The major side effects of the benzodiazepines are excessive daytime sedation, confusion, and disorientation, and withdrawal reactions. Withdrawal reactions usually occur after these medications have been prescribed for long periods, in high doses, and are then abruptly withdrawn. Signs and symptoms can include insomnia, anxiety, tremor, and tachycardia. In severe cases the resident may experience delirium, psychosis, or seizures. Treatment involves reinstituting the drug and then tapering it very slowly.

Other medications which are used to treat anxiety and insomnia include the antihistamines, neuroleptics, and buspirone (Buspar). The antihistamines such as hydroxyzine (Atarax) and diphenhydramine (Benadryl) are highly anticholinergic and should, therefore, not be considered agents of first choice in the elderly. Although neuroleptics can be helpful in treating severe anxiety and agitation, there are many risks associated with their use that have been described previously. Buspirone, a new nonbenzodiazepine anxiolytic, is nonsedating and nonaddictive, but its use in elderly patients has not yet been clearly established. At the present time, whenever pharmacological management of anxiety and insomnia is essential, the benzodiazepines should be considered the agents of first choice.

KEY POINTS

- Psychotropic medications are considered to be only one part of a multifaceted treatment program, and should only be initiated after a careful review of risks and benefits.

- Specific target symptoms should be chosen for monitoring, and reassessment of efficacy should occur regularly.

- Because the elderly are extremely sensitive to the side effects of psychotropic medications, staff should be vigilant for these adverse drug reactions.

REFERENCES

1. Avorn, J., Dreyer, P., Connelly, K., Soumeri, S.B. (1989). Use of psychoactive medications and the quality of care in rest homes. *New England Journal of Medicine*, 320:227-232.

   Important study concludes that a large percentage of residents in these long-term care facilities are elderly and psychiatrically disturbed. Raises the important concern that such institutions frequently use psychoactive medications without adequate medical supervision, using poorly trained supervisory staff.

2. Bezchlibnyk-Butler, K., Jeffries, J.J. (1990). *Clinical handbook of psychotropic drugs*. Toronto, ON: Hogrefe & Huber Publishers.

   Although not specifically related to the elderly, this spiral-bound handbook reviews the major psychotropic drug classes with numerous handy charts and tables.

3. Jenike, M.A. (1989). *Geriatric psychiatry and psychopharmacology*. Chicago: Year Book Medical Publishers Inc.

   This excellent brief text is easy to read, and provides numerous clinical vignettes.

SUGGESTED READING

1. Thompson, T.L., Moran, M.G., Nies, A.S. (1983). Psychotropic drug use in the elderly. *New England Journal of Medicine*, 308:134-138, 194-199.

   Two-part article highlights the unique needs and susceptibility of the elderly who are prescribed psychotropic medications; the major classes of medications are briefly reviewed.

2. Gerner, R.H. (1984). Antidepressant selection in the elderly. *Psychosomatics*, 25:528-535.

3. Wragg, R.E., Jeste, D.V. (1988). Neuroleptics and alternative treatments. *Psychiatric Clinics of North America*, 11:195-213.

   Excellent comprehensive review of the use of medication for the management of psychosis and behavioral problems in demented patients; reviews clinical studies which have examined the efficacy of these drugs.

4. Shulman, K.I., Mackenzie, S., Hardy, B. (1987). The clinical use of lithium carbonate in old age: A review. *Prog. Neuro-Psychopharmacol and Biol. Psychiatry*, 11:159-164.

CHAPTER

Behavior   **10**
Management Strategies

by Dmytro Rewilak

Yelling, screaming, hitting out, and progressive loss of independence are just a few examples of challenging behaviors common in institutions that care for the elderly. Management of such behaviors is difficult and emotionally taxing to caregivers. The problems are often magnified unnecessarily because staff do not have appropriate strategies for dealing with them. Behavioral approaches, despite their extensive use with children and younger adults in a variety of clinical environments, have been underutilized in geriatric and long-term care settings. This chapter presents the behavioral approach to the management of problem behaviors in cognitively impaired nursing home residents.

OVERVIEW

A comprehensive approach to the management of inappropriate behaviors of residents with cognitive impairments should include: 1. an assessment of the resident's cognitive deficits and spared functions, 2. a systematic behavioral assessment of inappropriate behaviors, and 3. a consideration of staff's perceptions of these behaviors. This approach recognizes the complexity of human behavior, and takes into account important factors within individual residents, their caregivers, and their physical environments.

Cognitive Assessment

Many factors within the individual such as various disease processes, sensory perceptual changes, and nutrition contribute to inappropriate behaviors in the elderly. The most important determinant in a nursing home setting, however, is the integrity of the brain. Generally, the brain can be thought of as an organ that allows us to interact with and adapt to our environment. When it becomes dysfunctional, as in cases of Alzheimer disease or stroke, this process of interaction and adaptation breaks down and results in impaired psychosocial functioning and inappropriate behaviors. Unfortunately, because the effects of an individual's cognitive deficits on his everyday functioning are often poorly understood, they are frequently misinterpreted or mislabelled. Terms, such as "senility," "dementia," and "organic" are too global and communicate little that can be of use in understanding specific behaviors. What once was called senility represents a multitude of different disease processes. Even in the case of Alzheimer disease, there is evidence pointing to different subtypes. It is crucial, therefore, to describe the individual's impaired as well as spared cognitive functions, as these will have an important bearing on the success of any management strategies that are implemented.

Description of cognitive functions is achieved through a neuropsychological assessment. A full neuropsychological evaluation is time-consuming and not warranted in every case of inappropriate behavior. In our setting, we have found that a comprehensive neuropsychological screening battery, which takes approximately 1 hour to administer, provides sufficient information that can be incorporated into a management plan. The battery assesses various aspects of the individual's orientation, attention, memory, language, constructional abilities, motor and sensory-perceptual functions, and abstract reasoning. If the services of a neuropsychologist are not readily available, valuable information about the individual's cognitive functioning can be obtained through a detailed mental status examination (MSE; see Chapter 2).

Behavioral Assessment

The next step in the development of an efficient management plan is a consideration of environmental determinants of behavior. This involves a detailed description of a specific problem behavior and the circumstances surrounding it. What is meant by behavior? Behavior is anything a person does that can be observed, measured, and monitored. It does not occur in a vacuum. The assumption in the behavioral approach is that for every occurrence of a specific behavior there are events that trigger it and events that encourage its repetition. Triggering events are called Antecedents, and events that maintain Behavior are called Consequences. In this model, every behavior can be subjected to a functional, or an "ABC analysis." An example is provided in Table 1.

Table 1
An ABC Analysis of Yelling Behavior

DATE:	February 3, 1987
TIME:	9:10 a.m.
ANTECEDENTS:	Nurse enters room to provide a.m. care
BEHAVIOR:	Resident yells: "What do you want, you (so and so) I don't belong here"
CONSEQUENCES:	Nurse responds: "What's the matter? You shouldn't use language like that.... There, there now." Nurse strokes patient's arm.

While behavior is always observable, antecedents and consequences are not. For example, a particular thought (e.g., "he's going to attack me") can act as the trigger for evasive behavior, and the "high" that comes after smoking a cigarette can serve as a very powerful reinforcer of smoking behavior. Through a behavioral assessment, an attempt is made to identify and measure the variables that control behavior. To illustrate, the antecedents that trigger the striking-out behavior of a cognitively impaired nursing home resident could include the nature of the resident's cognitive deficits, the time of day the behavior occurs, whether or not it is preceded by a stressful event, a particular location that is associated with the behavior, and the characteristics of the individual against whom the behavior occurs. Among the consequences that serve to maintain the behavior are the manner in which the behavior is handled, the amount of attention given to the behavior by staff, and staff's lack of attention to more appropriate behaviors. Only through a thorough and systematic analysis of a behavior is it possible to isolate the variables controlling it.

For the purpose of an "ABC analysis" of problem behaviors, it is important to define specific behaviors so that they can be measured. Terms such as "aggression," "dependence," and "agitation" are too vague and do not lend themselves to reliable measurement. They can be redefined, for example, as spitting or hitting (aggression), failure to self-feed (dependence), and pulling at hair (agitation).

Once the problem behavior has been defined in objective terms, a decision must be made about the best way to record the behavior. A number of different methods can be utilized. Continuous recording involves writing down everything a person says or does, a method which is not practical unless a highly specific analysis of a particular behavior is required. Recording the total length of time a behavior occurs is called duration recording. In interval recording, a period of time is broken down into blocks of 5 or 30 minutes, for example, and a record is made of whether or not the behavior occurred in that block of time. This type of recording does not measure whether a behavior occurred once or 50 times, it simply notes whether the behavior was present or absent during the stated interval. It usually is employed to assess behaviors occurring with a high frequency, such as constant yelling or screaming. Momentary time sampling involves checking for a behavior at the end of a predetermined block of time (e.g., at the end of every 10 minutes or every hour). The type of recording selected will depend on the behavior that needs to be assessed and managed.

Regardless of the recording method, the aim of the behavioral assessment is to obtain a baseline measurement of the problem behavior. Monitoring of the behavior continues throughout the treatment period. This helps determine the progress of treatment in an unbiased manner. If interventions are not monitored in this way, successful treatments may be overlooked and discontinued. In the case of yelling, staff might say that the individual is still yelling and conclude that treatment has failed. If close monitoring, however, reveals that yelling occurs only 20 times per week rather than 55, staff would have direct proof that the frequency of yelling has been reduced substantially.

Staff Perceptions

When confronted with problem behaviors in the cognitively impaired resident, it is crucial for the staff to examine their own perceptions, as these may be contributing to the problem. Under perceptions are included staff attitudes in general, staff interpretations of problem behaviors, and staff expectations of the cognitively impaired resident.

Attitudes are powerful determinants of behavior. For example, when an individual is introduced to somebody new she/he interacts briefly with that person, exchanges pleasantries, takes the person's phone number, and says goodbye, but not before having reached a conclusion about that person. The individual may label the person as a good or bad listener, as friendly or distant, as someone she/he could or could not trust. These conclusions, or labels, will determine whether the individual will call that person up on the phone and how she/he might feel (e.g., relaxed or tense) on meeting that person again.

One of the commonest forms of labeling relates to cognitive deficits. Many inappropriate behaviors are misconstrued as characterological when, in fact, they are the result of dysfunction in a particular cognitive domain. For example, consider the individual who has suffered a right hemisphere stroke and has difficulty attending to the left side of visual space. On his way to physiotherapy, he is wheeled along a corridor, attending only to the right side. On the return journey, what before was on the intact right side of space now is on the impaired left side. The individual begins to argue that this is not the way to his room, and staff try to convince him to the contrary. The misinterpretations of his environment lead to increased agitation, and he becomes labeled as "confused," or even "aggressive" and "paranoid." These labels become a self-fulfilling prophecy. In the future, staff may become wary of him and stop interacting with him, because their expectations are now based on these labels.

One of the functions of the cognitive assessment is to minimize the dangers of labeling, or rather mislabeling, by educating the staff about the nature of various cognitive deficits and their effects on psychosocial functioning. While it is recognized that the services of a psychologist are not routinely available to nursing homes, it remains crucial for staff to become more knowledgeable about cognitive impairments through different avenues, such as inservice education by invited professionals, attendance at workshops, or personal readings. A lack of understanding of cognitive deficits reduces the quality of life of residents and makes the job of providing care to them more difficult.

Staff attitudes towards the behavioral management program is another important consideration. A common reservation raised by staff is, "How is it possible to change the behavior of residents with memory problems, when they will not remember either their behavior or the consequences following it?" Recent research suggests that individuals with severe memory disorders are capable of learning complex new skills even though they do not remember the training to learn them. The fact is that most people can learn new and unlearn old behaviors. Take the case of the so-called screamer, constantly yelling out for cigarettes. Every nursing home probably has one such individual and the reader does not need to be reminded of the rebukes or commands to stop the yelling that follow this behavior. What happens when the individual is quiet? The first thought of staff is not to bother the individual, as this might trigger the screaming. The unfortunate result of these interactions or lack of interactions is that, through conditioning, the individual has learned that yelling is the only means of contact with the staff.

Another problem is the staff's reluctance to initiate behavioral management programs because of the additional work involved. For nursing home staff, who often feel overworked and perhaps unsupported, systematically recording problem behaviors and providing consequences for them on a consistent basis requires considerable time and energy. Behavioral programs are most successful in settings where staff perceive the program as a treatment intervention that is essential for improving the quality of life of the cognitively impaired resident, just as important as insulin injections for a diabetic, for example. Their success can result in a sense of mastery and self-perceptions of increased capability and effectiveness. At a practical level, staff often perceive their workload to have decreased.

When staff attitudes are not dealt with, they detract from the potential effectiveness of any behavior management program. Left unattended, they can result in inconsistent recording of problem behaviors and inconsistent application of consequences, which may lead to exacerbations of the target behaviors. This could lead staff to conclude that the approach is ineffective and should be discontinued.

The stress experienced by staff also has an important bearing on problem behaviors and the application of behavioral management programs. In order to reduce the level of stress in staff and enhance the effectiveness of a behavioral management program, it is helpful for staff to follow the stress inoculation paradigm [3]. In this paradigm, stressful situations are redefined as problems that require solutions. The solution is to break down a stressful event into a series of stages and use internal dialogue, or self-talk, to cope with the stress.

The stages are: 1. preparing for the stressful event, 2. confronting and handling the stressful event, 3. coping with feelings of being overwhelmed, and 4. evaluating coping efforts and rewarding oneself. An adaptation of this coping strategy in the management of an individual who is verbally abusive and hits out at staff is illustrated in Table 2.

Table 2
Examples of Coping Self-Statements in the
Management of a Verbally and Physically Abusive Resident

Preparing for Stressful Interaction

- I need to select an effective coping tape for my mental cassette player.
- What is it I have to do?
- We have worked out a plan to deal with this situation.
- Remember, stick to the task and don't take the verbal abuse personally.
- Watch out for his right arm.

Engaging in the Stressful Interaction

- I'm in the room, now; I need to remember, one step at a time.
- Focus on providing the care.
- There he goes, careful now, it's not personal.
- His brain isn't working right, that's why he does it.
- Take a deep breath, relax.
- This is working, it's easier than I thought.

Evaluating Interaction

- I almost lost it when he commented about my ....
- I could have become upset and angry.
- That deep breathing really worked.
- On the whole, I'd give myself 8 out of 10.

OR

- Didn't handle that one too well.
- Don't get discouraged. I'm new at this.
- Where did I become ineffective?
- What can I do next time?

CLASSIFICATION OF PROBLEM BEHAVIOR

Behaviors can be classified according to whether or not they need to be reduced or increased. Those in need of reduction are referred to as behavioral excesses, and those that need to be increased are referred to as behavioral deficits. Different behavioral techniques are applied, depending on this distinction.

Behavioral Excesses

In many instances behaviors may not be inappropriate in and of themselves, but become labeled inappropriate because of their high frequency of occurrence. Behaviors such as shouting, swearing, self-injury, constant demanding or ringing of the call-bell, verbal and physical abuse, are examples of behavioral excesses. Among techniques designed to reduce behaviors are extinction, reinforcement of alternative behaviors, and time out.

Extinction is the removal of reinforcement, where reinforcement is defined as any response to a given behavior. In the example in Table 1, the nurse's responses of inquiry, rebuke, and physical contact are all considered reinforcing of the yelling behavior. Being reinforcers, they increase the likelihood that the behavior will recur. Using extinction involves ignoring the yelling by walking away, for example.

Reinforcement of alternative behavior involves providing reinforcement on a consistent basis for any appropriate behavior that is incompatible with the problem behavior. Sitting quietly in the chair and saying, "Good morning," are examples of behaviors incompatible with screaming and verbal abuse respectively.

In time out, the resident is removed from the situation in which the inappropriate behavior occurs and placed in an environment devoid of any potential reinforcers. In settings where behavioral strategies are utilized routinely, there is usually a designated "time out" room. In nursing homes, where space may be limited, the resident's room may double up as a time out environment. Time out falls under the classification of "punishment procedures," and normally should be used only if other interventions have failed. Occasionally, however, it may be the most prudent intervention. For example, an individual who is constantly yelling in the corridor of a nursing home may upset other residents and provoke verbally and physically aggressive reactions. These reactions to the yelling, although negative, actually reinforce the yelling. Placing individuals in time out prevents this type of reinforcement and also serves to protect personal safety. When applying time out, the individual must be informed about the length of time he is to spend in the time out environment and that time out will be terminated if he is behaving appropriately at the end of that time. A time out period of 5 minutes should be the rule of thumb and is usually sufficient if applied consistently.

The general strategy in managing behavioral excesses is to eliminate the positive consequences that follow inappropriate behavior, while at the same time reinforcing alternative incompatible behaviors. It is unethical to simply decrease inappropriate behaviors without attempting to replace them with appropriate behaviors.

Inappropriate sexual activity and inappropriate voiding are other examples of behavioral excesses. Although they might not occur at a high frequency rate, they are labelled inappropriate because of the situation in which they occur. For example, voiding on the toilet is appropriate, but voiding in a public place is inappropriate. The general strategy aims to bring the inappropriate behavior (e.g., voiding) under the control of a particular stimulus (e.g., toilet) through repetition and training.

Behavioral Deficits

Behaviors that occur with a low frequency and are required for independent functioning are called behavioral deficits. Examples of behavioral deficits include loss of self-care skills, low activity level and decreased social interactions. A behavioral deficit that is frequently encountered in institutional settings is decreased independence. The institutional environment can occasionally foster this decrease in independence. The fact that individuals require institutionalization often implies that their ability to function independently has been compromised in some way. They enter an institution, however, with a repertoire of preserved skills for independent functioning. Unfortunately, many of their independent behaviors are not reinforced and fall into disuse. A good example is the individual who has suffered a stroke and is left with motor deficits. He may be able to put on and button his coat, but he requires half an hour to do it. Watching an individual struggle in this way elicits caring behaviors on the part of staff who are compelled to rush in and assist the individual and may, in fact, voice mild rebuke for the length of time that the individual requires to dress independently.

In this instance, what is reinforced is dependence on staff for dressing and independent behavior is discouraged by the rebuke. The individual's functional abilities decrease over time to the point of complete reliance on staff for provision of self-care activities.

The general strategy of intervention for behavioral deficits is to increase behaviors through gradual reshaping or retraining of absent or infrequent behaviors. The most frequent intervention for increasing appropriate behavior is the application of positive reinforcement immediately after the desired behavior has occurred. There are two main classes of positive reinforcers, primary and secondary. Primary reinforcers include such things as food and drinks which satisfy a primary physical need. Secondary reinforcers are social and include such consequences as praise, smiling, and verbal approval. When applied after the occurrence of a behavior, positive reinforcers increase the likelihood that the behavior will be repeated. In a typical behavior management program aimed at increasing a particular behavior, initially the behavior is reinforced each time it occurs and then later only intermittently. It is also common practice to provide primary reinforcers at the beginning of a program and substitute them with secondary reinforcers in the later stages of treatment.

The use of reinforcement depends on the individual emitting a desired behavior. Often, in the case of behavioral deficits, there is a need to intervene in order to elicit the appropriate behavior. Shaping and prompting are interventions designed to encourage the resident to emit a desired behavior. In shaping, a complete behavior which is not present in the behavioral repertoire of the resident, is broken down into its component parts, which are arranged in a hierarchical manner. For example, the final behavior of self-feeding can be broken down into the following steps: 1. looking down at the plate and fork; 2. touching the fork; 3. lifting the fork off the table; 4. holding the fork over the plate; 5. picking up a piece of food with the fork; 6. bringing the fork up towards the mouth; and 7. placing the fork in the mouth. Training begins with the first step, then the second, and so on, and the resident is reinforced for successfully completing each step of this behavioral sequence. Care should be taken not to progress too rapidly from one level of performance to the next, as the newly acquired behaviors may be unlearned.

Prompting is the use of physical or verbal cues to encourage a particular behavior. It is often applied during the steps of the behavior-shaping intervention, but is also applied as a discrete intervention. For example, individuals with frontal lobe dysfunction may have pathological inertia. While they have the desired or appropriate behaviors in their repertoire, they have trouble initiating them. It is not unusual for them to lie in bed for prolonged periods or simply stare into their plate without feeding themselves. Using verbal prompts (e.g., "It's time to get up") or physical prompts (e.g., guiding their hand to the utensil) helps them initiate functional behaviors.

CARRYING OUT BEHAVIORAL INTERVENTIONS

Regardless of the behavior targeted for treatment, a typical sequence of steps is followed in designing and implementing behavioral interventions. This sequence is outlined below and represents a summary of the more salient aspects of what has been discussed previously.

Defining Problem Behaviors

Problem behaviors need to be defined in specific and objective rather than vague and subjective terms. The emphasis is on observable behaviors rather than on assumptions about what the patient is feeling or intending. For example, the vague term "depression" can be redefined as the "resident does not leave the room," "does not smile," "makes derogatory statements about himself," and "talks of suicide." These specific definitions are amenable to measurement in terms of frequency or duration of occurrence.

Obtaining Baselines

This is a central part of any behavioral management program and serves a number of purposes. Baseline measurements yield objective evidence of the extent or severity of the problem. The frequency of occurrence of difficult behaviors is often overestimated by staff. This is not surprising, as the stress generated by these behaviors makes it seem as if they are occurring incessantly. Obtaining a baseline of a specifically defined behavior, however, gives a more accurate picture of the problem. A further function of baseline measurements is to provide a comparison for the effects of treatment. Behavioral charting continues during the intervention phase and helps determine the progress of treatment in an unbiased and objective manner, and whether progress is steady or fluctuates. Another purpose of baseline measurements is to provide important information about factors which are controlling the problem behaviors. Performing a functional analysis of antecedents and consequences of these behaviors via ABC charting provides details of events that trigger and maintain them. In many instances, it may also serve to highlight interventions that have been successful in dealing with the problem behaviors, and which can be incorporated into the management plan.

Planning Treatment

There are many important considerations before starting actual treatment. Decisions have to be made about who is going to be involved in providing treatment, who will be responsible for monitoring treatment, and what reinforcers are going to be used in changing behavior. If left unattended, these issues might jeopardize the potential effectiveness of a treatment program. An example of a plan of treatment is provided in Table 3. The plan should form part of the resident's chart.

Table 3
Behavioral Management Care Plan

NAME: Ms C

PROBLEMS: 1. Verbal abuse
2. Refusal of medications
3. Constant demands

ASSESSMENT: Cognitive assessment reveals problems in time orientation and estimation, attention and concentration, memory, construction, problem-solving and mental flexibility. There is evidence of left-sided neglect.

ABC charting over a 2-week baseline period reveals 7 instances of verbal abuse, 2 refusals to take medications, and 67 demands. The most frequent are demands for toiletting, followed by demands to be helped with feeding. There are no obvious triggers for these behaviors. Responses to them are inconsistent.

NB. The problem behaviors shown by Ms C are a function of the interaction between her cognitive deficits, emotional responses to her disabilities, and her premorbid personality.

Table 3 (cont.)

MANAGEMENT PROGRAM

1. **Behavior**:   Verbal abuse
   Intervention: Use extinction

   This involves withholding reinforcement by ignoring the behavior. Although it will be difficult, do not argue, reason, discuss, plead, or show that you are upset. Any reaction on your part will ensure that the verbal abuse continues.

2. **Behavior**:   Refusal of medications

   When Ms C refuses medications, use extinction (as above).

   Wait 1 minute, then offer medication again without commenting on her refusal.

   If she refuses again, use extinction.

   NB. Ms C does not refuse her medications all the time. It is important to reinforce all instances when she complies with your request. This means, for example, spending additional time with her, performing some activity with her, or simply smiling and thanking her for cooperating.

3. **Behavior**:   Constant demands
   Interventions: (for demands to be toiletted)

   Place Ms C on a 2-hourly toiletting schedule. Every 2 hours approach Ms C and offer to take her to the bathroom, using a verbal prompt (i.e., "It's time to go to the toilet.") Should she refuse the offer, comply with her request the next time she makes it, and then go back to the 2-hourly schedule.

   At all other times, apply extinction.

   Interventions: (for other repetitive demands)

   Anticipate Ms C's needs and meet them. Use extinction for the repetitive demands.

Table 3 (cont.)

Place food in her right visual space.

Use verbal (e.g., "It's time to eat now") and physical (e.g., guide her hand to the spoon) prompts to initiate self-feeding activity.

Reinforce compliance.

Use extinction for statements of inability to perform self-feeding (e.g., "I can't," "You feed me, please").

NB. Make sure you schedule sufficient time for Ms C to feed herself. If you do not, you will be pressured to rush in and help her, which will undo your attempts to increase her independence.

Remember:

1) Consistency of approach is the golden rule in managing difficult behaviors.
2) Reinforce all appropriate behaviors.
3) Be aware of how you label Ms C's behaviors and use coping self-statements in your interactions with her.

NB. The use of self-statements follows the format outlined in Table 2.

Beginning Treatment

Once treatment strategies have been planned, they are put into action. The golden rule of all behavior treatment programs is consistency. Consequences need to be provided immediately after the behavior occurs and every time the behavior occurs. In the case of behavioral deficits where the aim is to increase a given behavior, positive consequences are applied. In the case of behavioral excesses, where the aim is to reduce problem behaviors, positive consequences are withheld when inappropriate responses occur and are applied whenever incompatible appropriate responses are made. Consistency is difficult to achieve. It is made more difficult by the understaffing of nursing homes and the consequent use of on-call staff. This problem can be circumvented by instructing on-call staff about the treatment program.

Monitoring and Evaluating Treatment

As noted previously, charting of problem behaviors needs to continue during treatment. If applied correctly, significant changes can be seen after only a few days, although in the case of behavioral excesses it is usual for the problem behaviors to escalate before they begin to decrease. If after a few weeks of treatment there has been no change in the behavior, the protocol needs to be re-evaluated and adjusted. The consequences may need to be changed or may need to be applied more diligently to ensure consistency.

CASE ILLUSTRATIONS

Case 1

Mr J was a 77-year-old widowed gentleman admitted to a nursing home following a period of hospitalization and rehabilitation for a hip fracture. Prior to admission to hospital, he had been living in his own apartment, but had required considerable assistance and supervision by one of his daughters. There was no personal or family psychiatric history. He had a diagnosis of Alzheimer disease predating his admission to hospital. Over the course of the previous 2 years, he had shown progressive memory loss and inability to manage his finances. He was referred because of "increasing uncooperativeness and agitation."

Interviews with the staff revealed disagreement about the magnitude of the problem. The problem was perceived to be greatest and most urgent by the morning shift, while the evening shift did not perceive any major difficulties. The morning staff perceived the behavior as unpredictable and occurring "all the time." Whenever problem behaviors did occur, they were labeled as intentional. The staff had limited awareness of how Mr J's cognitive deficits were contributing to his problem behaviors.

Cognitive assessment

An assessment of Mr J's cognitive functioning was undertaken. He was disoriented to time and place. His passive registration of information was adequate (i.e., he could repeat five digits forward), but deficits were observed when increased demands were placed on his attentional resources. He could not repeat even two digits backward or recite the days of the week backward, although he could list them correctly forward. His memory was impaired for both visual and verbal information. His immediate recall was poor (i.e., two objects out of four), and he required repeated trials to register all the information. After a delay of 5 minutes, his recall was 0, and cueing failed to enhance his performance. His language was repetitious, he had naming difficulty, and his ability to generate words was impaired. His ability to comprehend staged commands (e.g., "Do x, then y") was deficient. Drawing tasks revealed severe constructional problems. The pattern of results was consistent with his diagnosis of Alzheimer disease.

Behavioral assessment

"Increasing uncooperativeness and agitation" were redefined more specifically as hitting, throwing objects, scratching, and screaming. Staff on all shifts were asked to chart these problem behaviors according to the ABC model. They were instructed to chart every occurrence of these behaviors over a 1-week period, with particular emphasis on their relationship to events preceding and following them. The aim was to arrive at a baseline of the frequency of these behaviors, together with the identification of factors that were triggering and maintaining them.

Results of ABC charting showed that the majority of Mr J's problem behaviors occurred when he was in the process of receiving help for some activity of daily living (e.g., bathing). He was often not told what was to happen, or the instructions were too complex. While engaged in one activity, he was sometimes asked to comply with additional demands (e.g., take medications while being toileted). Charting also revealed that staff responses to Mr J's problem behaviors were inconsistent and included reasoning with him, asking him to stop, or being critical.

Treatment program

The first step was to provide the staff with feedback from the cognitive and behavioral assessments. His cognitive deficits were explained together with how they affected his ability to function and cope with the demands of everyday living. Results of ABC charting were also given to the staff. Their attention was drawn to the fact that Mr J's problem behaviors were in fact quite predictable and usually occurred when demands were placed on him to comply with some activity of daily living. The inconsistency of their response was underscored as representing the kind of intermittent reinforcement that results in strong maintenance of a behavior.

The following interventions were utilized. The staff were instructed to inform Mr J of their intended action using brief, uncomplicated language (e.g., "Time for a bath, Mr J.") and to desist from making multiple simultaneous demands of Mr J in order to minimize the impact of his attentional, memory and language problems. The main intervention was that of extinction. This involved ignoring (i.e., withholding positive reinforcement) the problem behaviors whenever they occurred, while at the same time reinforcing appropriate behaviors.

Figure 1 illustrates the effects of treatment over a period of 3 weeks. Following one week of treatment, there had been an insignificant decrease of problem behaviors. Staff were encouraged to persevere with the program, and after three weeks there was a marked reduction in the incidence of problem behaviors.

Comment

An individualized treatment plan was developed to manage Mr J's problem behaviors. It was based on a clear understanding of how his cognitive deficits were compromising his ability to cope with the demands placed upon him and an awareness of how environmental factors were triggering and maintaining the problem behaviors. Results of the cognitive and behavioral assessments led to a shift in the staff's perceptions of Mr J's behaviors. Following the consistent and systematic application of reinforcement, Mr J's behavior improved dramatically.

Behavior management programs require consistency and perseverance. Mr J's problem behaviors resurfaced after several months. A reassessment of his cognitive functioning did not indicate any further significant decline in his abilities. A consideration of environmental factors, however, indicated that the staff had stopped applying the management program consistently. Once consistency was reestablished, Mr J's problems decreased.

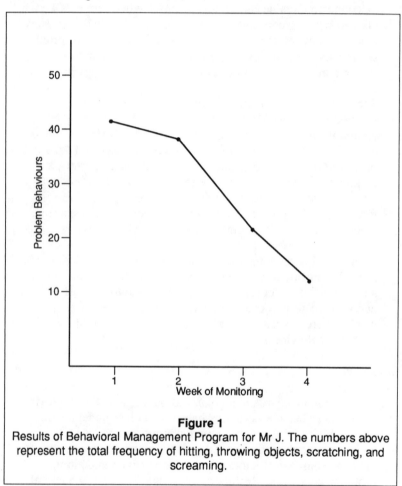

Figure 1
Results of Behavioral Management Program for Mr J. The numbers above represent the total frequency of hitting, throwing objects, scratching, and screaming.

Case 2

Ms C was a 68-year-old single woman, a former bookkeeper and secretary, who was living with her widowed sister and awaiting placement in a nursing home. Several years previously, she had suffered a right hemisphere stroke that had resulted in a left hemiparesis. Subsequently, there was evidence of further bilateral cerebral ischemic damage. Her sister was finding it increasingly difficult to cope with Ms C's problem behaviors. These included verbal abuse, refusals to take medications, and a complete dependency on her sister for all activities of daily living. The latter was expressed in constant demands to have her sister do something for her. While Ms C always had been somewhat dependent, the verbal abuse was out of keeping with her premorbid personality. The sister admitted that she could probably cope with Ms C's constant demands if only she were less angry, irritable, and abusive.

Cognitive assessment

Neuropsychological testing identified a number of significant cognitive deficits. Ms C was disoriented to time, having particular difficulties making judgements regarding recent events. Her attention and concentration were severely impaired. Her memory for both verbal and visual information was severely impaired and she had severe constructional deficits with evidence of left-sided neglect. Her capacity for abstract reasoning and problem-solving was deficient.

Behavioral assessment

The sister was asked to record the frequency of Ms C's verbally abusive and demanding behaviors using the ABC format. She was to try and specify events that preceded the problem behaviors, describe the problem behaviors as objectively as possible, and record her responses to the behaviors. When she returned after 1 week, it was obvious that the ABC format was either not sufficiently explained or she had misunderstood the instructions. Under the C column (for Consequences), she had been recording what Ms C was still doing following her verbal outbursts or demands (e.g., "sister continued to ask to be toileted"), and had omitted describing her own responses to these behaviors. She was reinstructed to record what she did in response to her sister's problem behaviors.

Results of ABC charting revealed that over the 2-week baseline period, there were seven occasions when Ms C was verbally abusive and two when she refused to take her medications. This

came as a surprise to the sister. While commenting that she may
have omitted some instances of verbal abuse, the sister admitted that their frequency was certainly lower than she had
thought. Charting failed to reveal any obvious triggering events
for the verbal abuse or refusals. Descriptions of the sister's
responses to the abuse, however, showed different emotional
reactions, including anger and sadness, and different behaviors,
including leaving the room and crying. A total of 67 demands
was recorded over the two weeks. Their frequency was underestimated, as the sister had not recorded all of Ms C's demands.

There was a perseverative flavour to many of the demands.
Perseverative behavior is a common behavioral disturbance
associated with damage to particular areas of the brain. It can
be defined as repetitive responding regardless of the situation,
or inability to shift one's attention from one activity or train of
thought to the next. In Ms C's case, even though her sister had
just complied with her request for toiletting or a drink, this
request was repeated within minutes. Toiletting demands were
the most frequent. While she was capable of feeding herself,
Ms C repeatedly asked to be fed. The sister's responses to the
problem behaviors were inconsistent. They typically included
pleading, bargaining, and reasoning with Ms C, and occasionally threatening her (e.g., "I'm gonna let you starve.").

Treatment program

Ms C's sister was provided with feedback of the cognitive and
behavioral assessments. The effects of her attentional deficit,
visual neglect, inability to keep track of information and events,
and perseverative tendency on her ability to cope with the
demands of her everyday environment were highlighted. She
was given reading material about the impact of brain damage
on the caregiver [2], and instructed in the use of self-coping
statements to reduce her own level of stress.

The behavioral approach was explained. A 2-hourly toiletting
schedule was planned in an attempt to bring Ms C's demands
for toiletting under the control of verbal prompts on the part of
her sister (i.e., "It's time for the toilet"). The sister also was
instructed to anticipate Ms C's needs and meet her demands
prior to them being made. The main intervention was that of

extinction. The sister was to ignore the problem behaviors, while reinforcing appropriate behaviors. To compensate for Ms C's left-sided neglect, the sister was told to approach her from Ms C's right and also to place objects (e.g., plate of food, a cup of drink) on that side. A detailed outline of the treatment program has been presented previously in Table 3. The results of treatment are illustrated in Figure 2, clearly demonstrating the effectiveness of the program.

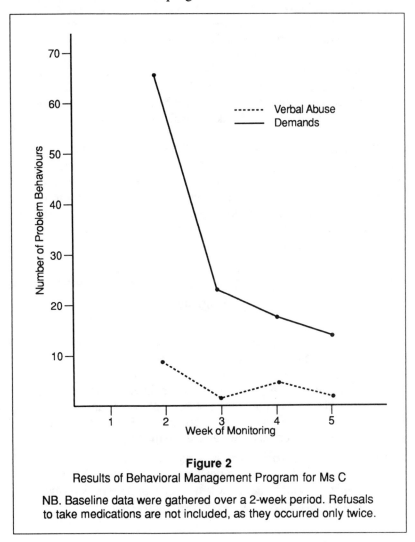

Figure 2
Results of Behavioral Management Program for Ms C

NB. Baseline data were gathered over a 2-week period. Refusals to take medications are not included, as they occurred only twice.

Comment

The sister had little appreciation of how Ms C's brain dysfunction was affecting her ability to cope with demands of everyday living, and was misinterpreting many of the resulting behaviors as intentional. She was also unaware of how her own inconsistent responses to Ms C's behaviors were compounding the problem. Educating the sister about the nature of Ms C's cognitive deficits and making her more aware of her inconsistent responses to the behaviors was essential in helping her manage them more effectively. Attention to her own levels of stress was also crucial and enhanced the effectiveness of the management program. Eventually Ms C was placed in a nursing home and the staff was assisted in the continued application of the management program. Ms C's behavior remained manageable and did not require additional interventions.

The specificity and objectivity of behavioral management programs make them easily communicable to other staff. Valuable information about successful treatment interventions can accompany residents should a transfer to a different floor or facility be required. As in Ms C's case, a clearly defined management program can also help the individual in the process of adjusting to a new environment, which is often a stressful experience.

KEY POINTS

- Effective management of problem behaviors in cognitively impaired residents requires consideration of the following: (a) their cognitive deficits and the manner in which these compromise everyday functioning, (b) environmental factors that trigger and maintain problem behaviors, and (c) staff attitudes, perceptions, and expectations. Failure to attend to any one of these can jeopardize the management program.

- Many problem behaviors arise as a consequence of specific cognitive deficits and are not intentional. Labeling, however, affects how staff interact with residents and determines their emotional response to the problem behaviors.

- Having cognitive deficits does not mean that residents have lost all capacity for change. While these deficits contribute significantly to the emergence of problem behaviors, they are not the sole determinants. Important environmental events trigger and maintain all behavior. Changing these environmental events results in changes in behavior.

- When confronted with a problem behavior, staff must adopt a scientific attitude. Problem behaviors must be defined in specific and objective terms and subjected to a functional, or ABC, analysis in order to determine the environmental variables that control them. Being scientific does not mean being uncaring or unsympathetic.

- An individualized management plan is instituted which is based on the results of the ABC analysis and knowledge of cognitive deficits. Problem behaviors require ongoing monitoring in order to determine the effectiveness of the program. Necessary adjustments are made as indicated.

- Staff need to examine their perceptions of the problem behaviors as these will affect their levels of stress. Problem behaviors must be viewed as problems that require a solution. It is helpful to break down stressful interactions with a particular resident into a series of steps, for which coping self-statements are developed.

SUGGESTED READING AND REFERENCES

1. Hussian, R.A., Davis, R.L. (1985). *Responsive care: Behavioral interventions with elderly patients*. Champaign, IL: Research Press.

   Excellent, easily readable book, presenting a practical guide for analyzing and treating problem behaviors in elderly institutionalized individuals.

2. Lezak, M.D. (1988). Brain damage is a family affair. *Journal of Clinical and Experimental Neuropsychology*, 10:111-123.

Provides information about the effects of brain damage on the individual's psychosocial functioning. Although it discusses different kinds of behavioral problems that confront families, the information it contains is relevant to all who interact with cognitively impaired residents in a nursing home setting.

3. Meichenbaum, D. (1985). *Stress inoculation training*. New York: Pergamon Press.

   Presents a model of treatment aimed at reducing and preventing stress. The model's principles are readily applicable to the stress produced by problem behaviors of nursing home residents.

4. Palmstierna, T., Wistedt, B. (1987). Staff observation aggression scale, SOAS; Presentation and evaluation. *Acta Psychiatrica Scandinavica*, 76:657-663.

   Presents a rating scale for the assessment of severity and frequency of aggressive behavior, which is among the most stress-producing behaviors in nursing home settings.

5. Nilsson, K., Palmstierna, T., Wistedt, B. (1988). Aggressive behavior in hospitalized psychogeriatric patients. *Acta Psychiatrica Scandinavica*, 78:172-175.

   Related to the reference above, this article highlights the clinical relevance and power of systematic observation and measurement of aggression. A 6-week observation period of aggressive incidents, in the absence of any planned interventions, resulted in a dramatic decrease of aggressive behaviors from week 1 (91) to week 6 (16), a decrease of 82%.

6. Vaccaro, F.J. (1988). Successful operant conditioning procedures with an institutionalized aggressive geriatric patient. *International Journal of Aging and Human Development*, 26:71-79.

   Presents the outline of a behavioral treatment program for an aggressive patient.

CHAPTER

Psychotherapy   11
for the
Institutionalized Elderly

by Joel Sadavoy

Psychotherapy, regardless of who conducts it and for whom it is used, is characterized by a complex interplay of verbal and nonverbal interaction between usually one therapist and an individual or group of patients. Well over 200 "psychotherapies" have been described from psychoanalysis to pet therapy. While there has been considerable debate about the efficacy of specific types of psychotherapy, the evidence is gradually accumulating that interpersonal psychotherapy of various types is effective in a variety of conditions, many of which afflict the aging individual residing in an institution. Other forms of psychotherapy including cognitive, group, and behavior therapy, and treatments based on learning theory, have also been shown to be effective in certain circumstances.

Institutions for the elderly contain individuals with a substantial degree and range of psychopathology, most often dementia, closely followed by a variety of disorders, including depression, anxiety disorders, psychosis, personality disorders, and others. Psychotherapy has been utilized for all of these disorders, although the few systematic studies that have been conducted in institutions have been primarily on patients with dementia. Additionally, most of the more rigorous work has been conducted in the area of behavioral and learning therapies.

While these treatments are often effective, the research suggests that behavioral change is most long-lasting when the "pure forms" of behavioral intervention are coupled with an awareness of the overall interpersonal needs of the patient and an attempt to engage the individual as a "whole person," rather than as a symptom in need of alteration. Indeed, with regard to management of the institutionalized elderly, it is clear that treatments which preserve the humanness and individuality of the patients will be both more effective for patients and gratifying for the health care team.

Group psychotherapy for the elderly encompasses many types of intervention including psychodynamic approaches, psychodrama, exercise groups, activity groups, current event groups, etc. Many patients, even those who have a degree of cognitive impairment, can be engaged in group therapy productively. This work has been described by numerous authors [1-5]. Often, it is only when individuals come together as a group that their previous levels of isolation, and sometimes hopelessness, begin to come to light, as they express to each other their perceptions of their current state. This point was made poignantly in a paper by Leszcz et al., [4] in which they described a men's group in a home for the aged. While individuals were initially wary about exposing their feelings and expressing their emotions, they gradually began to trust each other as group cohesion developed. Only then did they begin to admit tentatively how lonely and cut off they had felt, one resident stating that he had not known that there were men in the institution like himself who were not demented.

Individual psychotherapy has been used effectively for personality disordered residents [6] and for cognitively impaired residents [7]. An important component of many psychotherapies, especially individual, is the development of a detailed intimate understanding of patients, their development, how they came to be the individuals that they are now, and the system in which they live.

Goldfarb [8], demonstrated the effectiveness of his form of brief individual psychotherapy, characterized by short, frequent interactions with patients. His basic premise was that patients in institutions feel powerless and have suffered intense blows to their self-esteem simply by virtue of being cut off from their previous sources of gratification and interpersonal relationships. He suggested that patients will begin to feel a greater sense of value when they are able to experience the therapist as a powerful ally. In so doing, the patient is able to identify with the therapist's perceived importance and, hence, incorporate a sense of enhanced self-esteem which they have, so to speak, "borrowed" from the therapist. Goldfarb found that most patients, except for those with psychotic disorders or very severe depressions, would benefit from this type of intervention. He asserted that weekly sessions of approximately 15 minutes in duration were sufficient to induce the self-enhancing process and to modify behavior which was painful to the patient or troublesome to the staff.

INDICATIONS FOR PSYCHOTHERAPY

It is a safe assumption that the vast majority of individuals who live in institutions are forced to be there because of external circumstances beyond their control — physical illness, economic disadvantage, isolation, and so on. To the extent that this is so, many individuals who are forced to reside in an institutional setting are in need of various degrees of psychotherapy of one form or another. Clearly, it is patently impractical to suggest that all residents can be provided with what they need but, at the very least, an attempt must be made to establish what the needs are and respond at whatever level is possible within the limits of time, staff and expertise.

HOW DO I BEGIN AND HOW DO I UNDERSTAND WHAT I SEE?

The early contact with a patient is a delicate moment. The therapist's goal is to establish a relationship which is appropriate to the patient's needs. The more regular the contact and the more intimate the relationship between the therapist and patient, the more intense will be the relationship, and, hence, the greater the need for an intimate understanding of the workings of the patient's intrapsychic and interpersonal systems.

In general, in friendships, family relations and so on, feeling states are often observed, but rarely elicited or inquired about. One of the unique contributions that a therapist can begin to make in the isolated life of the institutionalized individual is to recognize his/her need for emotional contact. The beginning inquiry, therefore, should not stop at eliciting practical information. Residents should be asked, for example, what it feels like to be in bed all the time, how they experience not sleeping at night, what it means to them when visitors come or do not come, what it feels like to have given up their previous homes. In undertaking this aspect of the initial inquiry, the therapist may have to be prepared for early rejection by the resident who may not be ready to expose him or herself in this way. This does not mean, however, that the attempt should be avoided. On the contrary, if the initial response is to pull away from the therapist, the resident should be approached again later. It is helpful to acknowledge that it may be hard to talk about certain feelings and that he or she may not be ready to do so, but that you, the therapist, are available to listen. This availability should be active not passive, and the resident must be made aware of the therapist's willingness to talk and listen.

AREAS OF INQUIRY

The most critical areas of inquiry, in the early stages of getting to know the resident, are issues of interpersonal satisfaction or the lack of it; feelings of abandonment; fears associated with aloneness and pain; and alterations in the individual's self-perception. A longitudinal perspective of his or her life is of great help in understanding the individual's current behaviors and responses to the environment. While it is important to know who the person's family and friends were, what they did for a living and for enjoyment, it is of much greater value to both the resident and the therapist, to inquire about the nature of the feelings experienced in these previous relationships and activities.

One should not jump to conclusions about the feelings of another. For example, a former sculptor was admitted to a home for the aged. The staff initially assumed that he was sorry to lose his creativity because he loved his work. On closer inquiry it emerged that his main gratification came not from his creations but from the admiration which he obtained from others. Such specific pieces of information about an individual will often be enough to reorient the caregiving staff to a different stance. For example, the sculptor's need for gratification produced by the approval of others was addressed by providing him the opportunity of engaging in group activity where he was able to express his opinions and be heard by others. Without knowing the particular source of gratification which he obtained in his life, it would have been easy to erroneously assume that this man's lost capacity to engage in sculpting meant that he could no longer obtain any gratification in his life.

In many instances, of course, it is not easy to replace the lost sources of gratification. In fact, it is probably safe to assume that virtually every individual in an institutional setting has had to give up most of the major and crucial sources of self-esteem enhancement and sources of intimate relationships. The task of the therapist, around this issue, is to evaluate the particular sources of grief and loss with which the individual now struggles. This is a difficult aspect of the initial inquiry. It requires the therapist to be prepared to hear the patient's pain and to be able to listen to it without judgment, and, particularly, without withdrawing from the patient. One of the things that distinguishes the therapist from the friend, family or casual observer, is a willingness to engage with the person at the deepest level of understanding without being overwhelmed by the emotional pain or driven away by it. Naturally, not all residents want or need intense personal interaction. For some patients, such a relationship has never been a part of their life and they are often either afraid of it or unable to deal with other people. Even in these cases, however, the therapist must attempt to understand what factors lead the patient to push others away.

CASE ILLUSTRATION

A 70-year-old woman was an inpatient in a psychiatric hospital. She had a lifelong history of disrupted relationships beginning with her early family life and continuing throughout her adolescence and adult life. She had never held a significant job for any length of time, nor had she ever had relationships that seemed rewarding or in any sense stable. As she grew older, even the menial and intermittent household duties which she performed in order to earn a living, were no longer possible for her. She became increasingly "eccentric" in her behavior, withdrawn and uncommunicative. In addition, she developed combative paranoid behavior. A clear diagnosis was impossible because she would not communicate other than through her overt behaviors.

The staff were understandably frustrated in their efforts to deal with her. When left alone, she sat, isolated, smoking one cigarette after another, rarely speaking, and never confiding in anyone. With neuroleptic medication, her major symptoms seemed to settle down, but any attempts to discharge her ended in a marked return of symptoms and failure of all discharge planning. An external psychiatric consultation revealed that there were marked differences of opinion among staff on how to handle this patient. The consultant, upon reviewing the patient's history, and in discussing it with the staff of the ward, became aware that the central issue for this patient was her intense fear of living on her own. In contrast to the vast majority of individuals who end up in institutions, the institution became not only necessary, but highly desirable for this patient. She saw it as her home and resisted all effort to put her back out into the cold, rejecting, and empty outside world. Once all discharge plans were abandoned, and the staff accepted the patient as an individual in chronic need of "asylum," in the best sense of the word, virtually all her symptoms remitted. The patient's need for isolation was recognized — the staff avoided intruding upon her personal space, except when absolutely essential. This treatment plan not only relieved the patient, but it also relieved the staff of their ambition to "treat" and discharge.

Comment

This example is illustrative not only for psychiatric care, but also for care of individuals in any long-term institution. There are some people who welcome the environment and thrive within it, but only on their own terms.

Residents recently admitted to institutions must learn to cope with new and often unwelcome relationships, most of which they would not have chosen. Most people find it especially difficult when they are forced into a "roommate" situation. This is akin to a shotgun marriage, forcing two people, who are strangers and have virtually nothing in common, to live together in very close quarters, sharing space, bathroom facilities, and the other scarce resources of the ward. The therapist can be helpful by acknowledging the situation and not trying to unduly defend it, but rather, helping the patient to accept that it is a less-than-perfect solution. Caregivers in institutions, because they routinely see patients living in communal situations, often over many years, lose sight of the fact that this is an unusual and often unpleasant way to live, particularly when an individual is already struggling with physical and mental problems. Many residents react very intensely within the first month of coming into an institution - the so-called first month syndrome [9]. After that, behavior seems to settle down and the resident appears to "adapt." Most studies of institutionalized individuals are large-scale observational studies. In these reports there is rarely any data on the actual inner life of the individual, his/her conflicts, anxieties, or resentments. When one takes a closer look at newly admitted residents the adaptation is not nearly so felicitous. "Acceptance" is often more of a giving-up, grief process in which the individual comes to accept his or her situation and ceases rebelling against it.

Institutionalization is often provoked by crisis and once the person has been admitted to the institution, crises continue to arise. These may be personal assaults secondary to new illness, exacerbations of old problems, or external crises occurring in the family. These are particular indications for instituting psychotherapy, sometimes of a direct supportive nature, but, at other times, utilizing psychodynamic understanding in order to change the environment and the interaction with the individual. At times it may be helpful to attempt to understand the resident's inner psychological state via overt behavior [10]. The resident may be totally unable to explain verbally what she is experiencing. Especially for cognitively impaired individuals, new environments present a number of difficulties, not the least of which is that they are unfamiliar. While residents may attempt to continue to use well-learned patterns of behavior which stem from premorbid abilities, these are no longer adaptive within the context of the institution. For example, the woman who was a tidy, meticulous, and routinely involved housekeeper, may continue to try to maintain this type of activity in the institution. Unfortunately, this may lead her to move and tidy the belongings of other people, not realizing that she is not in her own space. The conflicts which inevitably arise, will exacerbate her feelings of unreality and agitation. It is only if the staff take the time and effort to understand the meaning of the behavior and attempt to channel it in more appropriate ways, that the patient will come to adapt appropriately to the environment.

While behavioral techniques may be used to extinguish such "inappropriate" activity, it is often much more humane and acceptable for staff to use the techniques of rechanneling and redirection rather than the more mechanistic approaches which may be inherent in extinguishing behavior.

In the medical institutional setting, caregivers are often faced with the long-term care of individuals who have suffered acute assaults to their cognitive functioning, for example, following a stroke. The sequelae such as dysarthria or paralysis, have an obvious impact and are readily understood by staff. However, there are other disabilities which are much more difficult both to diagnose and to understand. For example, the effect of damage to the frontal lobes may spare a variety of basic motor and cognitive activities, while damaging the most sophisticated centers of intellectual functioning. Similarly, damage to the nondominant hemisphere may produce subtle deficits in visual-spatial functioning which can only be demonstrated if carefully sought out. In both circumstances individuals will feel alien to themselves, their self-image dramatically altered by their awareness that they are no longer the person they once were. This state of discomfort can only be heightened if it is accompanied by a failure of the caregiver to comprehend the nature of the patient's experience. Such a failure will leave the patient not only impaired, but also isolated and often perplexed by the fact of his or her disability which no one else seems to recognize or understand. Under these circumstances, it is imperative that the caregiver carefully inquire about feeling states, as well as the patients' perspective on what has happened to them. A straightforward neurological or diagnostic stance is not sufficient at these times because it is the personal experience, not the objective findings which are crucial to the person's day-to-day adaptation.

WHAT ARE THE BASIC PROBLEMS WITH WHICH THE INSTITUTIONALIZED ELDERLY MUST COPE?

The basic psychological tasks of old age include dealing with grief and loss, intense anxiety, various forms of depression, and demands upon adaptational skills in order to deal with losses associated with physical, relational, and social decline. In the institutionalized, frail elderly particularly, these problems generally develop concurrently, and it is not uncommon to find an institutionalized resident who has had major interpersonal losses and recent disabling physical illness coupled with the task of coping with the dislocation of institutional life.

In addition to coping with loss, the elderly must often deal with a variety of fears and anxieties attendant upon facing the unknown, and an awareness of their own mortality. Interestingly, however, the elderly do not show a lot of anxiety about death. Rather, fears tend to focus on anxiety about living, uncertainties about what will happen in the future, and, particularly, whether they will have pain, disability, or loss of cognitive function if that has not already occurred.

The institutionalized elderly also must deal with adaptation to new and generally increasing, levels of dependency. Residents who are facing various physical and other disabilities in old age react with a variety of psychological responses. Some, for example, have a strong need to deny their problems. This can sometimes lead the person to resist taking necessary or appropriate measures or permitting caregiving staff to intervene. A gentle caring and educative stance on the part of the caregiver is necessary, and the therapist should be aware of the possibility of becoming angrily confronting and feeling frustrated because advice is not heeded.

Many elderly patients become acutely anxious, fearing, for example, that they are going to be abandoned in the face of their difficulties. They assume, sometimes correctly, that others do not want to tolerate their illnesses. Frequently, they will express the fear that they are a burden while underlying this fear is the more intense anxiety that they will be rejected. Indeed, in the face of often overwhelming illness or incurable disease, such as dementia or stroke, patients may become enraged both with themselves and their illness and may displace this feeling onto the caregiving system. Often these angry feelings cover more basic feelings of depression and hopelessness.

Caregivers must keep in mind that many elderly patients do not understand the nature of their problems, although, when cognitively intact, they are capable of forming an understanding if educated. Ignorance about disease will breed fears and fantasies which may become overwhelming and lead to undue anxiety and depression.

Especially with chronic illnesses, withdrawal and depression are a common accompaniment. Sometimes a major affective disorder develops, but more often withdrawn behavior accompanied by sadness is a reflection of a dysthymic disorder which resembles depression but, more accurately, should be seen as a struggle to adapt to loss and grief. Similarly, patients may develop anxiety states or even panic which can be characterized by sleeplessness, frequent calls for aid and assistance, or the development of a helpless importuning, sometimes demanding stance, which has been termed the "exaggerated helplessness syndrome."

INTERVENTIONS

Once the therapist has assessed the patient's presenting problems and determined some of the components of the psychological reaction that the particular patient is struggling with, the next question is how to intervene beyond the initial assessment stage. Naturally, any effective intervention for the elderly must incorporate complete and realistic physical diagnosis with the use of pharmacology as necessary. However, for many of the anxiety syndromes, depressive withdrawal and reactions that stem from ignorance, avoidance, or denial, psychotherapeutic intervention may be very helpful.

While concurrent medication is often necessary and useful, in the context of major difficulties of adaptation and coping in old age, the relationship between the caregiver and the patient may be the most effective "medication." Psychotherapy for patients at any age, but especially for the institutionalized elderly, is based on the tenet that everyone has a basic human need to be known and understood as an individual. Illness and other alterations of life in the final stage of human development all interact to create feelings of being lost, unacknowledged, and unknown.

Techniques of Psychotherapy

It is not always possible for caregivers in a busy institutional setting to provide residents with prolonged individual time. Often contacts are brief and focused on practical issues. Where, for specific reasons, more verbal interaction with residents is indicated, as already noted above, the caregiving staff can productively attempt to work out a schedule which permits 10 to 15 minutes of time for a particular resident. Brief interventions of this sort can greatly enhance a person's self-esteem as well as providing both the individual and the caregiver with a deeper understanding of difficulties experienced. Data on brief, intensive, individual, outpatient psychotherapy suggests that 3 to 4 months of weekly contact can produce symptom amelioration in many cases [11]. The institutionalized resident may similarly respond to grief work or other forms of therapy, but the contract may have to be long-term.

If regular psychotherapy, even if the sessions are brief, is going to be instituted, the caregiver should set aside a specific time which both he and the resident know will be kept free of interruptions. Other staff should be told that they cannot interrupt the session, except for true emergencies. Therapy is most effective if conducted in a setting outside of the resident's room, if possible. If the individual is bedridden, roommates should be asked to leave if they are mobile. If not, the therapist should be sensitive to the situation and hence the degree of confidentiality and openness may have to be restricted.

The therapist should expect to meet the resident. The elderly in institutions are highly vulnerable to feeling that caregivers may not want to see them, and that they are a burden. The therapist should make it clear that he or she wants to see the resident and, if the resident fails to come, he or she should inquire what has happened and make sure that the next appointment is clearly laid out. The concept of regularity and reliability of sessions is one of the most important elements in the psychotherapeutic endeavor, but one which is often paid insufficient attention.

What Techniques Are Useful for the Institutionalized Elderly?

There are three basic approaches which are practical in psychotherapeutic management of the institutionalized elderly, even by those therapists who are not schooled in formal psychotherapy. These are supportive therapy, cognitive therapy, and reminiscence or life review therapy.

Supportive psychotherapy

Supportive therapies are useful for all patients but are particularly important for the frail elderly. In using this mode of treatment, the therapist is most effective if he or she is active and interventive. The therapist engages with the patient frequently, asking questions which encourage the expression of feeling states, rather than eliciting practical information. For example, instead of simply asking "Did you sleep last night?" the therapist asks "How did it feel when you were not able to sleep?" "What do you think about and what do you do at night during those times when you are awake?" Supportive psychotherapy also requires the therapist to be available and regular. The goals of the contact can sometimes be spelled out, for example, that the therapist will attempt to help the patient speak about his or her problems and try to work on appropriate ways of dealing with them. Often, for institutionalized residents, supportive therapy is coupled with a need for changes in the environment, changes for which the caregiver may have to advocate.

An important component of supportive therapy is simple ventilation of feeling. Patients may be encouraged to talk about their feeling process which is enhanced by very simple questions around specific items such as "Do you feel angry when your daughter doesn't call? Tell me about your feelings of frustration when you wake up stiff in the morning from your arthritis. Are you afraid you are going to die when you become short of breath?" and so on.

There are certain themes which will continually recur in psychotherapy, especially if there is a degree of mild or moderate cognitive impairment. Repetition is sometimes the result of a patient's need to rework the same troubling piece of material over and over, or it may be the result of the patient's inability to remember the content of sessions from one time to the next. Such repetition must be tolerated, and indeed, encouraged, since this process of repeating feelings can often be healing.

The therapist may be helpful when simply repeating back, in different words, what he or she has understood the patient has just said. This simple feedback technique is strongly enhancing of the patient's self-esteem. It is also helpful for the therapist to present alternative ways of thinking or approaching problems, and the therapist should not hesitate to discuss practical interventions with the patient. However, the autonomy of the patient should be respected and they should be encouraged to offer their own ideas in solving their problems. Unfortunately, with institutionalized elderly, the degree of independent action, and hence problem-solving, is quite limited. However, to the extent that the person is able to think through his difficulties and come up with approaches, the accompanying sense of control over fate is most enhancing to his or her mental health. The elderly often feel that others, especially those who are younger, do not respect, value or seek their opinions, even on issues directly related to decisions about their own lives.

What is the role of reassurance?

Reassurance must convey realistic hope. Unrealistic statements may make the therapist feel better and may momentarily encourage the patient. However, patients are often exquisitely aware that reassurance may be an attempt by the therapist to "brush off" the problems. Indeed reassurance may stem from the therapist's wish to not get closer to the patient's fears and anxieties. Reassurance is most effective when it arises from a full understanding, both of the real issues in the patient's life, and his or her emotional reactions to them. To say "I am sure everything will be alright" without being sure, creates distance and may lead the patient to avoid speaking openly with the therapist.

Reminiscence therapy

The purpose of reminiscence therapy is to help increase the person's sense of self by encouraging what is probably a normal process of aging, ie., life review. Most older people do have a need to reminisce and to thereby retain emotional and mental contact with a part of themselves that, in the past, was healthier and perhaps more capable of coping. The process helps to work through losses and to put the person's current situation into a lifelong perspective. This therapy is effective for virtually all, although those residents who are highly anxious and focus only on bad memories of the past, those who have suffered massive psychic trauma, and those who are deeply depressed or whose reality perceptions are otherwise distorted, should be approached with caution.

Techniques of reminiscence therapy are varied. The most straight-forward and simple of these is to encourage the individual to talk about his past in vivid and emotional terms. Residents may also be asked to make audiotapes, prepare written records, or sometimes video records of their lives. This process may be even more meaningful if families are involved. Sometimes, when the resident is unable to actively par-ticipate, a family member or whole families may be interested in constructing a record of the person's life, both for their own benefit and that of the caregiving staff. The process is facilitated if residents or families contribute aids to reminiscence, such as picture albums, things they have written, or paintings, drawings, and other creative arts.

Cognitive therapy

Cognitive therapy has been used for the elderly in a modified form and is said to be most useful for dysthymic disorders and depression [12]. The treatment is based on the idea that thoughts produce feelings rather than the other way around. Various situations provoke distorted ideas about one's self which lead to depressive conclusions, producing hopelessness and lost self-esteem. The therapeutic approach is a step-by-step method of dealing with this process. The first step is to help the individual identify the major source of depressive conflict. For exam-ple, "I am bad and useless because I cannot perform the way I used to."

While there is an element of this statement which is true in that the person may not be able to do what he or she used to, there is another component which is a distortion, i.e., that they are bad and useless. The examination of the statement leads the therapist to move on to step two, that is, to evaluate, with the patient, the pros and cons of the idea and the reality component versus the fantasy. Part of the process helps the patient correct distortions and thoughts and introduces realities. For example, "this aspect of what you feel may be true, but perhaps this other element is not." In order to consolidate the learning process that goes on in cognitive therapy, the patient may be given homework comprised of testing out the truth of a new-found perspective. For example, in an institution, it may be helpful to ask a resident, who is convinced of her lack of value, to risk asking for feedback about herself in other forums such as a group situation or with her family.

While the three forms of therapy, supportive, cognitive and reminiscence are theoretically separate, in practice the models are often productively used at the same time and even in conjunction with more traditional, insight-oriented approaches. The three basic therapies are not difficult, nor do they require a great deal of technical expertise. As long as the caregiver and therapist attempt to understand and form a warm, caring relationship with the patient, all of the techniques are safe and useful.

Why Do Many Caregivers Avoid Engaging in Therapy with the Institutionalized Elderly?

Many individuals, including the older institutionalized resident, will at times idealize the therapist and form unrealistic expectations. Such magical ideas may cause the therapist or other caregivers to feel uncomfortable because of their awareness that they are limited in what they are able to do for the person.

Many problems of the elderly are not readily amenable to therapy. The problems often become chronic and the caregiver and therapist must beware that they themselves do not become unduly hopeless in the face of this chronicity. The therapeutic contract with the institutionalized elderly individual is indefinite. While formal sessions may become widely spaced and intermittent, the nature of the problems of this population is that they will flare-up and recur and the therapist must be prepared to pick up again at some time in the future, perhaps with a series of regular sessions.

All elderly residents, especially those in institutions, inevitably continue to decline. The success of psychotherapy must be viewed in the context of reestablishing the best level of emotional and psychological functioning for the person, rather than attempting to radically change the individual. Diminishing some anxiety, enhancing a sleep pattern, and encouraging interpersonal relationships may be all that the therapist can expect to achieve in certain cases.

Caregivers and therapists must be aware that guilt, anger and frustration will be normative feelings for them in treating certain of their patients, and must not let these feelings interfere with their attempts to carry on. Similarly, families will often be demanding and needy, placing these demands upon the therapist, demands which may, in certain instances, lead the therapist to want to withdraw.

Whatever the therapeutic approach, and regardless of the cognitive capacity or frailty of the patient, the therapist should avoid stereotyped "rules" and attempt to adapt technique to the patient's needs. For example, it has often been stated that the frail elderly require touching, sitting close, and a loud voice. However, such individuals show a range of tolerance for this kind of intimate involvement. One must evaluate the resident's need for touching versus their parallel need for maintenance of their personal space. Sometimes residents miss the intimacy of touching and close involvement, while at other times they may be resentful or even panicked by such intimacy and intrusion. Similarly, the use of familiarity (first names) should be employed judiciously. Residents have spoken of feeling demeaned, by the infantalizing implication of a too-casual informality imposed by caregiving staff who may view the frail elderly as "cute" or, in other ways, childlike. This stance fails to take into account the remaining "personhood" of the individual that lives inside the increasingly frail body and/or mind.

Special Problems of the Cognitively Impaired

With special regard to the cognitively impaired, the technique of reality orientation has been frequently used. Such individuals are often illogical, unrealistic, and inappropriately emotional in their communications, factors which may make it difficult for therapists to interpret the meaning of their behavior. When this happens, caregivers often wonder how to intervene and whether or not to correct a person's distorted reality and, if so, how to do it. Some residents are able to accept and allow interventions and are able to "borrow" the staff's reality testing. In other instances, corrections of reality may lead the individual to feel rejected or humiliated and, hence, not believed. This will often exacerbate paranoid or other psychotic misinterpretations of reality. Correction of the person's reality, therefore should be undertaken only after a knowledge of the individual's sensitivities is gained.

Delusional beliefs are particularly problematic for caregivers in institutions. They cannot be corrected by orientation-type feedback. In this situation, a rational first step is to make every effort to understand the nature of the delusion. A resident, for example, may misinterpret the presence of a nurse in the room at night, as being a thief coming to take the clothes which she has become convinced are being stolen from her. Such a concrete delusion is common in demented individuals, and may become entrenched and impossible to dislodge. In such circumstances, rather than trying to "reorient," it may be more appropriate to take practical and environmental steps, such as scheduling staff who the resident knows well, and who have not been incorporated into his or her delusion, to carry out the more intimate care. It is also important to keep the environment as predictable, structured, and simple as possible.

When residents become acutely agitated as a result of unrealistic beliefs, a simple technique of intervention may be redirection of their attention. In the case of the stealing delusion mentioned above, such a person may be responded to with reassurance that the caregiver will try to help locate the lost belongings shortly, but in the meantime, introduce another activity or interaction which will divert attention temporarily. Often, of course, despite the use of any techniques, overwhelming anxiety associated with reality distortions and cognitive impairment may require the use of medication as an adjunct. Such medications often make the resident more accessible to other interpersonal techniques of intervention and should be used appropriately.

When dealing with the cognitively impaired resident individually, certain basic approaches are particularly important. As noted above, the initial stages require the establishment of an accurate and empathic rapport. In addition, because of the communication difficulties of these residents, the therapist and caregiver will be aided by attempting to fully evaluate the nature of the communication. He or she will want to know the degree of the resident's level of understanding of language, their memory resources, and their ability to orient themselves. Often such individuals have difficulty comprehending verbal input, sometimes because of receptive problems, and sometimes because of other factors such as high levels of anxiety or fear. Most importantly, the therapist and caregiver must evaluate the person's capacity to utilize interaction. Some individuals cannot be readily soothed by contact with another person, while others are easily calmed when in the presence of a familiar caregiver. Indeed, the latter is probably the more common situation. This capacity for soothing is often the most important differentiating factor in determining whether a given demented resident will respond to interpersonal and, broadly speaking, psychotherapeutic interventions.

Psychotherapy of the cognitively impaired, or indeed any interaction with such residents, must take into account the often exquisite sensitivity of the person to nonverbal communication. Tone of voice, or body posture may be taken as anger or rejection, even though it is not necessarily meant in that way. For example, a caregiver who addresses the resident over her shoulder while walking out of the room, or uses a patronizing tone unwittingly, may agitate the person and lead to a breakdown of empathic rapport.

KEY POINTS

- The myth of aging is that the elderly, and especially the institutionalized elderly, cannot change and that psychotherapy and other forms of interpersonal intervention are of little effect. This is an erroneous concept, which has been disproved over and over again.

- Psychotherapy with the elderly can be a fruitful and rewarding experience for both patient and therapist, and is to be encouraged regardless of the setting, because of the impact which it has upon humanizing and individualizing the residents of geriatric institutions.

REFERENCES

1. Akerlund, B.M., Norberg, A. (1986). Group psychotherapy with demented patients. *Geriatric Nursing*, 7:83-84.

2. Cox, K.G. (1985). Milieu Therapy. *Geriatric Nursing*, 6:152-154.
3. Lazarus, L.W. (1976). A program for the elderly at a private psychiatric hospital. *Gerontologist*, 16:125-131.
4. Leszcz, M., Sadavoy, J., Feigenbaum, E., Robinson, A. (1985). A mens' group psychotherapy of elderly men. *International Journal of Group Psychotherapy*, 33:177-196.
5. Linden, M. (1953). Group psychotherapy with institutionalized senile women. Studies in gerentologic human relations. *International Journal of Group Psychotherapy*, 3:150-170.
6. Sadavoy, J., Dorian, B. (1983). Management of the characterologically difficult patient in the chronic care institution. *Journal of Geriatric Psychiatry*, 16:223-240.
7. Sadavoy, J., Robinson, A. (1989). Psychotherapy and the cognitively impaired elderly. In: D.K. Conn, A. Grek, J. Sadavoy, (Eds.). *Psychiatric consequences of brain disease in the elderly: A focus on management*, pp. 101-135. New York: Plenum Press.
8. Goldfarb, A.I. (1974). Minor maladjustments of the aged. In: S. Ariet, E.B. Moody, (Eds.). *American handbook of psychiatry*, 2nd Ed., pp. 820-860. New York: Basic Books.
9. Tobin, S.S. (1989). Issues of care in long-term settings. In: D.K. Conn, A. Grek, J. Sadavoy, (Eds.). *Psychiatric consequences of brain disease in the elderly: A focus on management*, pp. 163-187. New York: Plenum Press.
10. Cohen, G.D. (1989). Psychodynamic perspectives in the clinical approach to brain disease in the elderly. In: D.K. Conn, A. Grek, J. Sadavoy, (Eds.). *Psychiatric consequences of brain disease in the elderly: A focus on management*, pp. 85-99. New York: Plenum Press.
11. Lazarus, L.W., Groves, L., Gutmann, D., Ripeckyj, A., Frankel, R., Newton, N., Grunes, J., Havasy-Galloway, S. (1987). Brief psychotherapy with the elderly: A study of process and outcome. In: J. Sadavoy, M. Leszcz, (Eds.). *Treating the elderly with psychotherapy: The scope for change in later life*, pp. 265-293. Madison, WI: International Universities Press.
12. Gallagher, D.E., Thompson, L.W. (1983). Endogenous and non-endogenous depression in the older adult outpatient. *Journal of Gerontology*, 38(6):707-712.

SUGGESTED READING

1. Conn, D.K., Grek, A., Sadavoy, J. (Eds.). (1989). *Psychiatric conse-*

quences of brain disease in the elderly: A focus on management. New York: Plenum Press.

The authors discuss the management of neuropsychiatric disorders in the elderly from a variety of different perspectives; Chapters 4, 5, 6, and 8, in particular, focus on psychotherapeutic issues.

CHAPTER

Helping the Nursing Staff: 12
The Role of the
Psychiatric Nurse Consultant

by Alanna Kaye and Anne Robinson

The provision of high quality patient care and job satisfaction for personnel are two goals common to all institutions. The nursing staff make up the vast majority of professional caregivers and their work is often physically and mentally arduous and stressful. Although other mental health professionals can be of help to nursing staff, this chapter will address the unique role of the psychiatric nurse consultant with a particular emphasis on increasing the quality of patient care by the provision of clinical teaching and staff support.

Stolz Howard links the roles of nurse clinician and mental health consultant in an attempt to define the function of the psychiatric nurse consultant [1].

These functions include:

- Responding to staff requests for assistance with specific nursing interventions in the provision of care.
- Assisting staff to extract and co-ordinate information from their nursing assessments to further understand a problem.

- Assisting them to integrate their knowledge of the resident's behavior with the theory that behavior has meaning.
- Providing support for the staff around difficult clinical issues.
- Identifying aspects of a problem which may be systems-related and may be impacting on the clinical situation.
- Providing weekly supportive counselling to residents which then assists staff to care for the residents in their own milieu.
- Providing didactic teaching sessions to aides, registered nursing assistants, registered nurses and other multi-disciplinary team members in accordance with the biopsychosocial model.
- Helping staff to consider and identify possible underlying psychiatric syndromes.
- Helping staff to determine which residents may need referral to a psychiatrist or a psychologist. (We are aware that in many institutions such consultations are difficult to obtain).

Liaison is a central function of the nurse consultant's role. Liaison suggests the linking up of groups for the purpose of effective collaboration. Intimate knowledge of the conflicts and stresses that staff encounter working in institutions promotes a sense of collegiality and identification by staff with the consultant, which is essential to effective liaison work. The credibility of the psychiatric nurse consultant is enhanced when she conveys her clinical experience and theoretical knowledge in a supportive manner. This can have a calming influence during a crisis and should communicate to staff that their work is valued.

Case 1: "How Could She Say that to Me?"

Mrs B was a 79-year-old widow who had been admitted to the institution with moderate cognitive impairment. She had no family or friends. While staff had noted her to be "moody" at times, they had nevertheless taken an interest in her. As time progressed, Mrs B became more verbally abusive. Staff requested assistance from the nurse consultant as they were having increasing difficulty providing care and dealing with the insults. Investigation revealed a woman whose cognition was severely impaired. Although she was able to engage in brief conversations, she was disoriented to the time, place and person, and had little short-term memory. She was impulse-laden. Staff agreed to meet over a 6-week period to review her status and discuss strategies in the provision of her care.

The first three sessions were emotionally intense. Staff were offended by the resident's obscene and insulting remarks. They were angry and bewildered, wondering why she would attack those who had cared for and befriended her. They had difficulty accepting her increased cognitive impairment as the cause of her disinhibition, commenting, "But many times we can talk and I know that she knows me. She's not that impaired." These reactions were not unlike those experienced by family members who are unable to believe the person they love is irrevocably changed. When reviewing the case with the nurse consultant the anger and helplessness felt by staff was evident during various role-playing situations. The anger, once released, appeared to dissipate and subsequently staff began to report a change in Mrs. B's behavior. They noted a decrease in the number of insults and developed a higher tolerance of her salty language during the delivery of care.

Comment:

The clinical support groups facilitated expression and exploration of feelings, and helped the staff to provide a high level of care. Change is a slow process and often there is a disparity between intellectual understanding and integrated "knowing." The sharing of knowledge and mutual support fosters the integrating process, which results in changes in staff attitudes and responses.

Why Do Staff Need Help?

Nurses in long-term care are in a unique position. Their tasks are clearly defined, but the satisfactions are often nebulous. The nurse's inner sense of satisfaction is often derived from the knowledge and experience of giving within a highly sensitive, intimate, and therapeutic context. However, these positive energizing feelings can be severely diminished when the nurse is confronted with unrelenting racial slurs, aggression, accusations, sexual disinhibition, and perseverative noises. These have been described in the chapters on depression, dementia, suspiciousness, and characterologically difficult individuals. However, nurses are not dealing with these situations in isolation. Given the frequency with which these behaviors are encountered, it is not unusual for a nurse to have sole care for eight or more residents exhibiting these behaviors on a single shift.

In addition, staff assist and interact with the many family members on the unit. Since family dynamics, coping styles, and abilities will affect communication, staff must be prepared to deal effectively with a barrage of complaints, anger, and accusations that they "aren't doing enough." (see chapter on Understanding and Helping Families). Situations are often seen by both families and staff, in black or white terms. In reality uncertainty abounds during the process of clinical care and decision-making. Ethical, moral, legal, professional, and personal issues often blend to produce a total picture of great complexity. Nurses, therefore, need a highly developed sense of tolerance to be able to deal simultaneously with the varied physical and emotional demands, expectations, and ambiguities. These strengths and abilities to nurture are rarely valued by society or the institution in which nurses work. The nursing profession has traditionally emphasized technological skills and higher education rather than the less tangible personal qualities necessary to provide comprehensive, humane care to the elderly. Attitudes must change if gerontological nursing is to flourish and we are to retain and attract caring staff. To accomplish this shift in attitude, specific types of support are required.

TYPES OF HELP

Assisting with Crisis Management

One of the problems that arises in institutions is how to handle situations where a resident or family member is out of control. Understanding is not enough. The clarity, consistency, and follow-through necessary to contain certain unacceptable behaviors may be perceived by staff at all levels as punitive. It is important to assist staff to be consistent, while maintaining an empathic approach. The subjective sense of being out of control creates great discomfort, loss of dignity and may damage helpful relationships.

The following case of Mrs Q highlights both crisis management and the need for a structured plan of care.

Case 2

Mrs Q was a 92-year-old widowed woman admitted to the institution as a result of diminished physical activity following a myocardial infarction. A friendly, outgoing, and "feisty" woman, she soon made friends with members of the treatment team, sharing with them fascinating stories of her life and travels. Difficulties began for Mrs Q when a resident who was somewhat noisy was admitted. She took an immediate, intense dislike to him and demanded that he be moved to another part of the institution. When this could not be arranged, she was offered the opportunity to move to a different section of the unit, when room became available. She was incensed with the thought of being inconvenienced by this man and became more intensely agitated. She threatened to kill him if he was not relocated. The consultant, who had been seeing her regularly for some time, attempted to work with her and the staff with regard to the management of her anger. The necessity to control physical outbursts was explained and appropriate alternatives were reinforced. Despite these efforts, Mrs Q remained enraged with her co-resident and attempted to throw objects at him from afar. The need to set firm, clearly defined limits of acceptable behavior became critical.

She was then given the opportunity to work with staff towards the goal of maintaining her self-control. She was informed that the alternative would be possible certification and transfer to a psychiatric unit where she could be assisted in regaining her self-control. Two days later, Mrs Q threw a can of tuna at the resident screaming, "I'm going to kill you! I don't care what anyone says." Arrangements were then made for a brief admission to the psychiatric unit and she was placed on constant care until the transfer. Despite the need to follow through on limit-setting, staff became very uneasy, perceiving her admission to psychiatry as a punishment and questioning the validity of the decision. Several sessions with the staff were arranged to help them understand the management approach and Mrs Q was transferred.

Upon her return, staff felt more comfortable with the idea of setting limits in order to preserve an individual's dignity and comfort. Mrs Q was subsequently able to remain on the unit maintaining her relationships without further loss of control. As no medications had been used, it appeared that the management plan, with its clearly delineated expectations and consequences, had assisted her in achieving self-control.

Comment

In situations such as these, quick action is required to follow through on a particular care plan. As illustrated, Mrs Q had a good understanding of her situation, the consequences, and some degree of control over her actions. The dual interventions of applying external controls when necessary as well as supporting and educating staff were important factors in the successful outcome. These actions enabled the care plan to be carried out in a manner which left the dignity of all parties intact and promoted the continuity of the warm relationship between the resident and the staff upon her return.

Developing Consistent Models of Care

Provision of care in a long-term care setting differs from that in acute care settings. Although this may seem obvious, these differences are often a source of misunderstanding between residents, staff, families, and administrators. All four groups require help in identifying possible differences in goals if difficulties are to be minimized. The consultant can assist in clarifying some of the issues that arise. The difference between the "care versus cure" models of care combined with increasing desires of the resident (or substitute decision-maker) to participate in decisions creates the basis for a variety of potential problems.

Case 3

Mrs H, a severely demented woman, wailed loudly and incessantly, if left alone, even for brief periods. Despite all attempts to meet her needs, her wailing could not be easily diminished. The use of small doses of a phenothiazine was attempted and was successful in reducing the extreme agitation. Mrs H's daughter, however, began to berate the team physician for this use of medication, telling him that he and the nursing staff were "incompetent and unable to handle the simplest task of keeping mother company." Unable to tolerate her mother's cognitive impairment, the daughter continually harangued the staff until finally medications were reduced. The team began to withdraw from the situation and referred to Mrs H's daughter as manipulative and "wanting her own way."

The wailing escalated once again, sending the relatives of co-residents to the administrator to "do something" about the noise. Miscommunications and unrealistic expectations from all parties added to the confusion about Mrs H's management.

The consultant, liaising with all members of the treatment team and administration, facilitated a clarification of issues and the setting of realistic goals. Once these things had been accomplished, the team felt supported and empowered to help the daughter understand and accept the need for a transfer to a floor with other residents like her mother and the need for some pharmacological interventions to reduce Mrs H's agitation.

Comment

This vignette also raises the issue of whether it is acceptable for staff to have emotional reactions to intense situations, within the parameters of professional behavior. The fact that the problems encountered in chronic care facilities are long-term in nature cannot be overlooked. Unlike in acute care settings residents cannot be "cured" and sent home, for the institution has become their home. As a result, awareness and empathy among all parties concerned becomes a more critical aspect to the philosophy and expectations of those involved in long-term care.

Case 4: The Provision and Maintenance of Ongoing Front-line Support

The case of Mrs Y illustrates the need, not only for support of staff, but also the day-to-day intervention in the care of certain residents with multiple needs.

Mrs Y, an 80-year-old widow was admitted to a home for the aged when she became increasingly frail and incapacitated as a result of multiple physical problems. Although she had been a strong, successful woman, she had suffered many losses and traumas during World War II. She responded to her increasing infirmity by becoming needy, helpless, and clingy, and demanded to be "taken care of." She perceived the staff's attempts to encourage independence as rejection and lack of caring. This produced catastrophic-like reactions in her and increased the intensity of her demands.

She was often agitated, highly anxious and complained constantly of physical problems. Staff could no longer tolerate her incessant demands or determine which symptoms required intervention.

The nurse consultant was asked to assist with the management of Mrs Y's anxiety. Intervention and care planning required both individual counselling and increased staff support. Mrs Y was seen one to three times weekly for supportive counselling. Over the months and years, she found great comfort in having the consultant's complete attention. As the trusting relationship grew, she would save many of her complaints for the consultant, and reduced her demands on the staff. In addition, she was able to acknowledge her grief over the many losses she had suffered, both past and present. She was able to regain some sense of her strengths as she spoke of her past achievements and derived satisfaction from this.

Supportive sessions with the staff helped to increase their understanding of Mrs Y's behavior, balance the need for independence and dependence, and allowed staff to share their frustration and feelings of "never being able to do enough to please her." A consistent routine of care was implemented. Over the years, Mrs Y was able to attend programs and outings (albeit with much persuasion). Staff became attuned to the subtle changes in her behavior, which signalled a physiological change requiring medical intervention. Over the 4 years until she died, the long-term, mutual support between the staff and consultant enabled them to provide the necessary care for Mrs Y and to maximize her quality of life.

Comment

This case illustrates that the problems encountered in long-term care institutions are rarely short-lived. In order to maintain high quality care in the face of unremitting demands and demeaning personal slurs, support to staff must be available for as long as the problem exists.

The Acknowledgement and Management of Staff's Grief

While there are frequent discussions about the resident's and family's losses and grief, little attention is paid to the grief experienced by the staff. The long-term relationships formed with residents and visitors are highly valued and their loss can be understandably distressing. The perpetual decline and relentless losses can become overwhelming and affect the ability to work effectively with this population. There is a great emotional demand upon staff and unless the cumulative losses are acknowledged and managed, "burnout" can occur. Staff meetings to discuss recent losses can be an effective method of working through such losses.

Case 5

Mr M was an 81-year-old man living in a home for the aged. He had lived there for many years and was loved for his warmth and gentle wit. As the years passed, staff noted that he was becoming more demanding, forgetful, and needy. He required constant reassurance that staff would continue to provide care. As it became increasingly difficult to look after him, staff discussed the possibility of moving him to another floor with a higher staff-to-resident ratio. In discussions with the nurse consultant, staff shared their feelings as they watched Mr M's slow decline and their guilt around proposing his transfer. Several weeks after these discussions, staff decided they would not transfer him but would continue their attempts to care for him. They acknowledged that the open exchange and realization of their feelings had been a factor in their decision. Having developed a close relationship with Mr M, they would continue to provide their care and support until he died.

Comment

One of the risks involved in developing relationships with the elderly is the reality of eventual loss. In an attempt to "maintain professional distance," actual personal distancing in the form of avoidance of the resident, or precipitous transfers, may occur. By openly acknowledging sadness and grief within the safety of a peer group, this team was able to subsequently make decisions based on the resident's actual needs.

Identification of Educational Needs

Current trends indicate that the residents admitted to long-term care facilities are older, more frail, and more cognitively impaired than in the past. Consequently, increased knowledge of dementia is required to provide comprehensive care. As needs are identified by the nursing managers, the nurse consultant can develop and implement a unit-based educational package to meet these requirements. For example, didactic educational sessions are created to teach an understanding of how cognitive impairment translates into the behaviors seen on the unit. Management strategies are outlined, case examples are used, and role-playing is utilized as a mechanism to reinforce communication techniques.

SUMMARY

In the authors' experience, the consultant can be effective only when the delicate balance between assistance and preservation of the dignity of the staff is maintained. Staff must be able to experience the consultant as being committed to, and valuing, front-line work. One of the dilemmas faced by professionals other than nurses providing consultation to direct caregivers is that they may be perceived as being critical, with no knowledge of what it is like to provide intrusive, intimate care which often provokes intense reactions from the residents. The relationship between staff and the nurse consultant evolves over time and becomes a mutual learning experience. Thus, the role of nurse clinician encompasses teaching, support, and direct patient care via supportive counselling. As Tobin accurately points out, "Maintaining staff tolerance is not an easy task... it can only be accomplished if staff are supported and nourished by administration so that they can withstand personal abuse." [2].

KEY POINTS

- Working alone or in conjunction with other mental health professionals the psychiatric nurse consultant assists staff in the process of understanding and caring for residents, especially those with psychiatric/behaviorial problems. Extensive psychiatric clinical experience, education, and collaborative style contribute to the efficacy of the role. It is important that front-line staff feel understood, supported, and valued by the consultant.

- Types of help include:
  — Assisting with crisis management
  — Developing consistent models of care
  — The provision of ongoing support
  — The acknowledgement and management of staff grief
  — Identification of educational needs

- Assisting direct caregivers requires a long-term commitment from the nurse consultant to remain engaged and supportive as long as the problem lasts.

REFERENCES

1. Stoltz Howard, J. 1978. Liaison nursing. *Journal of Psychosocial Nursing and Mental Health Services*, April:35-37.
2. Tobin, S. (1989). Issues of care in long-term settings. In: D.K. Conn, A. Grek, J. Sadavoy, (Eds.). *Psychiatric consequences of brain disease in the elderly: A focus on management*, pp. 181-182. New York: Plenum Press.

SUGGESTED READING

1. Stoltz Howard, J. (1978). Liaison nursing. *Journal of Psychosocial Nursing and Mental Health Services*, April:35-37.

   Describes the process of establishing and defining the role of the psychiatric liaison nurse. Clear and easy to read.

2. Wasylenki, D., Harrison, M. K., (1981). Consultation-liaison psychiatry in a chronic care hospital: The consultation function; *Canadian Journal of Psychiatry,* 26:96-100.

   Focuses on the kinds of problems referred to a psychiatric consultation-liaison team and common interventions emphasizing interpersonal and environmental adaptations.

CHAPTER

Understanding and Helping the Family   13

by Etta Ginsberg-McEwan and Anne Robinson

Changing the model of care in a long-term care facility from one that focuses on the resident alone to one that considers the resident and the family means that members of the family are also considered to need care. Unlike an acute care hospital, a long-term care facility is a place where the individual goes to live. Here intimacies of family life, unknown to strangers become institutional knowledge. Family styles of interaction are divulged and discussed as families struggle to cope with the intrusion of the institution into family life and the demands of chronic illness. Staff become involved as observers and participants in the family's struggle to adapt. When care includes family members and it becomes clear that their contribution to care is valued by the staff, there is frequently a decrease in the worry, guilt, and anxiety of the family.

Gates suggests that shifting perceptions of care to all members of the family, leads to an increase in the overall quality of care [1]. This shift in focus assists staff in their struggle to understand, first, the family's ambivalence and pain in giving over care to strangers, and second, their struggle to encompass the idea of their relative as old and sick.

Burnside states that the mutual participating required by staff and families is often unfamiliar territory for both groups [2]. Misunderstandings and competitions occur as everyone struggles to work together and plan care. Social workers and nursing staff working collaboratively can do much to enhance the care of families and decrease the difficulties of institutionalization. The communicating of family history and observations of day to day interactions by the family allows staff to feel involved with their patient and the family.

INSTITUTIONALIZATION: A NEW PHASE IN LIVING

We are born, we go to school, we go to work, we marry, we have children, we have grandchildren, we retire: and we hope for a peaceful death. We move through these chapters of life prepared by preceding generations and by a whole host of rituals that mark the critical moments of passages in the life cycle. Institutionalization is the most recent phase of living; it is becoming a way of life as people live longer, develop chronic diseases, and as families are frequently unable to provide care at home. The entire family structure undergoes a reorganization. The forced removal of an individual from his lifelong context places him in an alien situation. Few enter an institutional setting willingly. Most enter because of complicated illness and the depletion of resources. There is no ritual to prepare us for this passage and what a passage!

Developing a New Institutional Identity

Upon entering the institution, the family enters a totally new developmental phase and moves slowly, cautiously, fearfully — and with trepidation. It is a time of crisis. It is the final chapter for the ill relative. Table 1 lists some of the issues facing the family when a relative is admitted. The family unit appears to be in an identity crisis. Their familiar roles, for example, husband, wife, son, daughter, do not seem to be easily understood by the institutional staff. The family member who is placed in the institution has never had a lesson in "how to behave as a patient." Preston discusses identity as being essential to orientation. "It tells a man, in terms of society, what he is and might be, how worthy he is and what he should do" [3]. Upon entering the institution, the individual and his family take on a "new" identity. There is a feeling of inner chaos, bewilderment, and apprehension. Whereas there may be relief in finally sharing the caregiving burden, family members are uncertain of what to expect.

Table 1
Issues Facing Families When A Relative
Is Admitted To The Institution

1. Feelings of guilt and anger for "abandoning" relative to strangers
2. Partial loss of role, as wife or husband, son or daughter, mother or father
3. Loss of supportive family member: e.g., parent's emotional support and wisdom; spouse's emotional, social and financial support, and physical tenderness
4. Fear of relative's impending death
5. Fear of relative's rejection and anger
6. Lack of knowledge about institutional, medical, and nursing care and fear of asking questions
7. Financial burdens

On occasion, families may encounter rigid institutional responses. Verbal and nonverbal messages to the family tell them to step aside, leave the room, go home, come back tomorrow at 11:00 a.m. and not before 11:00 a.m. You can remain until 8:00 p.m. and no later. You must leave the room when staff are giving direct care to your relative. Family members who have been the primary caregivers for years feel shut out. Hopefully there is some degree of flexibility and institutional rules can be discussed and negotiated.

The ill family member may be placed in the position of almost total dependency. He resigns himself to acquiescing to every recommendation of the health care team; he sleeps, awakens, attends to personal needs, eats; and struggles to live within the rules and regulations of the "world of the sick." In the "world of the sick," you are addressed by your first name, you are called "honey," "dear," — you are patted on the head, you are told to smile, brighten up. Staff and families wanting to comfort and reassure, instead, may become unintentionally patronizing. Sometimes you are dressed in a white gown which is in reality, symbolic of the shroud — that which is worn by the dead. In a way, part of you feels dead. If your body is twisted with disease, if your eyes have a vacant stare, if you utter something that is totally incomprehensible, if you cry out, all eyes avoid you or you are quickly reassured that all will be okay. But the individual and family know all is not okay. A strange environment; strangers speaking a new language — the institution language of "do's" and "don't's." Privacy disappears and the family have become part of the public domain.

The Patient Remains Part of the Family Unit

The ill member enters the institution with his family. At first this may sound overwhelming and unreasonable. Of course the entire family does not "live" in the institution. The family's lifelong relationships, values, conflicts, legacies, and loyalties enter the institution. This rich history impacts on the patient. Personal history should not be ignored by staff as it is crucial to care and treatment. Successful institutional adjustment is dependent upon maintaining the family's integrity. Staff reactions may reflect their own family backgrounds. Every staff member has a separate identity/uniqueness within his/her family history tree.

"Ties of kinship, marriage; and sustained intimacy create special psychological and moral bonds in our lives. Families, a term virtually impossible to define precisely in American society at present are composed of these ties and bonds, and constitute a distinctive social space, a space where rules and expectations apply that are somewhat different from those in impersonal, public places and in transactions among strangers" [4]. The institution is an impersonal public place and staff members are initially strangers.

"Family life, and especially the moral obligations that family members have toward one another, are challenged by severe chronic illness in two ways; first by the burdens imposed on families by chronic care; and second by virtue of the fact that severe chronic illness in a family can pose a crisis for our traditional moral expectations concerning family life" [4].

"Honour thy Mother and Father" is clearly and strongly stated in the Ten Commandments. The noted poet, Emily Dickinson, said: "Hold your parents tenderly, for the world will seem a strange and lonely place when they are gone" [5].

And the playwright, Marsha Norman stated: "One of the problems for daughters and sons is that you come into life with an unpayable debt, the mortgage of all time" [6]. The giving of life establishes an everlasting link with the past and the future. And whether it is said aloud or not, there is the traditional wedding vow: "In sickness and in health, till death do us part."

CASE ILLUSTRATIONS

Case 1

Mr and Mrs Y were married 50 years, when Mr Y's 10-year history of Parkinson disease necessitated nursing home placement. Mrs Y had provided her husband with personal care over the past 5 years when he could no longer attend to his needs. Mrs Y visited her husband every day and remained through lunch and supper to feed him. Staff were pleased with Mrs Y's feeding help. However, when Mrs Y freshened up her husband every night with a sponge bath and a change of pyjamas and stayed until her husband fell asleep, the staff became upset. They said that Mrs Y was disobeying the rules by staying beyond normal visiting hours. The staff felt that Mrs Y's behavior implied that their care was somehow inadequate.

Comment

These kinds of issues must be discussed and negotiated so that the family and staff can participate together in the best possible care, with staff understanding the threat that their "laying on of hands" poses to Mrs Y.

Case 2

Myra, aged 43, single, had to seek nursing home placement for her 75-year-old widowed mother, Mrs X, who suffered a serious stroke that left her paralyzed with impaired speech. She remained cognitively alert. Mother and daughter lived together all their lives and were devoted with strong bonds.

Mrs X was widowed at an early age and had raised Myra. They shared the same interest. Myra was determined to fix up her mother's room so that it resembled, in part, the home they once shared. Myra brought in pictures, a bed pillow, a favorite bed-side lamp, a blanket, a small chair, and numerous stuffed animals which belonged to Myra herself. Myra moved in a few items of her own clothing to place beside her mother's clothing in the closet. The staff were annoyed and politely asked Myra to remove most of the personal items. She could leave a picture or two and one or two stuffed animals. Staff said that this was an institution and all must be orderly and easy to clean. Myra refused and Mrs X was upset with the staff's anger and their threats to pack everything up in boxes.

Comment

The empathy that Myra required was an understanding that this was the last chapter in her life with her mother and that the separation, emotionally and concretely, was too painful for her at the time of admission. After several family meetings in which the focus was mutual understanding, it was possible to reach an acceptable compromise.

Staff sometimes take on a powerful and controlling role rather than a partnership of care with the family. Questions posed by families as a result of their anxiety may result in defensive and self-protective responses. It is helpful for staff to listen carefully and address with sensitivity the concerns of the family. Questions tend to be seen as challenging rather than indicative of family's fears and concerns.

Family System and the "Institutional Family System"

The family system has to interact with the "institutional family system." The latter is a highly bureaucratic and political system which takes staff months and years to comprehend. Yet, we expect families to negotiate the new system within a matter of a few days. Think of all the members of the "institutional family:" administrators, nurses, doctors, social workers, recreationists, occupational therapists, physiotherapists, language pathologists, lab technicians, X-ray technicians, dieticians, housekeeping staff, and maintenance staff. The patient and his/her family have suddenly taken on a whole new assortment of relatives.

There are now two family systems; the family of origin is at a vulnerable intersection of life. The ill member feels he or she has failed the family by becoming a burden, and failed society at large by being unproductive, and families feel they have failed the ill member by placing him/her in an institution. Family ties have been ruptured by illness.

The "institutional family" is equally vulnerable. They are mourning the loss of the patient who vacated the bed, almost always someone who has died. Staff is expected to start all over again, sometimes in less than 24 h. Staff have to direct their energies toward a new family without having grieved for the family that is gone.

The family of origin and the institutional family meet at a time of crisis for both. Staff are expected to be supportive and families are expected to be grateful that they are relieved of caring for their relative. Both groups report stressful encounters. Table 2 lists some of the major issues which potentially cause conflict between staff and families.

Table 2
Major Issues Causing Potential Conflict
Between Staff and Families

1. Institutional policies and procedures taking precedence over maintaining the family relationship
2. Tight scheduling for washing, dressing, feeding, bathing, and toiletting resulting in lack of flexibility
3. Lack of understanding the uniqueness of the family's relative
4. Staff feeling families ought to be grateful for their care
5. Poor communication around day-to-day events
6. Personal care given by families often discouraged
7. Strict adherence to visiting hours
8. Staff competing with staff for "the love" of the family

Staff may pass negative judgments about the family's behavior, becoming defensive, self-protective, and at times fearful of losing their jobs. Staff believe the family to be powerful because of their potential access to the administration. It is difficult in the face of threats of a lawsuit, but important to understand that a family's outburst may be due to feelings of helplessness. Staff's behavior of defensiveness and uncertainty adds to the family's fears of whether their relative is being provided with the best care. Their relative is now living in a community of "the many sick" and each must wait his/her turn to be washed, repositioned, toiletted, fed, etc. And the major change — "who will love my relative with tenderness and who will plant the good-night and good-morning kiss?"

Understanding behavior does not relate just to the behaviors of the families. It is equally important and at times more helpful for staff to understand their own behaviors and reactions. For example, it is possible to over-identify with a family or to be at loggerheads because of negative feelings about one's own family.

Dynamics of Family — Staff Relationships

The caring by the woman in the family is primarily taken over by the nursing staff who tend to every conceivable need of the husband. This includes physical needs and a special form of intimacy that may result from bodily care. We must be exquisitely sensitive to the threat that "hands on caring" poses to the woman. The reality is that the husband's care is managed, directed, and controlled by a host of staff, who are predominantly women: nurses, social workers, recreationists, dieticians, lab technicians, physiotherapists, occupational therapists, etc. The wife of 40 or 50 years feels as if she is an unwelcome guest. If she visits too often, the relationship is perceived as "enmeshed" or she is "controlling." If her visits are not frequent, she may be perceived as "rejecting." The adult children are caught in the middle having a mother who is "at sea without an anchor" and who is struggling to learn to negotiate with all these newly acquired concerns. The wife is potentially in conflict with the female staff for "the love" of her husband. The nursing and social worker staff, not understanding what is happening, may view the husband as a victim of an aggressive wife.

Staff Perceptions

In patient care conferences, the staff rarely discuss their own reactions in terms of identifications, cultural/ethnic differences, and expectations. Families are simplistically described in negative or positive terms. Team conferences need to reflect an understanding of the person and their family life, rather than being a discussion of medications and problems alone. We pathologize far too quickly and too much. Families enter a fish-bowl where every piece of behavior is scrutinized, discussed, and documented.

It is time for us to recognize that it is all right for both the institutional staff and the family to be unsure. Until this era of institutionalization families were generally in control and the primary caregivers. At the heart of every struggle with a family is the issue of who is in control. We need to move toward a partnership. We have to learn from families who are the socially evolved caregivers of the aged and from the ill themselves. Aging begins at conception and is a continual process from birth to death. This generation of older people and their families are the pioneers in institutionalization. We must learn to avoid singling out this end of the continuum as abnormal.

"It is difficult sometimes not to see the older person as victim, the family as enemy, and staff as saviors. Such a rescue fantasy serves only as an impediment to service. Instead, with the entire family as the unit of attention, focus must be placed on understanding the family's feelings about placement, on easing guilt if it is there, on lending a vision of help, that as partners, family and institution will do what must be done to ease the pain" [7].

HELPING FAMILIES

Funding to ensure more than basic physical care for residents is often not a serious priority for long-term care institutions. Mental health consultation and care and social workers are frequently unavailable. Nevertheless, direct care staff frequently possess a considerable degree of knowledge about the people for whom they provide care. Observations of family interactions, requests for care from different members of the family and social occasions within the facility all provide an opportunity for observing family dynamics and styles. Family differences of opinion abound! It is not uncommon for staff to overhear or be told:

DAUGHTER #1:   *Mother would like to be independent; she has always made her own decision.*

DAUGHTER #2:   *No, she's sick, she should have everything done for her.*

OR

DAUGHTER: *You don't visit often enough to know what is going on.*

SON: *Well, its better than wearing myself out like you and then not being of any use.*

OR

GRANDDAUGHTER: *I told the staff to get her up whenever she asks.*

DAUGHTER: *Oh no! She needs her rests, besides they won't put her back to bed.*

Families struggle with their new roles and are often unaware of the subtle pressure they exert on staff to favor their relative at the expense of other residents, for example:

You don't understand, my mother needs more help than the others. She never asked for help before, if she is asking now, you need to help her.

OR

My father says his food is always cold, feed him first.

OR

He's always the last to get up.

When the ramifications of what they are asking for are pointed out, families are surprised. They certainly do not mean for others to be neglected, they just want their relative cared for as they would care for him.

Distressed that their once independent relative is now dependent, families sometimes criticize or make demands for care that are not fully considered. To deal with the chronicity of a family member requires restructuring the image of the person that one has held for years. This is a painful process, no one willingly gives up the image of their parent as they once knew them. It is important to families that they share with staff who mother or father used to be — or "the person behind the illness." They want and need staff to know and understand that the person being cared for was once very different. Unless this is understood by direct caregivers, conflict and misunderstandings arise between staff and families.

How can this process be made easier? Families need assistance and education to understand the ravages of chronic illness.

MANAGEMENT

The family, once involved, need help in understanding the underlying disease, its progression, and what they can expect over the next months/years.

For example, in dementia:

- What is it?
- How does it manifest itself?
- Will the person get better?
- What are the stages?
- Does everyone go through every stage?

This knowledge helps families in understanding and surviving the changes in their relative. The information then needs to be translated into the very situations that they are likely to experience. They need to know that:

- Their relative will remember sometimes and sometimes not (and that this is not purposeful forgetting, it is part of the disease process)
- As a result of forgetfulness, the resident will perhaps begin to accuse staff of taking money, clothing, or not providing food.
- Family members themselves may be accused of neglect and not caring and of stealing or attempting to steal funds.

By arming families with knowledge of the nature of the illness and how it manifests itself, visiting itself may then become less anxiety-provoking. Concrete assistance in how to visit alleviates family distress, particularly when the resident is suspicious and accusatory.

Suggestions for Families when Visiting

- Use statements — don't ask questions of someone whose memory is impaired.
- Have a visitors' book or calendar that all visitors sign and comment that the particular person was visiting.
- Have a family album of pictures with names if possible (don't ask the resident continually — Who is this? or Do you remember..?).
- Just walk or sit together, it is all right not to talk.
- Listen to familiar music together, play cards.
- If suspicions are present, listen for a short time — do not argue or try to logically prove a point. Distract by suggesting a trip to the snack bar or a walk.
- Ask staff what they have found helpful.

During visits, family members often give idiosyncratic information to direct caregivers. This information needs to be valued, passed from shift to shift and written in the plan of care. For example:

> *But nurse, I told the staff yesterday morning that my mother never wore nail polish. She doesn't like it, she always said it made her feel claustrophobic. How could they let anyone put it on her — I told them!*

Such an oversight confirms the family's worst fear. The person behind the illness is not really known. The family feels that they must be vigilant and staff wonder what all the fuss is about. Understanding that family vigilance is designed to preserve the dignity of the relative, rather than reacting with anger or indignation helps staff to work collaboratively with the family in planning care and to work in partnership to provide this care. To facilitate collaboration it is useful to have one identified staff member on the day and one on the evening shift with whom the family can spend a few minutes. This contact reassures the family that they have someone to talk to about their relative who will know the details of their care. This is particularly helpful when there is an absence of resources and for those families who experience a great deal of difficulty with the institutionalization of their relative.

There are those family members whose difficulties in dealing with placement of their relative in a long-term care facility cause tremendous concern, anger, and dismay. Staff and the family unable to work together, struggle daily. These are the exceptions, but at times it can feel as if they are the rule.

Case 3

> *Mr A cannot tolerate his wife's deteriorating condition and he continually berates staff, barring some from entering the room and insisting on choosing the caregivers who will be allowed to provide care. He demands copious supplies and repeatedly insists that the doctor be called immediately. He accuses staff of not doing enough, but won't allow them to provide the necessary care. No matter what they do, it is never good enough. The entire team is tired and discouraged as this vicious cycle of behavior is repeated. Threats of lawsuits, rudeness, and racial insults become common place. Often heard threats include: "What's your*

name? — See I'm writing it down. I'm reporting you to the administration. You're negligent in your duty!"

Comment

It is important to understand that Mr A's behavior reflects his own feelings of helplessness with regard to being unable to help his wife. When these feelings escalate, he becomes abusive and out of control. The staff can help him to regain control by maintaining control themselves and by defining for him the boundaries of acceptable behavior.

Management suggestions

- A clearly written plan of care by the treatment team must be developed and adhered to by all — including the administrators. The plan must then be discussed with the family.
- A weekly update of the patient's condition by the physician may help lower Mr A's anxiety about his wife's condition.
- The social worker (if there is one) can provide active support to the husband.
- A contact staff member on each shift can be appointed to meet briefly with Mr A daily (5-10 minutes).
- Allowing rudeness to continue does not help Mr A. He will be hated by staff and will be seen not as a participant, but rather as an adversary in his wife's care. Tell him quietly that when he is calmer you will talk (but not now) and walk away. Do go back later in the shift when he is calmer. The same approach applies to rudeness over the telephone.

Misunderstandings arise if families, residents, and staff are not aware of and/or do not agree with the goals and plan of the treatment team. Understanding these goals, how they are arrived at, and, participation in the formulation of future goals 1. allows the family to be active participants, 2. helps to ensure a smoother working relationship, and 3. results in better care for all members of the family.

KEY POINTS

To understand and help the "institutionalized family," staff
need to:

- Consider the family system as the client.

- Recognize how disruptive chronic illness and institutionalization will be to the family system.

- Teach families about disease, its course and the possible
  effects on their relative and themselves.

- Support and assist families by teaching them in areas that
  are new for them, such as how to visit and respond to a
  demented or unresponsive relative.

- Encourage their participation in planning and providing care
  and the setting of goals for care and living.

REFERENCES

1. Gates, K. (1986). Dementia: A family problem. *Gerontion*, Jan/Feb,
   12-17.
2. Burnside, M. (1980). *Psychosocial nursing care of the aged*, p. 235.
   New York: McGraw Hill Book Company.
3. Preston, R.P. (1979) *The dilemmas of care: Social and nursing
   adaptations to the deformed, the disabled and the aged*, p. 38.
   New York: Elsevier North Holland.
4. Jennings, B., Callahan, D., Caplan, A.L. (1988). *Ethical Challenges
   of Chronic Illness*. Hastings Center Report, February/March,
   pp.1-11.
5. Luce, W. (1978). *Belle of Amherst* (A play based on the life of Emily
   Dickinson). Boston: Houghton Mifflin.
6. Gussow, M. (1983). Women playwrights — New voices in the
   theatre. *New York Times Magazine*, May 1:40.
7. Solomon, R. (1983). Serving families of the institutionalized aged:
   The four crises. In G.S. Getzel, M.J. Mellor, (Eds.). *Geronto-*

logical social work practice in long-term care, pp.83-96. New York: The Haworth Press.

SUGGESTED READING

1. Preston, R.P. (1979) *The dilemmas of care: Social and nursing adaptations to the deformed, the disabled and the aged*, p. 38. New York: Elsevier North Holland.

   This book addresses the health professional's adaptations to caring for the sick. It is a vision of the "world of the ill" viewed from that of the well.

2. Fischer, L.R. (1986). *Linked lives*. Toronto: Fitzhenry and Whiteside.

   Focuses on the enduring bond between mothers and daughters throughout the life-cycle.

3. Edelson, J.S., Lyons, W.H. (1985). *Institutional care of the mentally impaired elderly*. New York: Van Nostrand Reinhold.

   A book full of humanity and compassion, it demonstrates the art of making institutional life bearable for patients, families and staff.

CHAPTER

Legal and Ethical Dimensions   14

by Michel Silberfeld

Concern is increasingly being expressed to preserve the dignity of dependent adults by all involved. Irrespective of the source, this is a welcome development from which nursing home residents are likely to benefit. Clearly, respect for integrity of the person is an important part of chronic care contributing directly to well-being.

Respect for the integrity of the person means a concern for preserving to the utmost, that person's autonomy, facilitating the exercise of her self-directed choices to the limits of her ability. Tempered by a judicious evaluation of the person's best interest, respect also requires a protective attitude towards those areas of functioning where the person is impaired, and that best interest may not always be in line with the interests of the staff. It is difficult for caregivers to recognize themselves as having interests that are not equally shared in importance by those they care for. Staff are highly motivated to help. However, some of the reward in helping comes from the sense of mutuality that develops in the relationship.

At times it can appear that this mutuality is disrupted if there is no agreement on an area of common interest. This is regrettable and mistaken. Mutuality can be enhanced by "agreeing to disagree." This is a measure of greater respect.

Obtaining consent is the procedure designed to promote respect for autonomous choices. Some people are not capable of making such self-directed choices. Assessment of competency is the evaluation required to determine who requires a substitute decision-maker and in what circumstances. Substitute decision-makers for incompetent residents are not unconstrained in their endeavor. It is a common fear that if one becomes incompetent, substitute decision-makers will be free to do anything they please. This is not so. Standards are imposed to protect the incompetent.

There are circumstances where the wishes of residents can be overridden. This is necessary to protect them and to uphold certain values which have greater precedence. Some such circumstances commonly occurring in nursing homes will be examined. The object of this examination is to clarify the current directions that solutions to these thorny problems have taken. The issues remain controversial and incompletely resolved.

Sometimes residents wishes are overridden not by design, but inadvertently. The regulations and requirements of a nursing home can impose lifestyle restrictions which can be as intrusive as enforced treatment. Not enough attention has yet been given to the lifestyle implications of institutionalization. Nursing homes will benefit by helping residents deal with their fears concerning the restrictions they may have to accept, while having their dependency needs met.

These are general comments that require amplification for a number of specific issues.

CONSENT

The self-governing choices of all persons merit respect and freedom from intrusion. In obtaining consent, caregivers ensure that respect is given. The law imposes this requirement as a further safeguard and warning against unwanted intrusion.

The laws of consent derive from the common law on assault. None may touch another person without his/her explicit agreement. In the health care field this translates into: no treatment or procedures may be applied without explicit agreement. The nature of this agreement is made more explicit in the concept of valid consent. A definition will serve to illustrate the discussion here:

To give valid consent a person must understand the matter for which consent is being sought and must appreciate the consequences of both giving and withholding consent.

The general thrust is clear. A person must have the opportunity to make an informed choice, that is, to formulate his own intentions. In other words, a person makes a voluntary and considered choice. Persuasion on the part of others is part of normal caring, providing it is not intended to coerce.

There are frequent circumstances in the nursing home where it is difficult to ascertain whether residents have formulated their own considered choice. A sensitive caregiver will be alert to and respectful of a competent refusal, as well as open to the possibility of an incompetent assent. Agreement itself is not a sign of consent or competency. It is a mere jest to say that the competent are those who agree with us, while all others are incompetent.

Clearly there is a need for staff to exercise professional judgment and execute professional responsibility. Caregivers are always informal assessors of competency. They must determine whether there is any reason for doubt. If there is such a reason, it is their responsibility to solicit an expert opinion towards a formal determination of competency. Formal assessments of competency are medical-legal acts that have considerable implications. Decision guidelines regarding assessment of competency are outlined in Figure 1.

When people agree to enter into a long-term facility, it is sometimes considered that they have thereby given tacit consent, at least for routine care. Explicit consent need only be obtained for major interventions such as surgery. However, if routine care is opposed, consent and competency to give consent must be considered.

SUBSTITUTE DECISION MAKING

Someone else needs to make the choice for a person deemed to be incompetent. Who should that be? There is a growing consensus that in

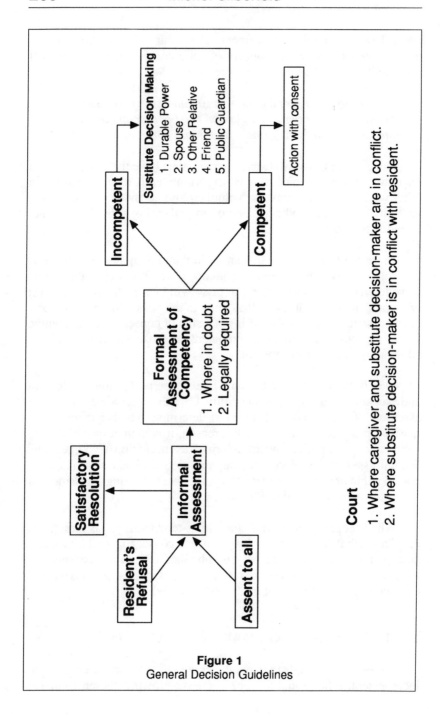

Figure 1
General Decision Guidelines

most circumstances people who are most familiar to the incompetent person should choose: spouse, family, friends, caregiver, and lastly, if none other is available, the public guardian. Familiarity with the person deemed incompetent will hopefully ensure both care (if not love) and a choice in line with that person's wishes or enduring values. In some circumstances, family have interests which come into conflict with this responsibility. Where this can be demonstrated, another substitute decision-maker should be appointed. More and more, it will become possible for people to leave advance directives specifying who shall serve as substitute decision-makers for them in the event that they should become incompetent. Where such directives exist, they should be honored for the most part. Sometimes conflict will arise between substitute decision-makers and caregivers. Such conflict, if it cannot be resolved by dialogue, should be taken to a higher authority. In some places a court hearing is required.

On what basis does one choose for another? Substitute decision-makers are enjoined by many to choose, "as the person would have chosen for themselves." This may be difficult to do with confidence in the absence of an advance directive. Caring and familiarity do help, yet a great deal of uncertainty can remain. This is felt as a burden by substitute decision-makers. Assistance can be received from caregivers. However, caregivers can feel at times that their authority is undermined by the presence of a substitute decision-maker. Sometimes the caregivers themselves have the responsibility of substitute decision making. The best health care interest of the resident is the required standard for their choice. Of course, the perception of best interest can vary.

When resolving discrepant perceptions, courts have considered whether due care is evident in the choice (in accordance with professional standards) and whether the choice is reasonable.

INVOLUNTARY INSTITUTIONALIZATION

A person who is found incompetent to choose her place of residence can be admitted involuntarily to a nursing home. In many localities, involuntary institutionalization requires sanction from a court even if there is an appointed substitute decision-maker. The impediments that exist to making this an easy accomplishment reflect the desire that the coercive route be the last option exercised. Often other less coercive solutions can work if patience is applied. Those admitted involuntarily often settle into their new environments to their own satisfaction in due course. Nevertheless, these are painful matters for all involved. The pain is acceptable only if the decision to admit is thoroughly justified.

It is important to distinguish as a separate group those who are admitted involuntarily to a psychiatric facility. Psychiatric patients committed involuntarily lose their freedom of movement. In contrast, people who are incompetent to choose their place of residence lose their right of choice with regard to that decision only. They are like minors (children) whose choice is governed by their parents.

DISCHARGING SELF

It is not uncommon for nursing home residents to express a desire to return to a previous familiar environment. This occurs most frequently soon after admission, during the adjustment period. If there is conflict and a friendly dialogue cannot resolve it, then a person who is presumably competent is free to leave. However, there are two provisos.

First, for persons putting themselves in serious danger by leaving, there is an obligation to protect them. This obligation is reinforced by statutes such as the Mental Health Act. Acts such as this provide the authority to detain persons at serious risk of harm. Acting on this authority would result in the person being transferred to a psychiatric facility for further evaluation.

Second, persons thought to be incompetent to make the discharge decision should be told so. An expert should be called in to evaluate the person's competency in this respect. If the person is competent and involuntary hospitalization is not warranted, he is discharged. If the person is believed to be incompetent by the expert, a substitute decision-maker has to be assigned. In some localities this will require a court application or the court itself may make the decision. For a person previously declared incompetent, the appointed guardian will decide. In some localities, however, even court appointed guardians cannot override the wishes of their charges without a court appearance.

It is important to be aware that expertise in medical-legal matters is necessary to deal with those situations which cannot otherwise be resolved. Knowledge of the law, expertise in assessing competency, and the need for involuntary hospitalization are required. Nevertheless, in most circumstances an informal solution can be found.

INVOLUNTARY INTERVENTION

Involuntary intervention is only required in two general circumstances: to preserve life and to restrain in situations of danger. In a non-emergency situation, involuntary treatment can occur even if consent is withheld only in the situations described above.

In an emergency where treatment is required to preserve life, involuntary treatment is given according to the same guidelines as would be followed in an emergency room. Can a competent person refuse life-saving treatment? In an emergency situation the potential for regret is heightened. Medical staff are duty bound by their professional oath to preserve life. And yet some people do refuse urgent life-saving treatment. On balance, giving treatment is preferred. Court decisions do not give clear guidance. Without these, physicians are likely to be concerned about being negligent of their professional duty if they do not act. If they proceed, they may still be liable to charges of assault. Financial penalties have been granted against physicians who have given life-saving treatment. The patient is compensated for the assault even when the court declares the physician to have acted properly.

Restraint, both chemical and physical, may become necessary in working with nursing home residents. Clearly, these should not become necessary solely because of a shortage of staff. Convenience is not sufficient cause for the application of restraints. Most facilities should have a policy in this regard that has been approved by an ethics committee. It should also be sanctioned by the lawyers for the institution. A small institution can borrow policies from another in the same jurisdiction and sometimes there are guidelines imposed by health authorities.

Restraint is the same as involuntary confinement, and the same criteria apply: presence of a serious risk of bodily harm (to self, to others, or both) and absence of voluntary solution. Restraint is a temporary measure until a better solution can be found. It may be required to properly evaluate an agitated patient so that a definitive treatment can be applied. When restraints are applied, it should be only for a specified period of time with a built-in mechanism for review after a set time.

FORCED FEEDING

Many residents in a nursing home are too debilitated to feed themselves and need assistance. Some of them may not even have a recognizable desire to eat. Helping with feeding is routine care so long as it involves feeding by mouth.

Some residents are not cooperative and may even reject feeding. For the caregiver responsible for feeding, this is a test of her abilities to care, perhaps in the face of "meaningless" opposition. Not only is feeding difficult, but there are risks of aspiration pneumonia and its sequelae. These risks are an additional burden to those responsible for feeding the patient.

A reason must be established when a resident is refusing food by mouth. If late stage dementia is the sole cause, forced feeding with a nasogastric tube is sometimes considered. This is an intrusive, though life sustaining, treatment. It is likely that such a resident would be deemed incompetent.

Substitute decision-makers have asked to discontinue nasogastric food and fluids on the basis of arguments made about the quality of life. The latest U.S. Supreme Court pronouncements on the Cruzan case have set a very strict standard. There must be clear and convincing evidence that the person requested (at some point) discontinuation. Inference from relatives and friends is insufficient. In the Conroy case, it was stated that the burdens of living must outweigh the benefits beyond a reasonable doubt. Furthermore, continuing treatment (feeding) would be considered inhumane in the presence of severe and uncontrollable pain. These decisions are recognized as controversial. Others prefer less restrictive criteria for withdrawing food and fluids from persons in a chronic "vegetative" state.

RESUSCITATION

Efforts to resuscitate a resident in a nursing home usually lead to the resident being transferred to an acute care facility. Most nursing homes have the expertise to provide basic life support, but it is rare for them to have the equipment to sustain cardiopulmonary functioning.

The model for medical care in nursing homes is frequently similar to acute care. The staff are geared to treat the onset of new illness in the same way as it might be done in an acute care hospital. There is some discontent with this approach. Nursing home treatment, it is said, should be modeled on palliative care. Care, comfort and quality of life should override simple prolongation of life. Resuscitation should not invariably be performed. It should be a judgment call. Residents and their relatives should be able to instruct the facility that resuscitation is not wanted after a certain point. Several studies suggest that resuscitation efforts in this population almost always fail to prolong life to a meaningful degree [1,2]. Some argue that resuscitation is a medical treatment that should not be offered if it is not indicated.

Some facilities would like to have blanket policies advocating no resuscitation for anybody under any circumstances. People would be forewarned about the policy upon entry to the facility. Unfortunately, residents do not have an alternative choice of placement if they object to a no resuscitation policy. Furthermore, statistical studies leave open the question of the outcome in an individual case. Medical discretion can be applied but perhaps not in a blanket fashion.

There is often a reluctance to discuss the desire for resuscitation with residents and relatives. This reluctance is both regrettable and understandable. These are painful choices to contemplate, especially on admission. Nevertheless, it is best if residents can participate and concur in these decisions. Significant others can be involved in the discussion if the resident is agreeable. The discussion and those present at the time of the discussion can be noted in the chart and the directive thereby made explicit.

Disputes may occur. A competent resident who gives a clear and informed advance directive should expect that directive to be honored when it comes to resuscitation. Relatives who object should be directed to the resident. A caregiver can facilitate that conversation, but the resident's wishes ultimately prevail. The substitute decision-maker should be consulted for an incompetent resident. Where the medical staff and the substitute disagree without resolution, an appeal to legal authority is the next step. Staff may indeed have the best informed and most reasonable views about the value of resuscitation. The resident or caring others should nevertheless retain the balance of discretion. How and under what circumstances people choose to die is not a decision which belongs to caregivers in the nursing home.

The most satisfying solutions are arrived at through dialogue and an openness to persuasion leading to mutual agreement. Where there is mutual respect, an adversarial resolution seldom ensues. Despite widespread publicity, the number of cases that have come to court is minuscule; the ones that do usually involve the withdrawal of life support after resuscitation has been instituted.

FINANCES

Persons entering a nursing home may request their personal finances to be handled by the facility. Sometimes a nursing home will require a person to turn over their personal finances as a condition of admission. The potential for a conflict of interest in these circumstances is great. The home may wish to spend "freely" on supplementary care; when staff is short, money for a private duty nurse or attendant makes this choice attractive. The resident may wish to preserve much of his estate for his family or other beneficiaries. This is only one of many potential conflicts of interest.

Personal finances are best handled outside the nursing home through assigning a durable power of attorney to a concerned person or some paid assistant such as a lawyer, or through voluntary assignment to the public trustee.

In trying to meet the costs of nursing home care, conflicts can arise for residents. Long-term care is often very long indeed; the accumulated costs can be prohibitive. Some residents feel that they should not be forced to divest themselves completely to meet those costs. There are also objections to relatives being coerced to underwrite the costs with threats of withdrawal of service. A resident who has to contribute to the cost of care may feel very guilty should this result in poverty for the spouse. How can nursing home care be provided to all those who will require it?

LIFESTYLE RESTRICTIONS

Nursing homes require structure in order to function, and programming of residents' activities is one of the components of such structure. However, scheduling people can remove their sense of discretion and effectiveness. Loss of control over one's daily activities has been documented as the most frequent cause of demoralization in nursing homes. Therefore it is important to be aware that good programming can go a long way to help residents continue to feel effective. Respect for residents can be demonstrated by flexibility and by allowing the resident to exercise discretion whenever possible. This should be the goal of programming. As with health care decisions, input from residents should be the rule rather than the exception when it comes to their daily programs.

Couples are often forced into separation when one member is admitted to a nursing home. This separation is as difficult and painful as any forced loss of a loved one. The loss of intimacy cannot be recovered by visits; nursing homes seldom permit enough privacy for true intimacy. Towards the end of life this is a sorry loss indeed. It is a shame that couples cannot be admitted as such more often. Many would be willing. However, very occasionally, a situation arises in which a couple is forced to live together on admission even if one partner's dementia puts the other at risk of abuse.

Sexual relations among the elderly residents of a nursing home cannot be denied. For consenting adults privacy should be possible. Concerns arise about new liaisons occurring in the nursing home. Children or a spouse may raise objections. Is the resident being exploited or exploiting others unwittingly as a result of his/her dementia? These are difficult questions. Most efforts are directed to finding the cause of illness or to specifying the abilities lost due to illness. How the elderly and demented construct their social world is very poorly understood. In spite of the handicap imposed upon them by illness, is the search for sexual intimacy a choice that they cannot make? Is this a competency that others can assess?

Avoidance of such questions has been the approach so far, but this cannot remain the case for much longer. As more people anticipate their old age, and the possibility of confinement to a nursing facility, the lifestyles they can expect will increasingly become a subject of public debate.

FEAR OF LIABILITY

Competency is not an issue that leads to litigation very often; the little litigation that occurs has mostly to do with estates. However, the fear of litigation remains among health care providers. This is remarkable since the most contentious difficulties usually arise in acute care settings and not in nursing homes. Residents themselves are unlikely to be able to launch a claim. The problem here is one of perception, for the primary fear is of families. If the family has been consulted, it cannot complain about a decision it has agreed to previously; this holds even when the family may not have had the authority to agree in the first place. This problem of perception can result in health care providers becoming reluctant to rely on the residents themselves, and the consequences for residents of the reluctance of caregivers to take risks leads to a further erosion of their autonomy.

Whereas legal suits are unlikely, regulatory sanctions are more frequently applied. Regional and local government authorities do regulate numerous aspects of care within nursing homes. Violations of basic standards of care can lead to penalties or closure of the facility. Perhaps regulatory sanctions have not been used sufficiently to advocate for better standards of care. For both the individual caregiver and the nursing home, the best risk management comes with the use of explicit protocols. Clear criteria for contentious situations need to be articulated and taught to staff. Documentation is one way to reduce the risk. The act of accounting in writing for the outcome of situations serves as a double safeguard. It gives a record that can be examined in the future, and it fosters in staff a thoughtfulness towards the interpretation of events. Unfortunately, it is sometimes seen as an opportunity to vindicate one's actions.

Another effective way to reduce risk, is the use of consultants. For example, a geriatric psychiatrist or other mental health professional who is not part of the health care team can serve a useful role in mediating a triangular conflict between caregivers, a resident and family. Even if the conclusion or action remains the same, the opinion of an uninterested party is reassuring. It indicates that the problem was recognized and due care was taken to come to a suitable resolution. The law does not require more, particularly in situations recognized as not having clear-cut solutions.

CASE ILLUSTRATIONS

Case 1

An elderly woman with Alzheimer disease had lost control of her ability to swallow effectively. The health care team was considering tube feeding because of the resident's otherwise good state of health. The resident's daughter was a single mother of three children who was very burdened emotionally and financially by her mother's care. She objected to starting tube feeding and sought legal assistance to impose her point of view. Prior to reaching a court battle, the daughter was offered financial relief, and was reassured that feeding her mother would be done by the health care team in a manner not requiring her additional intervention. The conflict was satisfactorily resolved.

Comment

This case illustrates the complex interplay between competency issues and the availability of resources. Once the resource problem had been addressed, the conflict leading to a competency assessment was resolved. The mother's choice was not the issue, but mistakenly became seen as a point requiring resolution.

Case 2

An elderly man was transferred to a long-term care facility from an acute care bed after the papers for admission had been signed by his family (two daughters). On admission it became apparent that he did not want to be in long-term care. In addition he did not appear to be incompetent to make his own decision. The administrator of the long-term facility requested a competency assessment. In the course of the assessment, the daughters admitted they had been precipitous. They withdrew their father's home from the sales market, and used his ample resources to provide the in-home assistance he required. Just invoking due process was sufficient to dissolve the conflict between this man and his daughters.

Comment

Estate issues are the visible expressions of family dynamics. The sale of the home was the daughter's way of settling emotional accounts with her father. They were persuaded by the challenge of the competency assessment to reconsider their indebtedness to their father.

KEY POINTS

- Respect for the integrity of the dependent adult means a concern for preserving the person's autonomy, tempered by a protective attitude towards areas of functioning where the person is impaired.

- The acts of obtaining consent and of assessing competency to give consent ensure that residents are given respect and are protected from unwanted intrusion.

- Standards exist for the appointment and behavior of substitute decision-makers in situations where individuals are not competent to choose for themselves.

- Involuntary admissions to longterm care settings are acceptable only if the decision to admit is thoroughly justified. Competent residents who express the desire to leave the nursing home are free to discharge themselves in most circumstances.

- Involuntary intervention is required only to preserve life and to restrain in situations of danger. Restraint may be physical or chemical. Institutions should have policies governing the use of restraints.

- The resident's personal finances are best handled outside the institution to avoid potential conflicts of interest.

- Many controversial issues that arise in nursing homes must be addressed at the individual level and as a subject of public debate. These include lifestyle and sexual issues as well as the use of forced feeding and resuscitation.

- Most disagreements can be resolved by an open dialogue between those involved. Consultants can play a useful mediating role. Conflicts that cannot be otherwise resolved can and sometimes must be taken to a legal authority.

REFERENCES

1. Bedell, S.E., Delbanco, T.L., Cook, E.F. (1983). Survival after cardiopulmonary resuscitation in the hospital. *New England Journal of Medicine*, 309:570.
2. Gordon, M., Hurowitz, E.(1984). Cardiopulmonary resuscitation of the elderly. *Journal of the American Geriatric Society*, 32:930-934.

SUGGESTED READING

1. Caplan, A.L. (1985). Let wisdom find a way. *Generations*, Winter 1985: 10-14.

   This paper reviews the ethical complexities of competency assessments. It is a concise clearly written statement of the major ethical conflicts with a proposal to consider the values of elderly residents as authentic.

2. Fader, A.M., et al. (1989). Implementing a "do-not-resuscitate" (DNR) policy in a nursing home. *Journal of the American Geriatric Society,* 37:544-548.

   This paper describes the introduction of DNR orders in a Nursing Home. As well it discusses the major considerations leading residents and their surrogates to their choices.

3. Arras, J.D. (1988). The severely demented, minimally functional patient: An ethical analysis. *Journal of the American Geriatric Society*, 36:938-944.

   This paper explores a description of quality of life considerations that may enter into a decision to withdraw food and fluids.

4. Kapp, B.M. (1988). Forcing services on at-risk older adults: When doing good is not so good. Social Work in Health Care, 13(4):1-12.

   The interplay between ethical principles is reviewed when social intervention is refused by residents. The rights of older residents are distinguished from the interests of professional caregivers.

5. Evans, L. (1989). Tying down the elderly, *Journal of the American Geriatric Society*, 36:65-74.

This paper reviews the controversial complexities of the application of restraints.

Index

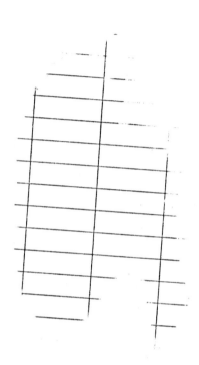